SO APPOINTED

QUO MONSTRAT DOMINUS

By the same Author:

The Problem of Gambling
Betting Facts
With Christ in the Bull Ring
Gambling and Youth
The Methodist Church Builds Again (jointly)
Gambling in English Life
Methodist Preaching Houses and the Law
etc.

THE REV. E. BENSON PERKINS, M.A., LL.D.
*from the portrait by Frank O. Salisbury
in the World Methodist Building, Lake Junaluska,
North Carolina, U.S.A.*

SO APPOINTED
an autobiography

by

E. BENSON PERKINS

Foreword by
the Rev. Dr Harold Roberts

WIPF & STOCK · Eugene, Oregon

Wipf and Stock Publishers
199 W 8th Ave, Suite 3
Eugene, OR 97401

So Appointed
An Autobiography
By Perkins, E. Benson and Roberts, Harold
Copyright©1964 Methodist Publishing - Epworth Press
ISBN 13: 978-1-5326-4635-5
Publication date 12/29/2017
Previously published by Epworth Press, 1964

TO ELSIE

CONTENTS

	Foreword	xi
	Preface	xiii
1	Early Background and Beginnings	1
2	On the Way	12
3	Ordination and Circuit Appointments	29
4	Temperance and Social Welfare	45
5	Central Missions	59
6	Unity and Citizenship	75
7	Widening Horizons	88
8	Church Buildings and War Damage	105
9	Appointments Extraordinary	124
10	World Methodism	146
11	The Ecumenical Movement	171
12	'Thinking Backward and Living Forward'	183
	Index	199

LIST OF ILLUSTRATIONS

The Rev. E. Benson Perkins, M.A., LL.D *Frontispiece*
from the portrait by Frank O. Salisbury

Facing page

Candidate for the Ministry, 1903; Ordination, 1910; Chaplain to the Forces, 1914; *Sheffield Telegraph and Star*, 1936   34

The Study in Birmingham, 1925-35   35

The Family in Birmingham, 1933   35

Mrs Benson Perkins, 1948   130

After the service preceding the Labour Party Conference, Margate, 1955   131

Dedication of Equestrian Statue of John Wesley, Washington, 1961   131

FOREWORD

By the REV. DR HAROLD ROBERTS

IT gives me great pleasure to write a Foreword to this volume, although no recommendation is necessary, since its merits shine in their own light. I first saw and heard Dr Perkins at a conference on 'Christ and Peace' at Somerville College, Oxford. He spoke two or three times during the discussion, and I remember hearing a lady member of the conference saying to him, 'I like a man who knows his own mind and can express himself with such clarity.' Those who know Dr Perkins hardly need to be told that he knows his own mind. His success in the various spheres in which he has been engaged throughout an illustrious life of service is due in part to the fact that he has deep convictions about the few things that matter. He has also the enviable gift of being able to communicate the content of his thought in language that is cogent and lucid. There are those who increase the volume of fog in any discussion by opening the window of their mind. Dr Perkins is not among them. He has a way of clearing the air whenever he speaks.

Readers of this autobiography will be impressed by the varied activities that are described. Dr Perkins would have gained eminence in many careers. When he entered the ministry the worlds of law and commerce were deprived of one who has unique forensic and administrative gifts. As prosecuting or defending counsel he would have created a great impression and most probably been burdened with more cases than he could manage. He would have had little sympathy with a judge or jury that disagreed with his views. Eventually he might have become a judge himself and gone on circuit in a sense other than that which was to be his chosen vocation as a Methodist minister. He would have looked the part and embodied the virtues which we associate with that high office. But Dr Perkins entered the ministry and the gifts that would have opened many gilded doors he gladly devoted to the service of the Church.

If you wish to see his monuments, take a look at the records of the Christian Citizenship Department, the War Damage Commission, District and Connexional Administration, and in later years the World Methodist Council. Let no one imagine that he ever allowed himself to become immersed in administration. He has never lost sight of the vision splendid. He has throughout his ministry maintained his interest in theology and kept abreast of sociological thought. He has had much to do with the erection of churches, and it has been his concern to bring before architects and re-planning committees the primary aim of worship. His preaching is eloquent, forceful, and evangelical in the best sense, and his conduct of worship suggests that he and the congregation are assisting at the most important of all events. Further, he has always cared for the work of the pastor of souls. Those who knew him as District Chairman and President of the Conference as well as a circuit minister will know that he has an understanding heart and a brotherliness that heals many wounds.

The name of Benson Perkins is well known throughout Methodism, and nowhere is it more highly honoured than in the minority branches of the Methodist family, where the sense of being linked with the World Methodist Council is a source of unfailing strength and inspiration. It is not an overstatement to say that the World Methodist Council owes more to Dr Perkins than to any other single man. His statesmanship of thought and action was available at a critical juncture in the history of the movement and the foundations are now well and truly laid. His ecumenicity is not limited to World Methodism, since he has a lively interest in the World Council of Churches and is no less ecumenical in outlook because he is eager that in the fellowship of Churches Methodism should bear its characteristic witness.

In all his endeavours, Dr Perkins has been supported by Mrs Perkins whose gracious influence extends far beyond their peaceful home. To them both we offer our gratitude and look forward with keen interest to the new and daring plans for Christian advance that are doubtless taking shape in the mind of the distinguished son of the Church whose recollections adorn the pages of this book.

HAROLD ROBERTS

PREFACE

IF my friends, at home and abroad, are responsible for the idea of this story, as indeed they are, I must relieve them of any responsibility for whatever ineptitude there may be in its telling. It had never occurred to me that my life called for a record though admittedly varied and interesting perhaps a little beyond the more normal course of the life and work of a minister of the Methodist Church. But when I heard one or another of these friends give a summary of the story it almost impressed me. It usually ran something like this: Superintendent of two of the largest central missions (Birmingham and Sheffield), Executive Officer of two departments (Citizenship and Church Buildings), Chairman of two districts (Sheffield and Manchester), Secretary of the World Methodist Council with travel in three continents, and along the way President of the Methodist Conference, Vice-President of the British Council of Churches and Moderator of the Free Church Federal Council. It certainly looked as though there ought to be a worthwhile story in this record particularly as from its very early beginnings it covers more than three-quarters of a century. The idea, once planted, was not to be resisted, and I can only hope that its publication justifies the anticipations of these insistent friends.

Does the title require an explanation? All Methodist ministers receive their appointments directly from the Conference. But the members of my own college will at once have in mind the words under the college crest, QUO MONSTRAT DOMINUS (Whither the Lord points). Very humbly I confess that through my life I have been conscious of the guidance—dare I say the appointment—of God. I have had my share of frustrations and seeming hindrances, but as events have worked out I have come to see that in these things also I was so appointed and disappointment has yielded to deep thankfulness.

None will dispute—least of all the members of my family —the fitness of my dedication of this book to one person. My wife has shared this pilgrimage with me in a comradeship of more than fifty years. Her love and companionship, her confidence and sense of right, her support when things were difficult, her necessary criticism on occasions, her creation of the peace and joy of home—all this and more lies behind what I have been permitted to do. This book is the incomplete record of what she made possible, often at personal sacrifice, for she recognized that we were so appointed.

The Rev. Dr Harold Roberts and I came into more intimate association in connexion with the work of the World Methodist Council, and his colleagueship and friendship have been to me a continual source of encouragement and help. I am indebted to him for adding to his many acts of kindness the writing of the Foreword to this book. The one about whom he writes certainly bears my name but those who read this Foreword will need to acquire a generous imagination like that of Dr Roberts if they are to discover other points of resemblance.

I am particularly grateful to the Rev. Wilfred Wade, who, when he left college, was for four years my intimate junior colleague in the Birmingham Mission. That began a friendship which has deepened through the years. He has been good enough to read the typescript as it became available, and, within the freedom of our friendship and out of his knowledge of experiences we have shared, to subject it to an objective criticism. The book is, in consequence, much better than it might have been, but I am responsible for whatever blemishes and errors still remain.

Dr Frank Cumbers and Dr William Strawson have been both encouraging and helpful and I am most grateful to them and also to other friends who have assisted in various ways and thus contributed to the accuracy and completeness of the record.

E. BENSON PERKINS

Birmingham, 1963

CHAPTER I

EARLY BACKGROUND AND BEGINNINGS

THE almost incredible contrast between life today and as lived in the late Victorian period stands out for me as I think back to my boyhood and youth in my home-town of Leicester. The setting was so vastly different from the city of this new Elizabethan age with its modern buildings, its great stores, its housing developments, its new lines of communication, its fast-moving traffic, its innumerable amenities, its University and its Lord Mayor. Even so, Leicester has, perhaps, retained more links with the past than seem to be allowed in the rebuilding of Birmingham where I now reside. The Leicester of my early days was very much the old market town, in spite of the increasing industrialization through the developing hosiery and boot-and-shoe factories. The slow moving carriers' carts came in from the villages several times a week. The horse-drawn trams on the main streets did not travel much faster. The weekly market, one of the largest open-air markets in the country, was then occupied by crude canvas-topped stalls lit up at night by naphtha flares. The safety bicycle was the fastest thing on the roads, and even faster when pneumatic tyres were invented in the early nineties. The main excitements were the annual Fair, which filled the wide area of Humberstone Gate and the regular visits of Poole's Panorama. The naked gas flame was the only illuminant, apart from oil lamps and candles, and the flickering light left in the street-lamps by the lamp-lighters did little more than emphasize the darkness.

What fascinated me as a boy were the many reminders of ancient history. Within sight of our home was a fragment of the old Roman wall, known as Jewry Wall, as it was believed to have association with the persecution of the Jews. Across the way were some cottages, since demolished, where John

Bunyan and John Wesley stayed. Shakespeare is said to have acted in the Corpus Christi Guild Hall, which served as the Town Hall for four hundred years. Every Sunday as we walked to church we passed the reputed burial-place of King Richard III after the Battle of Bosworth Field, some twelve miles away. Five miles to the north at Thurcaston a Methodist farmer lived in the old timber-frame house where Bishop Hugh Latimer was born, while thirteen miles to the south is Lutterworth where John Wycliffe was Rector, and from whence went the first English translation of the Bible. Of course, Leicester claims association with the death of Cardinal Wolsey and the exploits of Simon de Montfort, Earl of Leicester.

We were a small family. I was born in 1881 and was an insignificant schoolboy about the time my sister was born five years later. Another member of our family was an orphaned cousin who became 'one of us' in every sense. She remained at home and was a great help to my mother after my father's death, when my sister and I had homes of our own in other cities. Our parents came originally from Rugby, where I spent many a schoolboy holiday with relatives. It was a family tradition that our great-great-grandfather was disowned by his family because of his association with the Methodists. At any rate, the Methodist line continued through the subsequent generations.

Our home was in the central area of the town, for the reason that my father's business was that of a merchant tailor and, as was customary in those days, home and business premises were in the same building. This accounts for what is, literally, my earliest distinctive recollection. The oldest Baptist chapel in Leicester was quite near our home, and my mother was asked to entertain a visiting preacher for some days. I was barely three years old, but I retain a definite picture of the old man as he took his meals in our drawing-room, which was just across the corridor from his bedroom. He was Thomas Cooper, the Chartist, who was born in Leicester in 1805, when Mrs Charles Wesley had still seventeen years of life before her. During several days the old man held reception in that drawing room for the many people who wished to meet him and I suspect that it was the unusual procession of visitors which fastened the occasion on my remembrance. As I learned afterwards, our guest was delighted to find that my father possessed and had read his autobiography. That book and some other of his writings which he autographed are still on my shelves.

Another visitor in my early days was Commissioner Cadman of the Salvation Army. Until his conversion in the Wesleyan Methodist Chapel in Rugby, he was a notorious sweep well known to the police. He was then quite illiterate, and a well-known story about him is that he learned the alphabet by the little children in the Sunday School pointing out the letters and roaring with laughter when he held the card upside-down. My uncle, an elder brother of my mother, taught him to read. He joined William Booth's Christian Mission and was the first to speak of an army and to use military titles, an idea which 'General' Booth took over and developed. Whenever Elijah Cadman was in Leicester, he came to see us for a meal, a talk and always prayer. He rendered great service in many parts of the world.

One of the four statues on the Gothic clock tower in the centre of the city is that of Alderman Gabriel Newton, who lived in the early eighteenth century, and founded a charity school to bring some enlightenment into the squalor and ignorance of those days. The thirty-five boys of the foundation in 1760 wore green coats and bonnets, with breeches and yellow stockings. So it continued for a hundred years or more, when the old and then famous green-coat school was brought into line with progressive education and became a high school for 300 boys, with an emphasis upon science. To that school I gained a scholarship from the elementary school. We certainly travelled a considerable distance in branches of science under excellent masters. I recall that when Röntgen discovered X-rays in 1895 our physics master had himself been carrying out experiments with the Crookes tube, and was able to give us an immediate demonstration of the new and revolutionary discovery. Afterwards I came to regret that, while we did take English literature, French and other subjects, science predominated over the humanities. Within recent years the school has broadened out considerably. In all probability, the mental discipline of mathematics and the exact sciences had a permanent value, even though one's later studies took a different line. The school provided some quite outstanding scientists, including Sir Charles P. Snow, novelist as well as scientist. Others, however, turned towards the Church. A special friend of mine in my own form was the late Canon Harold Orgill, Vicar of Normanton and Rural Dean of Wakefield. From a rather later period came the late Dr Underwood, Principal of Rawdon Baptist College, and Dr Leslie Weatherhead of the City Temple and an ex-President of the Methodist Conference.

One of the extra-curricular interests which was of great value to me was the string orchestra under the direction of the Head Master, Mr J. W. Muston, who was a fine musician. My study of the piano began when I was seven, but during later schooldays I started with the viola largely because we had an instrument available at home. Because of its rather larger size, the use of the C, or alto, clef, and its seemingly inferior place in the string quartette, the viola is not a popular instrument, though Lionel Tertis has given it new distinction for solo purposes. I never came to play it very well, but a moderate viola player is welcome in an amateur orchestra. The school orchestra gave many of us great pleasure which the audience seemed to share on the few occasions of our public performances.

Another statue on that clock tower is that of William Wyggeston, whose charities were also used to establish schools. My sister gained a scholarship in the well-known Wyggeston Girls' School and later went on to Southlands College. She married the late Rev. Percy Ineson, whose distinctive work was done as Superintendent of the London Central and East End Missions, followed by a period with the Refugee Service of the British Council of Churches.

With schooldays over came the question of the next step. I was not conscious of any strong leaning at that time and the idea of joining the family business seemed almost inevitable. There was no compulsion about this, and on my part no reluctance, though I did wonder from time to time whether this was to be the final character of my future. However, I took it seriously and in business accounting and technical matters sought to equip myself for the position. Business in those days was very exacting and left little or no time for sport. I did manage to put in a few hours every week in the gymnasium and, of course, we cycled a good deal, which is better exercise than motoring. I was able to keep up musical interests as a

EARLY BACKGROUND AND BEGINNINGS

member of the New Musical Society—an outstanding choral association—and in playing both piano and viola.

As a family we were interested in politics and shared the radical liberalism which predominated in Leicester in those days. My father was a member of the Liberal Thousand—the official party organization. The first move to secure trade-union and labour representation in Parliament came by association with the Liberal Party with Lib.-Lab. Members, as they were named. Leicester was a case in point, for the members for the borough were, at that time, Walter Hazell of the well-known printing firm of Hazell, Watson and Viney, and Henry Broadhurst who was one of the pioneers in the trade union and labour movement. There were distinguished civic leaders amongst the Methodist laymen in Leicester, and the one who captured my imagination was the young solicitor, Arthur Wakerley. He was a brother of the Rev. John E. Wakerley, who was President of the Wesleyan Methodist Conference in 1922. Arthur Wakerley was one of the youngest Mayors of the town and created quite a sensation by insisting that all mayoral banquets for which he was responsible should be 'dry', an innovation at that time. One incident connected with him made a deep impression upon my mind. It has to do with his candidature for Parliament, and I told the story to the Methodist members whom I met at the Houses of Parliament when I was President of the Conference. On three successive occasions Arthur Wakerley contested the Melton Divison of Leicestershire and on the third occasion came within a very few votes of victory. There had to be a recount and there was great excitement in Leicester on that Saturday evening when the poll was declared. The following morning Arthur Wakerley was appointed to preach in our church, but I was quite sure that after weeks of electioneering and the excitement of Saturday night he would arrange a substitute. I watched the opening of the vestry door wondering who it would be. To my astonishment, Arthur Wakerley appeared and ascended the pulpit. With that distinction of manner and speech characteristic of him, he led the worship of the congregation and there was not the remotest suggestion of any carry-over of election excitement. The incident gave me an idea of relative values which I never forgot.

I had the inestimable advantage of a truly Methodist home. The predominant concern was neither business nor politics. They had their proper place, but the chief interest centred in the life and work of the Wesleyan Methodist Church. The mother church of Leicester Methodism was Bishop Street, which was also the head chapel of our circuit. That was the Methodist cathedral for us, and it was an event to sit in the gallery and see and hear some of the leaders of Methodism on the occasion of great central meetings. My father, as a young man, had been persuaded to leave Bishop Street and give his support to a new development on the King Richard's Road in the west end of the town. He became one of the first trustees of the new building and remained so, with frequent stewardships and other offices for half a century. Later my mother became a class-leader and held that position for a similar period. They had definite views about their children, with the result that my name was placed upon a Methodist class-book soon after I was born. The idea was that my ultimate decision should not be whether I would join the Church, but whether I would leave it. I suspect that this happened rarely, but there is nothing in the Methodist constitution to prevent it and much to commend it. It solves the problem of so-called junior membership. Of course, young people do not participate in the Church courts until they have reached years of discretion.

The King Richard's Road Church is a fine building of the Gothic type which in my time had a splendid spire. Unfortunately, it became unsafe and had to be reduced to a squat tower, much to the detriment of its appearance. It has a central pulpit with a gallery on three sides and seats about 800. It was a mile from our home, but we none of us regarded it as any hardship to walk there and back twice at least, but more often three times, on Sunday. The idea of the Victorian Sunday being dull and gloomy was very far from my experience. We younger ones did not attend the early morning prayer-meeting, but Sunday School was at 9.30, followed by morning worship. Then Sunday School or the Bible Class occupied the afternoon. Evening worship was at the normal time of 6.30, but before then there was the Mission Band. After evening worship there was always what was called an 'After Meeting', unless it was the monthly observance of Holy Communion.

Looking back, I can hardly realize how we managed to entertain our friends over the Sunday tea-table, but we did quite often, if not every Sunday. Then there was hymn-singing round the piano after supper. Actually, there was something bracing about this régime, and it was without doubt thoroughly interesting, whatever the cynic may say.

That Sunday evening Mission Band was typical of virile Methodism in the last century and the early years of this. I wish I could draw a vivid picture of the band of people as they came marching along, singing, most likely, 'O for a thousand tongues to sing, My great Redeemer's praise' to Lyngham which is a grand marching tune whatever other virtues it may not possess. The front line invariably comprised prominent members of the church, wearing their long frock-coats and silk hats. I am not speaking in any disrespect of the Salvation Army when I say that this was something quite different. They stayed at certain suitable points for a word of testimony, appeal, and invitation, reaching the church about ten minutes before the evening service began. The father of the late Rev. A. J. G. Seaton, one-time Secretary of the Sunday School Department and a lifelong friend of mine, was Leader of the Mission Band, and my father was one of the front rank.

Evangelistic enthusiasm touched the whole life of the church. The appeal for decision was frequent if not every Sunday. There was a prevailing opinion that a publicly declared decision for Christ was to be sought and expected from everyone. If I have wondered since whether that constant appeal was overstressed, I am sure that the neglect of a direct appeal in many of our churches today is a definite weakness. There came a Sunday evening when I went up to the front in response to the appeal. It was not for me an occasion of any radical spiritual change; it was a personal declaration. I had made my choice and was thenceforward committed to the way of Christ and to His service.

The life of the church was of one piece. There was a large congregation filling the building on Sunday evenings; there was a Sunday School numbering over 800; there were society classes, the choir, the Wesley Guild and other groups. They formed a real unity. We had a lively and interesting fellowship with many social events, and we were content within that limited community. The criticism that I feel I must make of the church of my youth, much as I value all that it did for me, is that we were too self-centred. Only very occasionally were we conscious of other branches of Methodism, not to mention other Free Churches. But I suspect that our attitude was also that of the other churches. Most of them were strong and flourishing, but they kept within their own fellowship, as we did. There were far-seeing leaders, like Methodism's own Hugh Price Hughes, who saw this weakness and were discussing the possibility of a Free Church Council. The first congress of the Free Churches was held in Manchester in 1892, but it was some years after that before the movement affected Leicester. This is the more surprising because it was often described as 'The Metropolis of Dissent'. I feel sure the ministers were being brought into closer touch, but the rank and file were slow in responding to any appeal for the most elementary expression of Christian unity. At that time, roughly sixty years ago, there were fourteen strong Methodist, Baptist, and Congregational churches in or near the central area of the town, with quite a few smaller churches. Today in that same area there are three. Six or seven have been rebuilt in suburbs or new housing areas, but I wonder whether we have not too easily deserted the central sites of the greatly enlarged city as we have done in other cities. Speaking on the same platform with a prominent Anglican incumbent from Leicester a few years ago, I heard him describe the city as the cleanest, wealthiest and most Godless city in the country. Allowing for platform exaggeration, the fact remains that, with its basic industries of shoes and hosiery, Leicester prospered even in the years of acute unemployment elsewhere, and nothing can kill religion more quickly than wealth and prosperity.

The situation regarding our association, or, rather, lack of association, with the Church of England was much worse. It might have appeared that we spoke a different language. Diagonally opposite our Wesleyan Methodist chapel was the Anglican Church of St Paul. It was the outstanding anglo-catholic church in Leicester. The incumbent was Father Mason, a fine-looking, bearded figure who was a very good man and a most devoted priest and pastor. He was never seen without his cassock. To our shame, we youths never seem to have regarded him as other than a figure of fun. On one occasion one of the numerous announcements of developing Catholic practices stated that after a certain date 'Incense will be used in this church'. The minister of our church had a large poster visible from the Anglican church announcing his subject for the following Sunday, 'Incense is an Abomination unto Me, saith the Lord'. At that date the story I am able to tell of Christian unity would have seemed to be quite impossible.

Within Wesleyan Methodism a movement was developing that was to spread throughout the country, with remarkable results. It was known as 'The Forward Movement' and in the 'nineties it was a chief topic of conversation around the Sunday evening tea-table. I little thought that years later I should have some part in two of its chief centres. It was the opening of the Central Hall in Manchester under Samuel Collier in 1886 and the West London Mission under Hugh Price Hughes the following year which marked the beginning of the Forward Movement. This was followed almost immediately by the work of F. Luke Wiseman and Samuel Chadwick in Birmingham and Leeds. The significance of the movement was that it combined personal evangelism with social reform. 'A social ministry of reformation which is at the same time a religious ministry of reconciliation', as I have seen it described. All this was a formative influence in my thinking, intensified by a similar, though more limited, development in Leicester, under the leadership of Joseph Posnett, assisted by a group of gifted ministers, of whom J. E. Rattenbury was one.

My first sight of the Wesleyan Methodist Conference was when my father took me to Nottingham on one of the days when the Conference was meeting in the Wesley Chapel, Broad Street. We sat in the gallery and heard a debate, the flavour of which has lingered with me through the years. Hugh Price Hughes was needing a permanent home for the West London Mission and had set his mind on a transformed Queen Street Chapel. Dinsdale T. Young was opposed to the idea of turning this grand old chapel into a modern mission hall. It was splendid speaking on both sides, but Hugh Price Hughes won the day and carried the Conference, though it was not until after his death that Kingsway Hall stood on the site of the old Queen Street Chapel.

The step that turned my way to the ministry was taken at the instance, I had almost said dictation, of one of our ministers whom I shall always remember with respect and affection. The Rev. George Harbottle was a man of virile mind and wonderful spirit. Otherwise he could not have sustained his ministry as he did against the background of domestic tragedy—the mental illness of his gifted wife. He gathered together a group of us in our late teens and formed a debating society. We had lively discussions, often on political issues, and I took a full part with growing interest and enjoyment. One day our leader said to me, 'Write me a sermon'. I protested that I did not know the first thing about such a business, but he would have none of it. As he insisted I had no alternative but to make the attempt, for none of us would have thought of refusing a request from one whom we so greatly respected. Ultimately the so-called sermon was written out and handed over. A few weeks later he said to me, 'You will be receiving a "Note to Preach" from the Superintendent,' and went on to explain that I should be appointed to go to one of the village churches with an experienced local preacher who would report on my effort. I thought this was going too far, for he had sought no permission from me, but once again there seemed to be no other course than to accept. The actual experience turned out quite different from what I had imagined. The moment of ascending the pulpit was terrifying, but once there I discovered an unexpected facility in declaring what I had so laboriously prepared. It was not at all a sense of self-confidence, but the feeling that here was something I could do if I would. I began to get the idea that I was committed to a new and surprising service from which there could be no turning back. It seemed that the insight of our friend and leader was justified.

The year 'On Trial' as a local preacher followed, concluding with an oral examination before the Local Preachers' Meeting. The Superintendent asked his young colleague, J. Ernest Rattenbury, to conduct the examination. I took the opportunity as President of the Conference, many years later, of acknowledging my indebtedness to Dr Rattenbury, but it was not that examination I had in mind. It was his inspiring preaching which fired me, and as I sat listening I became conscious of the call of God to me to be a preacher of the gospel. Doubtless, it is that early contact with Thomas Cooper, the old Chartist, that makes me remember Ernest Rattenbury's use, with tremendous force, of an incident just before the death of Thomas Cooper. He had been an avowed agnostic in his middle life and was fearful that people might say that he turned back to the Christian Faith in his dotage. He sent therefore for the Baptist minister, who recorded what followed. 'Yesterday,' said the old man, 'I worked through all the propositions in the First Book of Euclid, so my reasoning faculties are not imparied, are they? This morning I repeated the whole of the first part of Milton's *Paradise Lost*, so that my memory is not failing, is it?' Then, turning to the minister, he asked, 'Do I look like a person suffering from mental decay?' Being assured on all points, he raised himself up and declared, 'Then I testify that it is a faithful saying, and worthy of all acceptation, that Christ Jesus came into the world to save sinners.' Those who recall Ernest Rattenbury in his prime will know with what power and personal appeal he could and did use an incident like that from the life of the old Chartist.

The die was cast for me and I had before me the ordeal of a candidate for the Wesleyan Methodist Ministry. Looking back I realize that I must have worked pretty hard during those two years of preparation, for business life left all too little leisure. The Union for Biblical and Homiletic Study which pre-dated the present Study Centre was a great help, and I found, as I was writing, two prizes for theology and homiletics still on my shelves. Then I entered for the Local Preachers' Connexional Examination, and it was indeed a proud moment when I found my name included in the Honours List in the *Minutes of Conference for 1902*. The following year the *Minutes of Conference* contained my name as an accepted candidate for the ministry of the Wesleyan Methodist Church.

CHAPTER II

ON THE WAY

THE Conference of 1903 was held in Camborne, Cornwall, a part of the country with which I was to become very familiar a few years later. It was a deep satisfaction to hear from the Secretary that I had received the unanimous vote of the Conference. If not brilliantly, I had successfully passed the many tests lasting over some four months: written examinations, literary, biblical, theological; trial sermons; book lists; oral examinations before the Synod and the so-called July Committee. I was now 'On the Way'. There would be seven years to ordination, three of them in college, to which I hoped to go almost immediately. But a number of the accepted candidates were needed for a year of circuit work before going to college, and when the Conference concluded I learned that I was appointed to Jersey in the Channel Islands.

This year would count as one of the four years of probation, and it was not without some advantage, as it was possible to undertake certain reading and appointed studies in preparation for college. At the same time it was a test in itself to be lifted out of business life with little more than a months' notice and on the basis of spare-time study to face the duties and responsibilities of the full-time service of the Church. There was one valuable addition to my resources. In my last year at school I won an exhibition which had been wisely put aside to use, as intended, for some educational purpose. This made possible the acquirement of substantial additions to what I was beginning to call my library. It was an advantage thus early to have at hand the biblical and theological writings of Westcott, Lightfoot, Bruce, Fairbairn, and others. I am grateful for the wise advice I received in this connexion.

The journey to Jersey had a touch of adventure—at least that was my feeling during the night of sea-sickness when crossing the Channel in the old S.S. *Alberta*. I have never had such a dose since. Rupert Brooke knew what it was like when he wrote his sonnet on 'A Channel Passage', which begins, 'The damned ship lurched and slithered'. But the sun was shining when we reached St Helier. By then I had changed into a clerical collar and was prepared to sustain the dignity of the ministry with the clerical frock coat and silk hat included in my baggage. The superintendent minister who met me at the harbour was the Rev. J. A. Barrow-Clough. He was a grand man, a scholar of Trinity College, Dublin, and to me a real colleague and friend. As we drove along from the boat he pointed to the towering walls of Regent Fort and told me that some of my work would be with the Highland Light Infantry, who were stationed there. That did not help to reduce my preliminary fears to any extent. Everything was new and every experience without precedent. But the fears soon vanished through the unfailing kindness of everyone and the year on the lovely island was a rich and rewarding experience.

Methodism in the Channel Islands dates from the time of John Wesley. 1775 is the date of the earliest influence through laymen, but in 1787 John Wesley himself, then in his eighty-fourth year, visited Jersey. My appointment was to the English Circuit, with six churches. There were twenty-six in the French Circuit. In my time and for some years afterwards there was intense controversy between the traditionalists who clung to the French language and an increasing group who desired more use of English. I look back with real satisfaction to the fact that I brought together the Wesley Guilds at 'Grove Place Chapel', the head of the French Circuit, and 'Wesley Chapel', the head of the English Circuit, and organized with success the first Guild Rally held in the island. I still have the volumes of Hasting's *Dictionary of the Bible* presented to me as a joint gift from the Guilds of the French and English Circuits. This act of association across circuit and language boundaries was summarily suppressed a year later when a minister from the French Conference took over the superintendency of the French Circuit. But the traditionalists could not prevent the inevitable changes. The use of the French language gradually declined, and the German occupation during the Second World War led to its almost complete disappearance, except for the patois spoken in the remote farmsteads and hamlets. This is regrettable, but bilingualism is very difficult to maintain in the conditions of modern life. Today the whole of Methodism in the island is within one circuit, and I cherish the view that the first Guild Rally sixty years ago marked the beginning of the union now complete.

The Jersey people are rightly proud of being more English than the English, through their Norman lineage. On one occasion I was asked to introduce a minister from the Seamen's Mission in London to some of the prominent members in the French Circuit. He was seeking help for his special work. To the elect lady in one home he told an interesting story of the rescue of the crew of a French ship from both moral and physical disaster. Then he plunged straight into trouble as he said, 'This is very interesting, as it happened just before I was coming amongst French people.' I can still see that elderly lady as she rose to her feet with exquisite dignity and with scornful indignation reproved him for holding such an outrageous idea. Did he not know that Jersey was part of the old Norman dominion which conquered England? Was he not aware that the Jersey people were of the old Norman stock and not French at all? Could he not realize the insult he offered them when he called them French? Had he failed to understand that to speak French was one thing, but to be French quite another? I got him out of the house as quickly as possible, for there was no answer. He had committed the almost unpardonable sin against these kindly but proud folk.

Life on the island had many fascinating interests beyond the obvious opportunities for bathing, boating, and cycling round the lovely coast. These were the relaxations. In the course of the regular ministerial duties there were the attractions of the ancient forms and customs dating from Norman times and embodied in the government by the States, including the quaint voluntary police system. The simple Norman French was used for legal documents, including the Methodist Trust Deeds. The States Library was a boon for consultation and contained some show-pieces, including the very old polyglot Bible used by Dr Adam Clark when he was stationed on the island. What I recall with particular gratitude are the kindness of the people and the real friendships formed during that year. The boys' school in Charing Cross under Fred Ollivier and his gifted sister was for me a frequent place of call. He was a unique character and in constant demand as a preacher in French or English. A home I loved to visit in St Aubyns was kept by two elderly and charming sisters with the romantic Norman name of 'de Ste. Croix'. The circuit steward was Mr Davey, the head of the Oxenford House Boys' School. Every Quarterly Meeting he had my allowances ready in a pile of golden sovereigns—not a very large pile. So I might go on. All the people were not only kindly and friendly, but tolerant and even appreciative of the pulpit efforts of the raw probationer.

One of the boys in my Bible Class with whom I found common musical interests, Philip Syvret, became a lifelong friend. With him I paid my first visit to France before returning from Jersey. We spent an unforgettable night on the wonderful Mont St Michel. Arriving on the tiny island in the late evening, we enjoyed omelettes in the famous restaurant of Madame Poulard, and then the waiter with his paper lantern led us up the little narrow street to a building where we found the old French cupboard beds for our use. The following morning we went through the famous Abbey Church and refectory buildings. This is one of the finest examples of eleventh-century Gothic, with the glittering golden statue of St Michael surmounting the high central pinnacle.

I left Jersey with regret but anxious to begin the years of intensive study in college.

To my great satisfaction, I was given a place in Handsworth College, Birmingham. It would be invidious to compare the different Methodist college buildings. They were built at different periods and not all for their present purpose. Handsworth was designed for a Methodist College and opened in 1881. It is attractive because of its spaciousness and style. The campus is seventeen acres and the plan is an open quadrangle with modified Tudor architecture. Each student has two rooms —a study on the ground floor with a bedroom above. The modern study bedrooms have certain advantages, apart from economy, but I am satisfied that the two-room arrangement is much to be preferred. In my time the nearby Somerset Road Church served as the College Chapel, and so continued until the Jubilee extensions in 1932, when additional lecture-rooms, students' common-room, and a most beautiful Chapel linked up by cloisters were added. Some of my contemporaries of that 'year' which entered Handsworth in 1904 still remain in fairly active retirement. These include Douglas W. Lowis, who gained his London D.D. by a learned study in mediaeval Christianity, Francis B. James, well known for his devotional expository writings (both members of my 'Firm' as the college term has it), G. E. Hickman Johnson, for twenty-one years a missionary secretary, Albert J. Yorke (whose distinguished ministry was chiefly in the north of England) and Vavasor H. Griffiths, an experienced army chaplain. Edwin Finch, who served for fourteen years as Secretary of the Conference was a year our junior.

The Governor in 1904 was Dr Thomas Allen, an ex-President of the Wesleyan Methodist Conference and a man of fine presence and sterling quality, but failing in health in what was his last year. His successor was the Rev. Sylvester Whitehead, who had just completed his year as President of the Conference. He had served with distinction in China, but was entirely out of place in this new appointment. He had no understanding of a college community. When he was introduced to the whole College assembled in the Hall on the opening morning of the connexional year, he spoke of the evident laxness of discipline during Dr Allen's illness. This unexpected and astonishing statement was greeted by an emphatic 'No' like a pistol-shot from all the senior men. The new Governor could not realize that, while any of us were ready to commit a breach of regulations on occasion, there was an accepted and unwritten law that College discipline was rigidly observed when the Governor was ill. It was not easy for him to overcome that initial and serious mistake. Sylvester Whitehead was a memoriter preacher of the old school, much given to alliteration. I happen to recall part of a sentence from a well-travelled sermon on Joseph. It ran: 'The pit and the prison played their part in paving the path to the palace.'

Dr J. G. Tasker, President of the Wesleyan Methodist Conference in 1916 who was responsible for systematic theology, was a man we all revered, and for whom, as we came to know him, we acquired a real affection. When Mr Whitehead retired in 1910 and the office of Governor was abolished, Dr Tasker became the first Principal. The Rev. W. West Holdsworth came to lecture on New Testament language and literature and classics. He had spent seventeen years in similar service in India. The assistant tutor was J. Alexander Findlay, later to become one of the outstanding New Testament scholars. For all of us the predominant influence of the College centred in Dr W. F. Lofthouse, who, beginning in 1904, continued his distinguished service for Handsworth College until he retired as Principal in 1940. It is difficult to speak without seeming exaggeration, of his vitality, versatility, range of scholarship, and intense devotion. He was at first tutor in Old Testament language and literature and philosophy, but his actual range was even wider. I have often regretted not joining his class in German, which would have lessened the toil in more recent years to acquire some knowledge of the language for my many official visits to Germany. At the time I felt that Greek, Hebrew, and some Latin was as large a linguistic programme as I could well manage. In another field Dr Lofthouse was a pioneer. The churches were just beginning to wake up to their responsibility for social conditions. For the first time in any of our colleges we had the great advantage of a course of lectures from Dr Lofthouse on social history and economic theory. Sociology is now so much a recognized subject that it is difficult to realize the criticism that faced Dr Lofthouse from many of the Fathers of the Church. In their minds, sociology was only another word for socialism, and that surely was of the Devil. It was about this time that the Union for Social Service was started with that courageous man, the Rev. Samuel E. Keeble, as President, and W. F. Lofthouse as Secretary. It took its place with the Christian Social Union of the Church of England and similar societies in the other Churches. Very much resulted from this beginning—our Methodist Christian Citizenship Department, COPEC, the British Council of Churches, and in a sense the whole Life and Work movement. Dr Lofthouse was President of the Wesleyan Methodist Conference in 1929.

On his ninetieth birthday many of his old students and friends entertained Dr Lofthouse at a luncheon and presented him with a book containing several hundreds of signatures from his one-time students. The inscription of that book perhaps sums up as far as words can our thoughts concerning one who meant so much to us all. Addressed to Dr W. F. Lofthouse, it says, *inter alia*: 'The consistency of your devotion: the unstinted giving of your scholarship: the courage of your application of the truth; and your concern for and comradeship with the least gifted of your students have all left their mark upon the lives and service of those who have had the privilege of knowing you as tutor and friend. The influence of your dedicated life has pointed the Way of the Lord to so many.'

Those who had the privilege of knowing Mrs Lofthouse will not forget her grace and charm, nor the contribution she made to the life of the College.

Handsworth College has been served through the years by a succession of Principals and Tutors of notable scholarship. It will be understood if by way of tribute, I mention a later one of that number who in a rather special way became a personal friend. Wilbert F. Howard retired as Principal in 1951 after some thirty years service. He was a New Testament scholar with an international reputation, a trusted Methodist statesman who had influence in ecumenical Methodism, President of the Conference in 1944 and one of the few to secure the distinction of F.B.A.

In the American theological seminaries there is an arrangement of student-pastors under which a student gives three days a week to the pastoral care of a small church. Nothing of that sort is found in our British Methodist colleges. The whole time is given to college work, but on Sundays there are preaching engagements in the churches of the surrounding district. Often two Sundays out of three are occupied in this way. On one such occasion, when I was preaching at the King Street Chapel, Dudley, I made a most valuable discovery. When I came to prepare myself for the evening service, I found that I had accidentally left behind in my study at the College both manuscript and notes of the new sermon I had been preparing. This looked like sheer disaster. However, I went over in my mind the main points of my sermon and faced the congregation without any paper support. To my surprise, I found that I was maintaining a closer contact with the congregation and communicating the message more effectively than if I had been depending upon my notes or reading from the full script. That experience determined for me my future practice. For more than the fifteen years Phillips Brookes, in his well-known lectures on preaching, advised preachers to write out their sermons fully. I wrote out every word. Then I left it all behind when I went into the pulpit. I would not suggest that this is necessarily the right course for everyone, but, if I mistake not, there is far too much reading of sermons or the slavery of notes even in Methodist pulpits. When writing has clarified the thought, the preacher ought to be able to deliver the Word in crisper sentences than in any attempted reproduction of the written style. Whatever one may say, the script or the elaborate notes constitute a barrier between the speaker and the hearers. If preaching is, as has been said, 'truth through personality', then the personality needs to be set free from every kind of bondage.

Before I left College I burnt all my sermons beyond the one or two most recently made. There was quite an accumulation from my days as a local preacher and the regular preaching in Jersey. I had the feeling that if I was to make good I must start afresh with the advantage of the background of the years of study. So they went into the furnace. I was undoubtedly right in recognizing that preaching must be contemporary, not in its shallow catch-words, but in its definite and courageous application of the truth. If we had not discovered it before, the experience of two world wars has taught us how completely dead old sermons can be.

Free Sundays in a city like Birmingham gave us opportunities of hearing other preachers. At Six Ways Baptist Church we sometimes heard Samuel W. Hughes before he went to join and ultimately follow Dr John Clifford at Westbourne Park Church, London, and still later to become Secretary of the Free Church Federal Council. As I said when speaking at the memorial service after his death: 'We were interested in his Johnsonian language, so characteristic of him throughout the years, but much more in the vitality, sincerity, and deep conviction conveyed by the man and his message.' Our chief pilgrimage was to Carrs Lane Chapel to hear that prince of preachers, Dr J. H. Jowett. He seemed to deny by his practice all that I have been saying, for he read every word with studied effect. And yet the occasion I remember most vividly was when, putting aside his prepared sermon, he brought a letter into the pulpit and used the moving story of the letter as the basis of a powerful exposition and appeal. We were glad to walk the nearly four miles each way on those Sunday mornings, and not the least valuable of those occasions were the discussions on the sermon as we walked back. Occasionally we went to hear Luke Wiseman at the Central Hall, always to admire his command over that great congregation and his skill in conducting the choir. One characteristic incident lingers in my mind. He was using the story of the war between Rome and Carthage to illustrate a point in his sermon. With dramatic force, he strode the platform declaiming, *'Carthago delenda est.'* The congregation had not a clue as to its meaning, but it sounded effective. I little thought that twenty years on I should be in his place.

There is much more to college life than lectures and study and preaching. There was great value in the community life, with its personal contrasts of background and experience, sometimes even with the clash of personality. Out of it came those more intimate friendships which were of abiding value. In my view, the ragging—and it was pretty severe in my time—is worthwhile. We learned to take it without resentment. I doubt very much whether the exclusion of competition between the junior and senior years and the virtual absence of ragging, especially of the first year, is really an improvement. Over-softness does not develop character or personality. Sport had its place, though I was never a sportsman. Occasional tennis and racquets satisfied me. We had an excellent football team, but the rest of us were required to turn out from time to time for purely College games, often between the years. Rumour has it that I scored a goal on one occasion, but I doubt it. It must have been an accident.

The Cassowary, the College magazine, was started in my time, with Francis B. James, the College Chairman, as editor. My task was to report the proceedings of the Literary and Debating Society, of which I was Secretary. The reference in the first issue to the opening concert includes this comment: 'The orchestra revealed finer technique and increased power. Though one of the youngest of the College institutions, it is always appreciated—except when rehearsing.' If I wrote that, as I probably did, I was giving a little boost to one of my own contributions to the life of the College. I started this little string orchestra and played or conducted as occasion demanded.

One incident gives me the opportunity to pay a tribute to the domestic staff, to whom we owed so much. On returning after the Christmas vacation, 1904-5, we had to walk from Handsworth Wood Station in thick snow, and did not look forward with any pleasure to our cold studies. Then, and for many years afterwards, coal was delivered to each study and we were responsible for lighting and maintaining our own fires. Judge of our intense pleasure when we arrived at the College and found that the maids had been round and lighted a blazing fire in each one of the nearly seventy studies.

One aspect of College life, and that the most important, cannot easily be described. In a theological college particularly, the devotional life could easily become formal or even artificial. On the contrary, to me—and I think to most, if not all of us —the daily prayers, the weekly preaching service, the Quiet Day each term, the Friday evening Class Meeting, all had a refreshing quality which was spiritually stimulating. The brief opening prayers in the lecture-rooms kept the main purpose of our work clearly in mind. The still more intimate occasions with our own friends in our studies were an important part of that devotional life.

It has been to me a great privilege to be associated with the College through subsequent years—to be a member of the College Committee, to have served as one of the official visitors, to enjoy the friendship of the Principal and Tutors and to be given the right of 'Tables', from time to time, by the College as a whole.

The first appointment after college had an important difference from that pre-collegiate year. One was still a probationer, but it meant the beginning in a definite way of the work to which we were committed. I thought the Governor knew my desire for central mission work or work in a city circuit. When I knew that I was being sent to Helston in the far west of Cornwall my spirits fell. This was frustration indeed.

What could I do in a scattered farming country when I was completely town-bred? When the circuit plan arrived my depression deepened. Seventeen churches distributed over an area stretching down beyond the wild Goonhilly Downs to the Lizard Point, northward halfway to Camborne and eastward toward Falmouth. Three, often four, and sometimes five services between Sundays in different villages, with up to a hundred miles travel in a week by horse and trap or push-bike. What opportunity for concentrated work or study with a weekly routine of this kind? A probationer has to carry further his college work on stated lines, with reading and examinations. Ordination depends upon successful reports. For me it meant parts of the Old Testament in Hebrew and New Testament in Greek, with essays on church history, theology or philosophy and the presentation of a book-list showing fairly wide reading. What a prospect! Yet it was probably the best thing that could have happened to me.

I was so appointed, and I am thankful to remember that I managed to leave all signs of depression behind when I met my new colleagues and the good folk at Helston. The express carried me from London to Plymouth, and then came the tortuous line passing the more populous parts of Cornwall, St Austell, Truro, Redruth, and Camborne. At last I detrained at the seemingly deserted frontier station of Gwinear Road, from whence the little branch railway carried me through Nancegollan to Helston. This ancient borough, with a population of some 4,000, has a Mayor and Corporation, and once returned two Members to Parliament. It was—and I presume still is—a sort of capital and market centre for the Meneage district, which stretches eleven miles south to the Lizard. Three things remind one of the ancient character of the little town. One is the name of the main street, where I lived—Coinage Hall Street, which carries our thoughts back to the days of tin-mining, it being a stannary town. Another is the sound of water running down the 'kennels' on both sides of the street. This is the constant accompaniment to the life of the town, and is said to be due to the arrangement made by the monks of long ago. The third is the traditional celebration of Flora Day on 8th May, with the 'Furry Dance', which is an undoubted survival of a primitive spring festival.

I had most excellent rooms, a study and bedroom, on the second floor of a large house belonging to two cultured spinster ladies. Once they conducted a preparatory school in the house, but now rooms were let to a member of the staff of the secondary school and myself. We had meals together in the dining-room on the ground floor, and I had the use of the drawing-room, with its piano, on the first floor. Probationers today will be amazed to learn that for this excellent accommodation, including meals and laundry, I paid £1 sterling per week. Of course, I received only the recognized minimum for probationers of £80 a year.

The outstanding event in my remembrance of the beginning of my work is the first drive out to a village service. The horse and conveyance would be brought to my door immediately after lunch and I would have to drive up through the town to collect my colleagues. Hitherto horses had no place in my life, but I disliked intensely the idea of looking the novice I knew myself to be. Fortunately, I found an article on horses in an encyclopedia, with illustrations of driving—the very thing I wanted. With a piece of string, I practised the correct way of holding the reins and handling the whip when driving. When we set off I felt sure the horse knew what to do and I could concentrate on preserving the correct style with the reins. My colleagues made no comment, and the day passed uneventfully. The sequel came later. I was out for supper one evening and introduced to the wife of the Borough Surveyor, who belonged to one of the other Methodist churches. She said, 'Oh, I have seen you before,' and noting my surprise went on to explain. 'I was looking out for you on your first drive out, as you had to pass our house. I wanted to see what the new minister looked like.' 'Well,' I said, 'I hope the verdict was favourable.' 'Oh quite,' she said seriously, 'I said to my husband that you would be all right, as you knew how to drive.'

As the days passed I acquired a reputation as a furious driver, which was largely based on another incident. The man from whom we hired the outfit had bought another horse, which was a real high-stepper until tamed down by hard work. I was out with this fresh horse and supposed to pick up the Superintendent on my return from a village further away. He was not to be seen at the appointed place, and I went along the next morning to enquire about him. 'You want to know where I was last night?' he asked indignantly. 'When I heard you coming along like a fire-engine, I got into the hedge out of harm's way.' He wanted to make out that the horse was running away with me. Actually, I was enjoying myself driving an animal with some life. That horse could travel.

It was our invariable custom, whether driving or cycling, to leave town immediately after lunch, and reach the village with three or even four hours for visiting before the evening service. Thus we came to know our people in their homes. This pastoral duty was not easy, with the scattered farmsteads, but it was vital to the success of our work. The advent of the motor-car and motor-cycle has made travel easier but not always to the advantage of rural work. There is such a temptation to dash out in time for the service and back immediately afterwards. That is fatal to Methodist ministry amongst the rural communities. I was trained, as all probationers should be, by both the example and the precept of my senior colleagues.

In those early years I learned that part of the distinctive genius of Methodism lies in the circuit system with the grouping together of town and village churches. The demand for concentration is understandable, and I had sufficient experience of it in later years to know its value. But for the minister there are opportunities of a different but equally valuable kind in the travelling ministry of a country circuit. I soon found that the point to avoid is that of being a slave to the inevitable and necessary routine. I could have managed very well with one new sermon each fortnight, but I saw the mistake of that and resolved that I would never preach a formal sermon at the week-night services. Instead, I would take Bible studies of a different form. This sometimes had surprising results. At one period I was taking a series of studies of the Minor Prophets. A tall, well-known farmer stopped me in the street one day, and said, 'I was not at the service you conducted at Cury on Tuesday, but if I had been I should have walked out.' 'Yes,' I said, 'I noticed your absence, but why ever would you have walked out?' 'You were using the pulpit to advocate small-holdings,' he replied. It was the time when Lloyd George's land reforms were under acute discussion. I denied his assertion and explained that I was expounding the message of the Prophet

Micah, which I advised him to read. Then I added, 'If you or your friends can tell me of anything I said which was not a proper comment on the word of Micah I will make a public apology.' I heard no more about it, but I do not suppose that he was convinced.

The opportunity for a special piece of work was not to be resisted. On Saturdays the country people flocked into Helston, the farmers and their womenfolk travelling behind their own horses, and the others in the horse-drawn buses. By about five o'clock there were crowds of men standing around waiting for the women to finish their shopping, ready to leave at six o'clock. What an opportunity for open-air meetings! It had to be a lonely venture, but I took the risk of announcing a series of meetings at five o'clock during the summer. They were really lectures on stated subjects, followed by questions. During the three summers I was in Helston I spoke on the theology of the Gospel, the social teaching of the New Testament and its implications and on many other themes related to Christian life and work. They were certainly an attentive audience. I suppose it was intended as a compliment when one man said to me, 'I do like to hear a good talker: I don't mind much what he's talking about.' There were one or two slight brushes with the police for causing obstruction, which added to the interest. The meetings were evidently successful, though it was impossible to assess their permanent value. Many years afterwards, when in Cornwall, I heard references to them. For me it was an invaluable experience. I learnt many things about open-air work which stood me in great stead when I had to undertake more exacting tasks of this kind. I have often wondered why none of my successors, as far as I know, made use of this unique opportunity.

Few people in these days have had the experience of an old-fashioned Cornish revival. Unless I am seriously mistaken, they have practically died out in the Cornish Methodism of the mid-twentieth century. There was one such revival in the Helston Circuit in my time. It occurred in a scattered village with an old, gaunt, stone chapel very unattractive and poorly attended. A general decision had been taken to close the chapel. One loyal family started prayer meetings in their home. They were soon transferred to the chapel, and with increasing numbers went on every night for eight weeks. The building was generally quite full, and the intense emotionalism very trying to a person like myself. No one conducted these meetings except on the occasions when one of the ministers was present. Almost one hundred conversions were recorded. The people came from a wide area, and many of the genuine converts would be connected with other churches. The remarkable thing to me was that within our own circuit five local preachers came out of that revival. Here was another task. I started a Bible study class for these and other young preachers in particular. It had to be held on Saturday night, which was the only free night available. It ran through the greater part of one year and certainly started these young recruits on sound lines.

The Superintendent asked me to conduct a ten days' mission in Helston, and I agreed on condition that I conducted it on my own lines. It was to be a teaching mission and I had an immediate objective in the senior boys of the Boys Brigade Company, with which I was closely connected. On the first week-night a group of the old stalwarts came up to the front ready to take charge in the old, familiar way. They found no such opportunity, and in the midst of the service four or five of them stamped out of the church in disgust. I took no notice and never referred to it afterwards—nor did they. The mission served its purpose in bringing to definite decision a group of young men, some of whom proved to be a strength to the church in following years.

Some of these old-fashioned men were wonderful characters, and I could only wish that our more liberal ideas and modern methods produced results of similar quality though in different form. One could only endure their rigidity and ofttimes intolerance in silence and with understanding of their sincerity. But they were not all like that, old-fashioned as they might be. One whom I remember with real affection was a true 'father in Israel'. He was a class leader, and it was always a pleasure to visit his class. He and his wife lived in a tiny cottage, which they had made most attractive. The gracious lady would talk about their family with justifiable pride. How had they done it when he had never received in his life wages in excess of 15*s.* a week? What a condemnation of our social and economic system at that time. The secret of their triumph was to be found in their love, their abstinence, their thrift, and above all their robust Christian faith. What so many have failed to realize in these later days is that no amount of money is a substitute for those virtues and that faith.

There were many interests in Cornish life in addition to Cornish cream, Cornish pasties, and saffron cake. A political election had some of the old flavour about it in which I delighted. Then I played hockey for the town team—a fact more surprising to me than to anyone. The May Synods were more leisurely than is customary today and included such items, not on the agenda, as a coach-trip from Penzance to Land's End and a boat-trip up the River Fal. Cornwall holds some very happy musical memories for me, particularly associated with my oft-repeated lecture on Handel. One of my special friends, the Captain of the Boys' Brigade Company, had a passable tenor voice well up to some of the oratorio solos. The bass soloist in the choir was extraordinarily good. He was a bootmaker and made me the best pair of boots I ever had, made to measure and hand-sewn for 18s. The bandmaster of the Boys' Brigade Company was an excellent cornet-player and accustomed to play with the organ at the regular services. Here was almost ideal material to illustrate the lecture. These three accompanied me on many occasions in the villages and even to Penzance and the West Cornwall College. The illustrations included 'The trumpet shall sound' from *Messiah* and 'Sound an alarm' from *Judas Maccabaeus*, with the trumpet obligatos. We included the dramatic duet from *Samson*, 'Go, baffled coward, go', and other excerpts. In addition to lecturing, I accompanied and played some movements from Handel's harpsichord suites. It was a very popular event and gave us great pleasure. We enjoyed driving out together, and there were no complaints about my furious driving.

At the District Synod in Bodmin in 1910 I preached the required trial sermon, prior to ordination, at the uncomfortable hour of 7 a.m. The trial sermon remains for all ordinands, but a kinder age has revised the time. I received from the Synod a unanimous recommendation for ordination at the forthcoming Conference in July. From Helston friends I received quite a few presents, mostly related to another event, which was due to follow shortly after ordination.

It may appear strange to some that I count myself fortunate to have had these three years in Cornwall. The feelings of disappointment and frustration which possessed me when I first heard of the appointment seem very foolish in the light of experience. I was beginning to learn something about the wonder of the guidance of God, if we are prepared to follow. These three years served to establish health, to extend and test available resources, to open up hitherto unknown possibilities of service and to mature and balance personal judgement. I had in truth come a considerable distance 'on the way' and now new tasks and new experiences awaited me.

CHAPTER III

ORDINATION AND CIRCUIT APPOINTMENTS

I WAS ordained in the Carlisle Road Wesleyan Methodist Church, Manningham, Bradford, during the morning of the last day of the Ministerial Session of the Wesleyan Methodist Conference, which was assembled in Bradford in 1910. It followed the reception into the full order of the ministry by the solemn standing vote of the Conference. There were sixty-five ordinands that year and the service lasted well over three hours. According to the Constitution, the President of the Conference, the Rev. John Hornabrook, conducted the service, and the charge was given by the immediate Ex-President, the Rev. William Perkins—a friend, but not a relative of mine. Other ministers joined the President in the imposition of hands.

This is the form of ordination today, with incidental changes consequent upon the Union in 1932. It is the whole Methodist Church in this country participating through its representatives in the ordination of each of its ministers. It is a part of the universal Church of Jesus Christ giving to each ordinand 'authority to fulfil the office of a minister in the Church of Christ'. Speaking in the name of the whole Church, the President, or one of the Ex-Presidents, makes this solemn declaration, 'In the Name of our Lord Jesus Christ, the only head of the Church, I hereby declare you to be ordained to the office of the Holy Ministry.' It is necessary and important to realize that in any working out of deeper and wider unity there cannot rightly be any denial nor repudiation of this ordination.

For good or ill, the regulations in regard to marriage have been so relaxed as almost to disappear. In my day there could be no marriage until after ordination, except by special permission, which was given reluctantly and only on the ground of unusual circumstances. I should be prepared to argue that we have lost something as a Church through the almost complete absence in these days of the celibate and flexible ministry of unmarried probationers. I fear that it would be an unpopular argument.

My bride was the daughter of Mr and Mrs Arthur J. Bull of Leicester, and our wedding took place in the Saxe Coburg Street Wesleyan Methodist Church, to which the family belonged. As in my own case, my wife's Methodist ancestry goes back four generations. Her forebears came from the Isle of Wight and were associated with the introduction of Methodism into the island. I should find it very hard to say when I first met my wife. There was some association between her parents and mine, but a closer contact was through relatives on the Benson side, who were members of the same church and friendly, especially the young people, with my future wife and her sister. Christmas parties linger in my memory as having something to do with the beginning of things. Elsie Bull took a noticeable place in the church life and was leader of a fine class of girls, the members of which scattered rose petals as we left the church after the wedding ceremony. Like my sister, my wife is an old girl of the Wyggeston School.

The church where we were married no longer exists, having achieved the distinction of being the only church in Leicester destroyed during the war. The fellowship continues in a fine new structure further out from the centre of the city.

The Wesleyan Methodist Conference confirmed the invitation I had received to the Sheffield, Ellesmere Road, Circuit, and by the first Sunday in September we were settled in our new home in the Yorkshire city. Sheffield is a city with distinctive characteristics which my wife and I came to appreciate, not only during the three years of this first appointment, but twenty-five years later, when I was appointed to the superintendency of the Sheffield Mission, with its centre at the Victoria Hall, and Chairman of the District. Sheffield is noted throughout the world for its cutlery and plate. These industries were originally carried on largely in homes and tiny factories along the mill streams in the valleys. The city had the feeling of maintaining something of the advantages of village life, where everyone knows everyone else. We appreciated greatly the friendliness and equally the outspokenness of the people.

The city today is less insular than it was, and even the Sheffield dialect, which is different from that of West Yorkshire, is fast disappearing. Within the city boundaries there are amazing contrasts. On the eastern side, in a valley running out towards Rotherham, are the great furnaces and rolling mills of the heavy steel industries. This development dates from the first half of the nineteenth century, and unfortunately included some of the worst features of the Industrial Revolution. Keir Hardie must have been seeing the quite amazing sight of the furnaces at night when travelling through the east side by train when he said, 'If the entrance to Hell is anything like the entrance to Sheffield by way of Attercliffe and Brightside I have great sympathy with the Devil.' My work was located in that area. On the western side hardly any city has more beautiful country within its borders, and stretching out to the glory of the Derbyshire moors and hills. We found relief and exercise when we took the tram to the terminus and walked on along the Rivelin Ridge to the old Roman road leading to Stanage Edge and round by Fox House. By the time of our second period in Sheffield we had degenerated and travelled by car, which certainly had the advantage of taking us still further into the glories of Derbyshire.

The Methodist Church has from the earliest days been strong and extensive in Sheffield. This applies to all the branches prior to the Union of 1932. It still comprises the greater part of the Free Church life of the city. The Bishop of Middleton, writing as a result of his experience as industrial missioner in the Sheffield Diocese,[1] describes the Methodist Church as only drawing to a small extent from the industrial population up to the turn of this century. Unfortunately, he makes no reference to the more recent development in the establishment of the Sheffield Mission and the building of the Victoria Hall. But this fine work did not make any real impact on the great East End area, where lived in my time a quarter of the population of the city. I was faced with the virtual religious desolation of that district. There were twenty-five Wesleyan Methodist ministers in Sheffield when we went there, and only two of them, myself and another, in an adjoining circuit, appointed to this quarter of the population and attempting to deal with

[1] E. R. Wickham, *Church and People in an Industrial City*, Lutterworth Press.

an appalling situation. The few Anglican and other Free Churches in that area were in a like state. I found that I was appointed one of the two secretaries of a commission set up by the District Synod to work out constructive proposals. When the Rev. John Hornabrook, General Secretary of the Chapel Department, met the commission after visiting the area and examining the facts, he said that no problem he had been called upon to consider had left him with a greater sense of depression. All that the commission could do immediately was to provide my colleague and myself with deaconess assistants. Later, steps were taken in various ways to meet the situation. It is almost impossible, however, to overtake the inaction of half a century.

I was in pastoral charge of three churches, with a deaconess working with me at the largest of the three, which was placed at the point of acute difficulty. When I have been asked to speak about the experience of those three years, I have felt that the only appropriate title was 'Apparent Failure'. We were surrounded with the social problems which impinged upon the church work and seemed to defy solution. These external conditions were bad housing, overcrowding, low wages and a total absence of all that we know today in the provisions of the Welfare State. The results were a debased moral standard, sexual vice, wife-desertion, suicide, and attempted murder. When I have spoken of these things with personal stories, I know that I have been accused of exaggeration. But that was the setting of our work. Of course, this was not the whole story. We were able to secure a response to our appeal from within a limited fragment of the population. During those three years, and in the three churches in my pastoral care I received 150 new members. At one we had a splendid Boys' Brigade Company; at another my wife's class of girls achieved a lasting work. But with all this encouragement there was the colossal background of entrenched evil.

One illustration will suggest the task confronting us when we tried to break into this immense problem outside the limited fellowship of the church. The deaconess working with me found a number of girls who were employed searching the middens and refuse-heaps. They had lost whatever self-respect they may have had, and no religious influences of any sort had touched them. Many were under police supervision, and so bad were their characters that if accused of any offence their guilt was at once assumed. No church had made any attempt whatever to reach them. The ordinary artisans looked down upon them as almost untouchables. The deaconess gathered a number of these girls together in a club on our premises. Some of the women workers of our church volunteered to help, but only went once. They were thoroughly frightened of these rough, vulgar, uninhibited girls. The deaconess had not only the difficult task of running the club, but of protecting the girls afterwards from those who would victimize them. With great courage and patience, the deaconess certainly made a beginning during those years towards a better state of things.

In February 1912 the great coal strike began. Practically every mine in the country was closed, and over a million miners laid down their picks. The principle involved was the reasonable demand that every miner, including those working on a poor seam under difficulties, should be assured of a minimum wage. By April that principle was embodied in the Coal Mines (Minimum Wage) Act, 1912. Our experience in the East End of Sheffield was not with the miners directly, but with the steel-workers who were thrown out of work through absence of the necessary coal. These labourers were receiving a wage of 21*s*. a week. They could have no reserve and by the second week were starving. We provided soup kitchens and bread distribution. It was an unforgettable experience to distribute loaves of bread to starving men with the knowledge of the conditions of their wives and children. I stopped a member of our Brotherhood whom I knew and asked how he was getting on, with a view to helping him. He was a fine type with a clean home in that overcrowded area. He broke down as I talked to him. They had had no food the previous day and he had walked the streets because he could not bear to see the sufferings of his wife and child. It is one of the tragic facts of our social history that mine-owners and steel companies had to be forced by Act of Parliament to grant elementary justice to their workers.

The definite line I felt compelled to take on these issues of social and personal life was by no means popular with everyone. How thankful I was and always have been for our Methodist polity whereby the minister is appointed by the Conference and is not the appointee (I had almost said the servant) of the local congregation or church court. I had authority to act which none could gainsay, however much they might disagree with my judgement. The Methodist polity is based on the democracy of the whole instead of the dictatorship of the local group. But how splendidly I was supported by some of the finest characters I have ever known, who were bearing a courageous witness in home and workshop in face of much opposition. They were by no means educated men, but they had the Grace of God in their hearts. At an open-air meeting I heard one of the best of them declare, 'As David the Psalmist says, The proof of the pudding is in the (h)eating thereof, O taste and see that the Lord is good.'

I started a class for the study of sociology, and one session we worked through the massive report of the Royal Commission on the Poor Law, which was the basis of revolutionary action in following years. One of the regular members was a tram-conductor. I recognized his quite remarkable mental calibre and advised him to enter public life if the opportunity occurred. He took my advice, and the way opened through his trade union. When I returned to Sheffield more than twenty years later he was Lord Mayor of the city.

It was here in the East End of Sheffield that I came face to face with the ramifications of gambling, not realizing to how great an extent it would occupy my thought and action in years to come. I found it impossible to avoid the challenge of this evil thing. One day I was attending the police Court in the interest of one of our members and heard another case which preceded the one in which I was concerned. A young man was charged with failing to support his wife and two young children. He was receiving a good wage for those days, but had provided no home and given his wife a mere pittance only. The evidence showed that he was neither a drinker nor a smoker but absolutely absorbed in gambling. He remained quite unmoved by the words spoken to him in the Court and showed no sign of any regret. As Joseph Conrad says of a character in one of his stories, gambling was just 'eating him up'.

Late one Sunday night I was stopped in the street by a man whom I had met previously. He spoke of acute difficulty

*Candidate for the Ministry
1903*

*Ordination
1910*

*Chaplain to the Forces
1914*

*Sheffield Telegraph & Star
1936*

The Study—Birmingham, 1925-35

The Family—Birmingham, 1933

and I went along to his house. He worked on the tram track, receiving 21s. a week, with half kept in arrears, according to custom. Behind with the rent, he heard of a 'dead cert' on a forthcoming race-meeting and threw up his job so as to put the half-week's pay on this horse. That was his tale, and, of course, he lost his money and his job. Would I write to his firm, explain that he was in urgent need of the money and ask for his job to be given back? They feared being turned out of the house. There was another problem, for on the table was a pint glass full of ale. I began there and pointed out that if he was going to reform he would have to give up the public house and the drink as well as the gambling. At that stage he was ready to promise anything, and I said that I would begin. I threw that pint of ale into the street, almost expecting to have to follow it. I wrote to his firm, but not his sort of letter. That failed of its purpose, but I got him another job.

Personal cases of this kind were a frequent occurrence and something had to be done. I announced three addresses on gambling at the Brotherhood, and then found how limited and ineffective was merely book knowledge. If I was going to reach these men, I must get close to the problem and know as much about it as they did. Amongst other lines of enquiry and investigation, I set in operation statistical research into the forms and extent of gambling amongst the steel-workers. Through those I knew in different works and various departments I was able to secure confidential information. The results were startling. The overall figure was 81 per cent. regularly gambling in one form or another. The highest return for any one department was over 90 per cent., while the lowest did not fall below 65 per cent. More than half were regularly betting on horse-racing, while the rest, in addition to occasional bets on horse-racing, were betting on football by fixed odds through the bookmakers and participating in the frequent sweepstakes and gaming.

When I had tested the facts and figures, I secured a full column in the *Sheffield Independent*, with editorial comment. Then the armchair critics got going and I was vigorously attacked. My friend, the Rev. George H. McNeal, at the Victoria Hall, wrote to me fearing I had laid myself open to a humiliating exposure. He indicated, however, that he was testing my figures, and he soon found to his astonishment that they were well within the truth. Then he was ready to co-operate in a bold attack through meetings in the Victoria Hall and articles in the Press. For me it was the beginning of complete and scientific research into the whole problem, and I shall have occasion to refer to its place in my continued ministry.

Absorbing as the work was, and often depressing, relief was possible and necessary. How great a mistake it is to allow oneself to become stale through over-concentration even on one's primary task. During the slightly less exacting summer months I spent some hours every week in the University library. I was particularly interested in the study of the fourteenth century, which marked the beginning of modern England with the emergence of the labour movement. There were great figures in that century, John Wycliffe, Geoffrey Chaucer, William Langland, and it was the latter who attracted me. He might be the last of the old Middle English poets, but he had an amazingly modern outlook as he viewed the social conditions and recognized the Christian condemnation of so much in the customs and practices of his time. All this comes out in his massive poem, *The Vision concerning Piers the Plowman*, and it may well be that his songs inspired the social movement of that century. I could not fail to be interested in the fact that the name 'Piers' is a contraction of 'Peterkin', which in another contraction appears in the poem as 'Perkins'. I often lectured on the poem at that time under the title 'The Plowman Christ', and my wife declares that in those years I never preached a sermon without quoting Langland. That is a wifely exaggeration, but who could desist from some quotation? Here are a few lines in modern English from the message of 'Long Will' as he was often called:

> *'For our joy and our health, Jesus Christ of Heaven,*
> *In a poor man's apparel pursueth us ever,*
> *And looketh upon us in their likeness, and that with lovely cheer.*
> *To know us by our kind hearts and casting of our eyes,*
> *Whether we love the lords here before the Lord of bliss.*
> *For all we are Christ's creatures and of His coffers rich,*
> *And brethren as of one blood, as well beggars as earls.'*

Another relief came through music. Sheffield is one of the cities where choral music is a chief delight. Sir Henry Coward did much to cultivate that. One might almost come to believe that Handel wrote *Messiah* especially for Sheffield. A small choir and a few very amateur instrumentalists were rehearsing this oratorio in the smallest chapel in our circuit. I said to the conductor, 'Don't you think it would be a good idea to take a simple cantata first and then come on to the oratorio later?' 'Ah no,' he said; 'we'll tak t'*Messiah* fust and then we'll cum on to summat else.' They were all sure that they knew everything there was to know about *Messiah*, and most choir members could sing their parts in the more familiar choruses from memory. I enjoyed taking part in choral music, but it was a different musical experience that I particularly remember with pleasure. We had in Sheffield during those three years a ministers' piano quartette, and provided a substantial section each year of the ministers' concert at the Victoria Hall. The quartette consisted of Valentine Ward Pearson, Principal of Wesley College, Rutland Spooner, Superintendent of Carver Street Circuit, A. J. G. Seaton, junior minister at the Sheffield Mission, and myself. We rehearsed in the studio and under the direction of Miss Lily Foxon, an outstanding musical figure in the city. It was invaluable teaching and great fun. She found evident delight in having four ministers under her dictation. During the three years we played a number of the great classics in this field. I am inclined to think this was unique, for I have not heard of another ministerial pianoforte quartette.

With the three years' system operating at that time I had accepted an invitation to the Wakefield Circuit. Five churches in Wakefield city and five village churches comprised the circuit, with four ministers. My particular charge was an attractive church opened in 1902 in Outwood, a suburb of Wakefield, and known as St John's. I had two village churches also under my charge. It was a happy pastorate and in some measure a respite from the three strenuous years in Sheffield. Less than a year after coming to Wakefield, war was declared, and in a few weeks I was in uniform, beginning a limited period of chaplaincy service. I never felt that Army work was my particular *forte*, but we were all anxious to do our part as far as we could in the difficult circumstances. The position of a temporary full-time chaplain had not been ordered and organized at that time, as it was later, and many of the details, especially regarding Wesleyan and other Free Church chaplains, had to be improvised. Even certain of our allowances were only discovered after considerable search.

I was gazetted to a West Riding Brigade, particularly for the organizing of social services. At that early period of the war many of the Regular Army customs were still being observed, and I was quickly faced with the temptation which has led to the sad downfall of chaplains as well as many in all other ranks. On my first attendance at the Mess, the Colonel invited me to sit by his side. As the dinner proceeded the waiter came round with a seemingly official request that hardly permitted of a refusal. 'Will you take port, sir, with Captain X?' The Colonel turned and explained to me that it was the custom in the Mess for any officer who became engaged to be married to treat the Mess to port wine. My decision had to be taken immediately, and I claim no credit for taking the only course my training made possible. Within the hearing of the Colonel, I said to the waiter, 'Will you please give my compliments to Captain X and say that I wish him all the best, but that I am sure he will allow me to drink his health in water?' How easy, under those circumstances, to find oneself committed to a course that has possible disaster in its train.

The formal parade service is now a thing of the past, but I wonder whether it has been relinquished too easily. Everyone says that the present voluntary system, with Chaplain's Hours, Moral Leadership Courses, and the like, is a great advance. Perhaps so, but the parade services I conducted in those early days of the war were a real inspiration. I had under my influence some 700 men, mostly Yorkshire miners, and how they could sing. One story related to those parade services must be told.

A draft was pushing off to the front line, and a man came to see me for what was his first and proved to be his last talk with me. He told me of his home in a Yorkshire city, of his father who was an agnostic, and of his boyhood and youth, from which all religious influences and associations were rigidly excluded. When he joined up, as was required at that time, he had to have a religion, and as his chum was 'Wesleyan' he had himself put down under the same heading, though he did not know a thing about it. The parade services he had to attend were the first religious services he had ever known. He went on to tell me of the extraordinary effect they had upon him. First, that there was clearly something in this religion after all. Then that these men had got something he had not got. Finally, that it was something worth having and he must find out about it. The way might have been easier if he had come to see me at that point, but instead he sought out a quiet spot one day and knelt down to pray to find out whether there was anyone to listen. At that moment in this story I jumped in with my question, 'Well, what happened, Dawkins?' 'Nothing like I expected,' he said, 'but having once commenced to pray I could not leave off.' Then he added quietly, 'Now I know.' Actually he knew very little, for at that time he had not even read the New Testament for himself, but he knew the essential fact that there was a God and that He was in touch with his life. It is not often one comes into contact with a person who has started from complete ignorance without any other person's help, and has found his way to God. I kept in touch with him by letter and Dawkins helped many a man along that way in the following months and then died in the trenches during the second year of the war.

Others can tell stories of Army chaplaincy service far more exciting than mine. I found the Army routine rather difficult to endure, and I never got over the absurdity, as it seemed to me, of every orderly springing to attention when I entered an Army hospital ward. It was my firm conclusion that it would be far better if Army chaplains had no officer rank, but, like naval chaplains, had their own uniform and designation as 'chaplains', with direct access to all ranks, from the commanding officer to the private soldier.

After my period of Army service ended, there were but a few months to complete my three years as a minister of the Wakefield circuit. I had enjoyed my work at Outwood during the very shortened period, but I should regard the situation very differently if I were appointed there today. Methodist Union has brought together into one circuit all the Methodist churches of the area. Instead of ten churches with four ministers, there are now thirty-one churches with six ministers. Of course, there should have been the uniting of churches in the different sections. In Outwood there are three, one erected since the Union which has no young people and must soon cease in any case. A commission has visited the circuit and worked out a constructive policy, but the rigid mind of people with a limited vision blocks the way. Taking the country as a whole, the Methodist Church has done a great deal toward solving this problem of redundancy and at the same time extending in the new towns and housing areas. Since Union over 3,000 church buildings have been closed, some, of course, through war damage, and in the eight years from 1954, when more widespread building became possible, has opened on the average two new buildings every week. But there are still pockets of resistance and the Wakefield Circuit is not the worst example.

Our next move was to Nottingham, but with a difference. During the Wakefield period our daughter, Mary, was born and we had the joy of taking with us to Nottingham a little lady, one year old, who was making a vast difference to our home. I was appointed to be Superintendent of the Nottingham, Halifax Place, Mission, and it was an appointment very much to my mind. This was the mother church of Nottingham Methodism, though not actually the first building so used. It was opened in 1799 and had remained a fine example of a Methodist Preaching House. About the turn of this century it was detached from a circuit arrangement and made a centre of aggressive mission work with quite remarkable results, which continued even after the opening of the Albert Hall Mission in the city. But what a location! The lace warehouses had developed around it and, with war-time blackout, I had to arrange a series of stewards with cycle lamps to guide the congregation through the dark streets to a main road.

They were a splendid people and the services full of interest. We had an excellent choir, with paid principals. The organ was old, with tracker action, but a gifted organist used it to fine effect. We were able to offer first-class music both in regular worship and on special occasions. As the war drew to its close I started a club for returning service-men which became very popular and established a fine group of men in association with the Mission. If the work was not spectacular it was most satisfying and in the true sense successful. I had a lay assistant to help with the open-air work, the pastoral visitation and the fellowship classes. One such colleague who remained on in Nottingham for many years was F. J. Boughey, to whom I must pay an affectionate and grateful tribute of remembrance. If a man is to be known by his family, he was blessed indeed. His older son is a most loyal voluntary worker in our Church; his second son is a minister in America, while his eldest daughter is the wife of one of our ministers.

Various extra duties came my way, in particular the Assistant Secretaryship of the District Synod and the Presidency of the Free Church Council. In the latter capacity I spoke at a great united peace meeting on the Nottingham 'Forest' to mark the conclusion of the First World War. It was said that 25,000 people were present and it certainly looked like it from the platform. They could all join in the singing led by a band and united choirs, but I have often wondered how many heard the addresses, for at that time there were no microphones and loudspeakers. I was told that I was heard better than anyone, but even so I do not think I can claim to have rivalled John Wesley in being heard by so vast a company. He affirmed that he had been clearly heard by fully 20,000 in Gwennap Pit, Cornwall, but were his calculations correct?

Research into the gambling problem continued, and in 1917 I was called to represent our Church in giving evidence before the Parliamentary Select Committee on Premium Bonds. An agitation had developed pressing this means of raising money to meet war finance. It was my first experience in giving evidence of this kind—the first of quite a long series. It is a testing situation to sit isolated before a semicircle of Members of Parliament, including, always on such occasions, several experienced lawyers. After the Chairman has taken one through the précis of evidence, previously submitted, comes the cross-examination by each of the members in turn. I was certainly nervous, even if I did not show it. Sir Charles Henry commenced, and it was a question of his which gave me confidence. We had been supplied with a blue-print of a possible scheme as the basis of argument, and I had pointed out that the chance of winning the chief prize was ten million to one. Now let me quote the official record:

Sir Charles Henry: I should like to correct one point. You said that anyone who held these bonds would only have a ten million to one chance of winning a thousand pound prize. It is extended over ten years and there is a drawing or two drawings a year, so that chances would be much larger.
Rev. E. Benson Perkins: No, pardon me! On the question of the principle of chance one drawing has no effect on the chance of another; there is one in each case who can win the £1,000 prize and that draw has no possible effect on the next. It is a ten million to one chance every time.

My positive answer settled it and Sir Charles Henry had no further word to say on that point. It was just what I needed to make me feel that I was on top of the situation.

To the surprise of many, the Select Committee reported against the desirability of an issue of premium bonds, and members of the committee encouraged me to believe that my evidence and argument was a helpful factor, in securing that decision. Sir Robert Kindersley, as he was then, Chairman of the War Savings Movement Committee, gave very strong evidence against the proposal. It is impossible to think of Lord Kindersley as Chairman of the National Savings Committee in recent years agreeing to accept or operate Premium Bonds in connection with the National Savings Movement as did his successor.

Shortly after this I was urged to write a book on gambling, as there was no comprehensive study available. Dr F. H. Neave, a well-known London solicitor and a member of our Church, agreed to provide a section dealing with the law relating to gambling. In the early autumn of 1918 I had finished writing the main part of the book, which stated the facts of the problem, analysed the wrong involved, and suggested lines of action to combat the evil. Unfortunately, Dr Neave was seriously handicapped through the illness of his partner, and had been unable to make any progress with the legal section. Seeing him one day, I made what he could only have regarded as a preposterous suggestion: that I should work over the ground and prepare a rough draft for him to revise. In his kindly way, he agreed, and supplied me with a large volume written for lawyers on this aspect of the law. I am sure he must have had some quiet amusement when he wondered what I should make of it. I soon found that it was quite impossible to make a précis without understanding fundamental definitions and principles of the law. Further, the understanding must be exact; a merely general idea was no use. I could make a long list of the perplexing points that emerged—fundamental questions, like the difference between the Common Law and Statute Law, and more detailed points, like the nature of a contract and the doctrine of consideration. It was a seemingly impossible task.

It is strongly against my nature and temperament to admit defeat—certainly not until the last ditch. Even in this instance I was not inclined to give up until I had discovered that no other course was possible. During that autumn and winter all my available leisure was given to the attempt to master these fundamental legal facts and principles and to digest the volume Dr Neave had handed to me, and other legal volumes. I soon acquired a deep interest in this field of study, and by the spring of 1919 I was able to submit to Dr Neave my summary of the law on gambling. He altered a word here and there, substituted a more exact phrase in a few instances, but virtually accepted my draft and allowed it to be published under his own name with his professional authority. I can only hope that I deserved what was a very great compliment. The book was published in the middle of 1919 with a Foreword by the Rev. Henry Carter and in association with the Temperance and Social Welfare Department. It led to a succession of articles and pamphlets on different aspects, with other books to follow.

Entirely unforeseen consequences arose from those months of close legal study. It gave me added confidence when dealing with the intricacies of the problem before other Parliamentary Committees and Royal Commissions, as also in other discussions and in writings on the subject. Another result was more remote. Years later it gave me the legal background when, charged with the responsibilities of the Department which deals with all our Church buildings, I had to handle the legal issues and relevant documents associated with property and trusts. It is my profound conviction, which this volume illustrates in several directions, that to go forward with the work that presents itself, however seemingly impossible, is to find years afterwards that it fits into the appointed pattern. Events do not correspond so exactly unless there is an underlying purpose. It is there where I have found the guidance of God.

Early in 1920 the Committee of the Temperance and Social Welfare Department decided to ask Conference to sanction my appointment as an assistant minister on its staff. I was completing four years in the Nottingham appointment and had no thought of leaving, but this was obviously a call that could not be resisted. It was along the line of my special interest and experience. At the same time, I could not bring my happy work at Nottingham to an end without real regret. Those good folk understood the situation and, while sharing my regret, sent me up to London with their good wishes.

CHAPTER IV

TEMPERANCE AND SOCIAL WELFARE

THIS new appointment involved a radical change from regular pulpit ministry and the routine of pastoral work to that of departmental leadership. The significance of a 'Department' should perhaps be explained. While the supreme legislative and administrative authority of the Methodist Church resides in the annual Conference, which meets for ten days in two sessions, Ministerial and Representative, the authority during the other 355 days is multipartite. The Conference delegates its declared authority to a General Purposes Committee and a series of Departments which act on behalf of the Conference under their appointed committees and within their appointed spheres. Certain of these departments have a long history. 'Overseas Missions', which is the whole church acting overseas, really began as a society in 1813, while 'Chapel Affairs' dates from 1854, and 'Home Missions' from 1856. During the past hundred years other departments have been established as the work developed.

The department in which I was to serve is now known as 'Christian Citizenship', but in 1920 bore the name 'Temperance and Social Welfare'. There had been a Temperance Committee appointed by the Conference in 1875, and in 1891 it became a department with a ministerial secretary. At that time the drink problem was the only social problem which, in the minds of many people, needed to be considered by the church. But great changes were taking place. I have referred to the Wesleyan Methodist Union for Social Service. Its first publication, *The Citizen of Tomorrow* dealt with issues such as labour and poverty as well as drink and gambling. This new concern found expression when, from the floor of the Conference, a young minister named Henry Carter was appointed Secretary of the Temperance Committee, with anticipation of what might follow. In 1918 he persuaded the Conference to enlarge the scope to 'Temperance *and Social Welfare*' and such subjects as gambling, League of Nations, minimum wage, and the drug traffic were remitted to this extended department. Two years later I was appointed to serve with Henry Carter. My interest in social problems and particularly work done on the gambling problem were mainly responsible for this appointment. There was definite attraction for me in having a share in this responsibility of the Church. It was also a privilege to work with a chief of the mental and spiritual vigour and driving force of Henry Carter. I should hardly be true to the situation if I did not add that the privilege carried difficulties, for the strength of my colleague could create tension.

The personal change from a definite pastoral office is very far-reaching, as all the twenty-five or so departmental ministers would readily affirm. Office hours and methods have to be adopted and whether the office is in London or Manchester it is necessary to join the army of commuters. We lived in South Croydon, so my journey from home to our offices in the Central Hall Building, Westminster, did not exceed three-quarters of an hour. The work is by no means confined to correspondence, agendas, committee minutes with deputations and interviews. It includes a great deal of research and writing for publication in various forms. The week-end comes into the overall pattern. There are preaching engagements all over the country, with associated meetings and conferences. This involves journeys, sometimes very long journeys, on Saturdays and Mondays. The result is that one sees very little of home and family, and the Methodist joke about 'departmental widows' is too near to reality to be funny.

The new situation created for us some family problems which were only resolved after a time. We were unable to secure a house for four months, owing to the serious housing shortage. Our daughter, Mary, was just over five years old and ready for school. Fortunately, Croydon ultimately provided what was necessary in that direction. The major difficulty arose from my almost regular absence from home over the week-ends. Ultimately we secured a companion-help in Miss Elizabeth Preedy of Ross-on-Wye. She moved with us to Birmingham in due course and entered very fully into the work of the

Central Hall. She was married from our Birmingham home to Mr F. C. Truman, who later became one of the Treasurers of the Birmingham Mission. Her untimely death, as it seemed to us, though many years later, was a sorrow to us all. I could not pay too high a tribute to one who became a real friend within the family circle.

Against the background of departmental routine there were many events and incidents which are worth recording, as they all illustrate the work and influence of such a department acting throughout on behalf of the Church. My immediate responsibilities were the gambling problem, which was increasing in importance, and the questions of social purity, which included the international drug traffic then claiming considerable attention from the League of Nations. Beyond these issues, I shared in the activities on the temperance question, to which my chief was devoting his principal attention. During the war he had served with distinction on the National Liquor Control Board, which had dealt with the desperate situation arising from the excessive indulgence in drink among the munition workers. When that ended, Henry Carter wrote an authoritative account of the effective results achieved, under the title *The Control of the Drink Traffic*. There was widespread feeling that the lessons of this wartime experience ought not to be lost, and when I entered the department Henry Carter was almost exclusively occupied with the legislative effort which secured the Licensing Act, 1921. This made permanent some of those reforms, particularly the drastic reduction in opening hours for licensed premises and the break secured by several hours closing in the afternoon. The invaluable work done by my senior colleague in this connection was recognized by a wide circle of Parliamentary and other social reformers.

With this Licensing Act on the Statute Book, the mind of Henry Carter turned to the need for more comprehensive temperance reform, particularly the policy of local option. It seemed as though the mind of the country was open to receive this proposal, and certainly the licensed trade were alive to the danger from their point of view. We became vividly conscious of this at the Middlesbrough Conference of 1921. The President was Dr John Alfred Sharp, who was Henry Carter's predecessor as Secretary of the Temperance Committee. He had announced his intention to make temperance reform the significant note of his presidential year. A new organization of the liquor trade, the Fellowship of Freedom and Reform, opened a temporary office in Middlesbrough. It was my responsibility to arrange a series of open-air meetings in reply to the challenge of this organization. At one such meeting held by the side of the Wesley Church in which a Conference public meeting was in session I was replying to the statements of their chief organizer. The crowd responded vociferously and we were having an exciting time until word was brought that our noise was upsetting the more stolid official meeting indoors.

Turning aside from the temperance question for a moment, reference should be made to a Conference meeting in the interest of the League of Nations held in the Bondgate Methodist Church, Darlington, which is still remembered. It was stiflingly hot, intensified by the crowd which filled the building, attracted by the distinguished platform—Sir Robert Newbald Kay, who presided, and the two speakers, Dr Hensley Henson, Bishop of Durham, and the Right Hon. Arthur Henderson, M.P. The Chairman and the Bishop read most excellent speeches, but it has to be admitted that they were not sparkling. Then, to everyone's surprise, and contrary to his usual style, Mr Arthur Henderson read an address which sounded like a *Times* leading article, except that it went on for nearly an hour. The audience settled down into bored somnolence. Nearly two hours after the meeting started I was called on for certain announcements on behalf of the Department. I began with a humorous quip and the audience woke up and roared with laughter. They had waited two hours for something in lighter mood. My prepared impromptus were seized upon, and for ten minutes the audience and I had a wonderful time. I dared not continue longer. Forty years on there were still Darlington Methodists who talked of that meeting, and I am not likely to forget it.

One of the wisest things Henry Carter did was to create the Temperance Council of the Christian Churches with its four Presidents, the Archbishop of Canterbury, a Free Church leader, the Roman Catholic Cardinal and the Salvation Army General. He had now devised a five-year plan to carry national temperance reform beyond the provisions of the 1921 Licensing

Act. It was for the Temperance Council to lead this effort, and an invitation meeting was arranged in the Egyptian Hall of the Mansion House to expound and press for local option, which was the spearhead of the campaign. By some ingenuity, a group of representatives of the licensed trade secured seats in the hall. The Archbishop of Canterbury, Dr Randall Davidson, presided, and opened with an admirable speech in unqualified support of the policy. He then called upon the next President, the Roman Catholic Archbishop of Westminster, Cardinal Bourne. His alleged support of the proposal was so hedged about with qualifications and limitations that it lost all value and played right into the hands of the brewers. The temperature of the meeting fell to zero, and under these conditions Dr Scott Lidgett, the Free Church President, was called upon. With graceful courtesy, he complimented the Cardinal upon his address and proceeded to interpret and embellish what had been said. In the skilful hands of Dr Lidgett, the audience could not fail to realize that the Cardinal had done a great service to the campaign. I have never heard anything more masterly, and it must have been impromptu. The meeting was saved and the forthright words of the General of the Salvation Army, the fourth President, formed a fitting climax to the statesmanship of Dr Lidgett.

Another story about Dr Scott Lidgett is worth telling. He had been brought specially to a meeting of the Temperance Council of the Christian Churches in the anticipation that he would resolve a situation of rather acute tension. Henry Carter explained the position with meticulous care. Gifted speaker as he was, he could be boring when he over-explained a complicated matter. This was such an occasion, and immediately he had finished Dr Lidgett was called upon to speak. Instead of healing the rupture, he said all the wrong things and left the issue worse instead of better—to the complete dismay of those who had arranged his presence. A few days later I met Dr Lidgett in one of the corridors of the Central Hall at Westminster. He looked at me rather quizzically and said, 'I'm afraid I did not help things very much the other afternoon.' 'Help!' I said. 'Why, you put both feet into the trouble and stirred it up.' 'Well, I'll tell you a secret,' he replied, 'but you must not pass it on. Henry Carter sent me to sleep and I did not wake up until I heard my name called and had to get up to speak.' The interesting thing is that no one had guessed that as the possible explanation.

I had been asked to take as full a part as possible in the organizing of the campaign under the Temperance Council, and this led to several quite exciting experiences. At Alford in Lincolnshire an open-air demonstration had been arranged for the afternoon in the Market Place, with an evening meeting in the Methodist Church. I arrived to find the local people in a state of great trepidation. The brewers had given their staff and workers a half-day holiday to attend the demonstration and the Alford people in charge feared the worst. I had difficulty in persuading them not to abandon the meeting. The crowd were not in militant mood at all, and when I explained that every opportunity would be given for questions after my address they listened with seeming interest. Their spokesman had his questions ready and I immediately recognized their source. It was a handbook issued by the Fellowship of Freedom and Reform for use by supporters of the licensed trade. I brought out my own copy and when the crowd saw that I knew the questions beforehand they appreciated the joke. We went on with the discussion and had a thoroughly interesting time, so much so that, to the astonishment of the Methodist folk, quite a few of the brewery people came to the evening meeting.

On another occasion the members of a registered club came to the meeting *en bloc* and filled the centre of the hall. This frightened away some of our supporters, for the club members were in excited mood, under the leadership of a man who was the degenerate son of a well-known churchman. They gave me a most difficult time with their interruptions and I made a serious blunder which I learned to avoid in future. I tried to make a bargain by offering one of them the use of the platform if they would hear me in silence. They agreed, but failed to keep quiet, and abused the freedom of the platform when it was given. I was surprised to find in the local paper the following morning a fuller account of my case than I thought had penetrated through the disturbance. At that time, forty years ago, there was a real enthusiasm for the temperance cause indicated by the organized opposition of the 'trade'. Today comparatively few are concerned and the licensed trade are quite indifferent. Their lack of antagonism is a measure of our lack of conviction.

My most embarrassing experience was at Torquay, where a full day's programme had been arranged—luncheon, women's demonstration, teachers' conference, and Town Hall meeting. The Bishop of Exeter, Lord William Cecil, was to preside, and the speakers were the Bishop of Croydon, the Right Hon. Walter Runciman, M.P. (as he was then), Lady Victor Horsley, and Mrs Pereira. Owing to a threatened railway strike, not a single speaker arrived, and I reached Torquay that morning from Cornwall to find only the Bishop of Exeter available. I managed to persuade the stewards to go through with the arrangements as though nothing had happened. Lord William Cecil was splendid and prepared to be discreet, though he assured me he had only one speech, which I asked him to reserve for the evening. At the luncheon I apologized for the absence of the rather elderly Bishop of Croydon and deputized for him. Somehow I fixed up the women's meeting with local talent and spoke myself at the teacher's conference. When the Town Hall meeting began, not even the Press knew that Mr Walter Runciman would not be there. The meeting had hardly started when the Fellowship of Freedom and Reform made their presence known. I whispered to the Bishop of Exeter, who was presiding, that this was going to save our meeting, as undoubtedly it did. They were kept in abeyance until the time for questions following my address. There was quite a group of them and they went ahead, one after another, with their prepared questions. Fortunately, I knew their case and the answer to it. Though it sounds like unpardonable egotism to say that I bowled them out every time, people assured me that I did. Of course, I was living with this concern at that time and had all the information at hand. The meeting got more and more excited and finished up with a sense of triumph. The licensed trade could not have given us greater help. Owing to the enemy, what might so easily have been a humiliating flop was turned into a genuine triumph.

There were outstanding figures in the temperance movement of that time. Lord and Lady Astor were most active. Philip

Snowden, as we shall always think of him, was particularly forthright. Speaking with him at a meeting in Portsmouth, with an election in the immediate future, I heard him say, 'I will not support a candidate of my own party who is not sound on the temperance question.' There was a strong group in the House of Commons who could be relied upon, including such leaders as Isaac Foot, James Hudson, Arthur Henderson, Walter Runciman, Sir Ernest Lamb, and others. It would be impossible to find such an outstanding group today as could be depended upon for the fight at that time.

The technical details of both the drink and the gambling problems—operative, statistical, and legal—required constant study, but in view of my interest in statistical and legal matters I do not think I was often caught out. I do remember that even a barrister who was checking a legal statement of mine missed a mistake I had made in bringing 'welshing' under the Gaming Act, 1845, instead of describing it as an offence of larceny under the Common Law. But mistakes were much more likely through an error of judgement in respect of propaganda or administration. On one occasion I very nearly involved the Temperance Council of Christian Churches in a libel action as well as myself. I had been asked to see a play which had just appeared on the London stage and, we understood, justified gambling and made light of alcoholic indulgence. I wrote a caustic, well-deserved, but unwise review of the play, and someone else added to the mistake by having it published in the *Quarterly Journal of the Temperance Council*. No one imagined that the playwright would take it so seriously, but it certainly got under his skin. The outcome was a threatened libel action against the writer and the Council. For me it meant a very uncomfortable hour in the office of our advisory solicitors, with the senior Secretaries, while they considered the best course to avoid the consequences of my rashness. The claim that this was proper matter for public comment did not settle the issue. Eventually it was settled on the publication in the *Quarterly Journal* of the correspondence, which included their long letter analysing the so-called libel. It is almost impossible to avoid risks of this kind if an aggressive line is to be taken in combating these evils and I must admit that anything short of definite aggression would not appeal to me.

TEMPERANCE AND SOCIAL WELFARE

Isaac Foot and Henry Carter both hailed from Plymouth and were friends from schooldays. To me it was a privilege to acquire the friendship of Isaac Foot in and through the work of the Department. We came into very close association through the Parliamentary Select Committee on a Betting Duty. In appointing this Committee in the spring of 1923, the Government had responded to pressure for the imposing of a tax on betting. Mr Isaac Foot was selected as a member of the Committee and in agreeing to serve looked to me to work with him throughout the inquiry. He knew the temperance issues from A to Z, but had not the same detailed knowledge of the gambling problem. Before each sitting of the Committee, I spent an hour or more at the House of Commons with Isaac Foot, going through the papers for the day, including any précis of evidence to be given, and discussing the points to be watched and brought out in the cross-examination. I attended the public sessions of the Committee and made my own notes of the way things seemed to be developing. I was also one of the witnesses, and it proved to be more exacting than when giving evidence before the Premium Bond Inquiry. Then the questions addressed to me numbered 170, but on this occasion 246. We were opposed to a betting tax because it was the wrong way of securing a reduction of betting and instead likely to give it greater respectability and to fasten it more firmly on the country as a revenue-producer.

In the late autumn of that year a dissolution of Parliament was announced. Had this been a royal commission it would have continued its work until completed. A select committee, however, though working in an exactly similar way, comes to an end with the ending of the Parliament of its appointment. All the evidence had been taken, but the report had not been considered, and little more than a week remained before Parliament dissolved. The Chairman of the Committee, Sir Henry Cautley, had drafted a report which was known to be favourable to a betting duty as both 'desirable and practicable'—the two points of the terms of reference. When this draft was submitted to the Committee, Mr Isaac Foot wanted to submit an alternative draft which would embody our point of view against the proposal, and in any case would be printed in the Blue Book if only supported by a minority. He was not able to prepare such a draft and urged me to do it for him. He sent across the pile of Committee minutes for my use. It was Friday and the draft must be in his hands by Tuesday evening. I had Sunday and Monday engagements in the North of England, but I had to make the attempt. Every available minute during those three days was spent on the task, and the final writing was only completed in the train as I travelled back to London. I still have the pages of a large loose-leaf book which were used for that writing. As soon as I could on returning to Westminster, I rushed them into the office to be typed. The draft went across to the House of Commons that evening. Beyond adding the correct form of address, Isaac Foot made no other alteration and it stands in the Blue Book exactly as I wrote it, but under the name of Mr Isaac Foot. This alternative report received good support from members of the Committee though not a majority. It had the effect of preventing the Committee reporting that a betting duty was 'desirable', though they admitted that it was 'practicable'. When the *Manchester Guardian* described this document as being 'a most workmanlike report' I felt that I was repaid for those days of concentrated effort.

It was about this time that I had managed, after much difficulty, to secure a representative committee of the Christian Churches on Gambling, of which I acted as Secretary. At the urgent request of this Committee, I undertook to make available the mass of evidence on different aspects of betting which had been submitted to the Select Committee. This book, entitled *Betting Facts*, was published by the Student Christian Movement and ran into a second edition. Mr Isaac Foot wrote a most interesting Foreword. It is in a sense now out of date, as it describes the situation as it was forty years ago. There was a mass of betting on horse-racing and on football at fixed odds through the bookmakers and much illegal cash betting. There were, however, no football pools, no dog racing, no totalisators, no premium bonds, no bingo clubs, no legal gaming houses and casinos, and no licensed cash betting offices. Yet even then it was regarded as a great social mischief. Today it is accepted and provided for officially as a social amenity. In their hearts, most people know that it is part of the false and shady side of life, but it is increasingly difficult

TEMPERANCE AND SOCIAL WELFARE 55

to persuade them of the fundamental truth that gambling in all its forms is wrong.

I had been feeling the strain of the strenuous months during 1923, and the offer of a months' chaplaincy in Switzerland was most opportune. This was our first visit to Switzerland, and my wife and I both recall, as everyone must, the exciting experience of the first sight of the high, snow-covered mountains. Of course, we travelled by train across France, and I wonder whether the present-day journey by air does not take away some of the thrill. I have made many air-journeys in recent years, but I still remember the first sight of the mountains from the train in the early morning, the coffee and rolls after the night journey, and the beauty of the Swiss valleys with their chalets as we saw them for the first time. A fortnight in the hotel on the Rigi-Scheidegg, 5,500 feet above sea-level, made us both feel on top of the world in every sense. From Brunnen, where we stayed for a second fortnight, we set off on a walking trip over the Furka and Grimsel passes, staying one night by the Rhône Glacier in the Belvedere Hotel, which is 7,500 feet above sea-level. It is never possible to repeat the intense pleasure of a first experience in any field, and especially in making acquaintance with Switzerland.

By the twenties of this century the various social service unions had come together in repeated conferences at Swanwick and were turning their thoughts to the next major step to be taken by the churches. I am particularly thankful to remember that I was present at the joint meeting in London under the chairmanship of Bishop Charles Gore. At that meeting, Malcolm Spencer, a friend of us all, with the Edinburgh Missionary Conference of 1910 in mind, asked, 'Why should we not have an Edinburgh Conference on Social Questions?' It was at that moment that the Conference on Christian Politics, Economics and Citizenship—COPEC for short—was born. It came to fulfilment in the Birmingham Central Hall in April 1924. Through many months preceding, I worked as a member of the Executive Committee and as a member of the Commission on 'Leisure'. The report of this Commission forms Vol. V of the twelve volumes of *Commission Reports*, and it contains the statements on 'Drink' and 'Gambling' which it had been my responsibility to draft. Henry Carter was a member of the

Commission on 'The Social Function of the Church', Vol. XI. These twelve volumes constitute the first comprehensive achievement of a blue-print of a Christian sociology in this age of civilization.[1]

The Conference was chaired throughout by William Temple, then Bishop of Manchester. Who can say what the Churches owe to that great man, who later became Archbishop of York and then of Canterbury? He was not to see the fruition of his work in the first assembly of the World Council of Churches at Amsterdam in 1948. Other figures who played a distinctive part in the long months of preparation for COPEC and in the conference were Canon Charles E. Raven, Dr Hugh Martin, and Miss Lucy Gardner, the Secretary. Among Methodists taking a prominent part were Dr W. F. Lofthouse, Dr Russell Maltby, and the Rev. Samuel E. Keeble. Henry Carter spoke when the drink question was before the Conference, and I participated in the discussion on gambling. The Rev. F. H. Benson, who was then Superintendent of the Birmingham Mission and Chairman of the District, asked me to speak at the weekly open-air meeting in the Bull Ring. Having COPEC in mind, I spoke, I remember, on 'The Cross in the Market Place'. I little thought that a year later I should be residing in Birmingham, Superintendent of the Mission, and in charge of that Bull Ring meeting.

When I went to the Temperance and Social Welfare Department, I was invited for a term of six years, with the possibility of extension beyond that period. Early in my fifth year the senior officers of the Department intimated to me that it was desirable that I should leave at the end of that connexional year. No reason was ever given to me nor to the Departmental Committee for that decision. The meeting of the Committee in January 1925 was most disturbed by reason of unexplained undercurrents and the failure of the members to secure satisfactory answers to questions asked especially about my removal. Naturally, it was for me a most perplexing and anxious time, but I was enabled to take it quietly. I am profoundly thankful that I did not allow my deep sense of an injustice to get out of control, though it would have been understandable if I had given the reins to my resentment at this

[1] See *infra*, Chapter XI, p. 172

unexpected and inexplicable decision in which the responsible committee had no part. Instead, I acquiesced, not humbly I fear but wisely, in the suggestion of a move if appointed.

As no other appointment, however, had emerged by the time of the Conference, I went down to Lincoln, where the 1925 Wesleyan Methodist Conference was being held, assuming that I should, after all, be staying on at the Department for a sixth year. There was a reception in the public gardens in Lincoln before the opening of the Conference, and as I went through the gate I came face to face with Dr Scott Lidgett. He said, 'You are going to the Birmingham Mission.' The Stationing Committee, which had just concluded its session, had taken the matter in hand, and I was so appointed. I received a warm welcome from the Chairman and representatives of the Birmingham District, who were attending the Conference, and once again the unexpected turned out to be the providential course for me. I had yet to discover that it opened the way to one of the happiest periods of my ministry.

A fortnight after the conclusion of the Wesleyan Methodist Conference in Lincoln I was due to leave for the International Life and Work Conference, which was to be convened in Stockholm. I refer to this important assembly when I am dealing with the Ecumenical Movement in a later chapter. There was much to do in these two weeks to clear up both departmental and domestic matters, in view of this unexpected move to Birmingham. House and furniture were a personal and not a departmental responsibility and the shortened term and brief notice added greatly to the financial as well as other difficulties. My own personal commitments had to be adjusted. However, we struggled through, and, impossible as it seemed, before I left for Stockholm we had cleared the way for removal three weeks later.

Hobart Stacey, a ministerial friend and splendid travelling companion, was coming with me to Stockholm, and we had resolved to add a few days' holiday before and after the Conference. We travelled through Norway—to me a most delightful first visit. We stayed at Stalheim, visited the Suphelle Glacier at the head of the Fjaerland fjord, and had a wonderful day sailing up the Sogne fjord. We had the company of the Bishop of Lichfield and his wife, Dr and Mrs Kempthorne, who were going to the Stockholm Conference and whose friendship I already had occasion to value. Up the Flaam Valley we travelled by *stolkjaerre*, a drive which took over four hours. I said 'drive', but we had a stiff walk up the steep part of the ascent out of the valley. Its charm and simplicity as we saw it seems to me to have been partly spoilt by the electric railway which I regretted to see on a later visit. I greatly dislike travellers who mark the stages of their journey by the meals they have enjoyed, but at the Vatnahalsen Hotel overlooking the valley, where we arrived in the late afternoon, we had salmon which had just been caught in the mountain lake. I still think I have never tasted anything to equal it. Joining the train at Myrdal, and travelling on through Finse, the highest station on the railway, over 4,000 feet above sea level with perpetual snow, we spent a day in Oslo, and then travelled by the night express to Stockholm. After the Conference we took that fascinating three days trip along the Göta Canal and through the great lakes to Gothenburg. From there we travelled by train south to Denmark, joining the boat at Esbjaerg for Harwich. We ran immediately into a head-on storm and for twenty-five hours had to endure the North Sea at its worst. If I feel some satisfaction that I was not sea-sick, the honest truth is that I lay on my back only just *not* sick. We were hours late reaching London from Harwich, and I got home in South Croydon by means of a rather reluctant taxi-driver well after midnight. There was one day left before we set off for our new home and work in Birmingham, ready to begin a new chapter in our lives.

CHAPTER V

CENTRAL MISSIONS

THE Forward Movement, of which I had heard so much as a boy, had now come alive for me through this dramatic change. For the next ten years in Birmingham, followed by four years in Sheffield, I was to exceed my early dreams by having the responsible superintendency of two of our great central missions. The Birmingham Mission belonged to the first group, being established in 1887. Contrary to the gloomy predictions of some of the Methodist prophets, the old hall, which seated a 1,000, was crowded week after week under F. Luke Wiseman, and a second congregation was gathered in the hall of the Midland Institute. In 1903 the present spacious hall, seating 2,000, was opened and able to accommodate both congregations. After twenty-six years, F. H. Benson became Superintendent, continuing for twelve years, when my appointment as third Superintendent completed forty-eight years before another change. Being Midlanders my wife and I fitted easily into the life and spirit of Birmingham and came to like both the city and its people. Whether we shall appreciate the modern city which is wiping out the familiar streets and buildings is at present very doubtful. The Sheffield Mission, started in 1901, belongs to a sort of second generation. The fine Victoria Hall was built in 1908 under the Superintendency of George H. McNeal, who served for nineteen years. P. M. Medcraft followed for eleven years, and in 1935 I succeeded for a much shorter term. For me it was a case of going back to a city in which I had already worked and knew very well indeed.

The most striking evidence of the success of the central missions was seen in the large congregations which were gathered, though it would be a mistake to think of that as the only special feature. The Birmingham Sunday-evening congregation, filling the Central Hall, was by far the largest in the

Midlands, while the Sheffield, Victoria Hall, congregation, only slightly less, was one of the largest in the North of England. It is a challenging responsibility to face week after week a congregation approaching 2,000. In a sense, it is the same responsibility if the numbers are two hundred or even twenty. But the larger crowd does create its own atmosphere and expectancy. The structure of the hall offers an open door to those who are not accustomed to church-going and at that period did constitute a great attraction, greater than is the case to-day, thirty-five years later. The fact of a hall did not mean that anything shallow or cheap belonged to the form of worship, though a real friendliness was associated with it. The Birmingham Central Hall has a dignified beauty of its own, with a fine organ and high musical standard, due mainly to the creative influence of Luke Wiseman, and when in the development of the years the large and excellent choir were appropriately robed there was nothing incongruous in the result. I was more than glad to follow the Wiseman tradition in the music of the Central Hall.

The nature of a hall offers the opportunity for departure from the purely conventional. One such departure which achieved considerable popularity during my ministry was that of question conferences following sermons on specially announced subjects. While some of these were on social and what are called topical issues, some of the most appreciated were on theological and ethical problems. Almost all the questions were written and anonymous. They were handed up by the stewards. Thus there was no hesitation in submitting the most pertinent questions—sometimes even impertinent. I shall refer later to the more definitely personal work, but it is still the case that many people, shrinking from the more intimate contact, find great help in having their problems discussed, if not always resolved, in this more general and impersonal way. There was much evidence to reveal the value of this departure from the conventional, and from time to time other forms of change from the normal were introduced.

In my second year we had an unexpected visit from Mr Leslie Hore Belisha, M.P. (later Minister for War and still later in the House of Lords). He was representing the *Daily Express* and writing a series of articles on 'Living Churches'. In his published article on the Birmingham Central Hall he described the unity created by the congregation as they joined in the opening hymn and 'transformed a hall into a church'. He went on: 'The minister and his people have made an atmosphere. The congregation brought the smouldering faith. He struck it into fire. . . . Here is a service which all can understand and which all can combine instinctively to make. Here is a great democracy of faith, each citizen of which has an equal voice in prayer and praise.' Our visitor came into the social hour for young people, which was held in the smaller hall following the service. He seemed to enjoy the music and discussion and was astonished that 'the minister who had already conducted two services was fresh and vigorous enough to play accompaniments on the piano'. But he understood an essential fact: 'Spiritual influence in the Wesleyan community is not the breath of Sunday only, but of life. There is no human activity in which the message of the Mission is unspoken. The spirit which the Sabbath has engendered overflows into a series of clubs and social gatherings.' This is an interesting comment from a stranger who came without previous knowledge, and certainly without prejudice. Mr Hore Belisha did not forget his visit. I had a charming letter from him after he had listened to one of our broadcast services, and I shall refer later to an occasion when my contact with him was of very great value.

The great hall was fully occupied, not only on Sundays, but on Saturday evenings. The weekly concerts during the autumn and winter, which included the celebrity concerts, were a popular feature of the musical life of the city. In recent days in Birmingham I am constantly meeting people who tell me that these concerts were amongst the most enjoyable occasions of their lives. Quite a few of the concerts were on the radio in whole or in part. My place on the programme was announced as 'Events of the Week'; invariably a humorous story, a Christian judgement on things that were happening, and a reference to the following day. This contact was invaluable. In Sheffield we also had concerts on most Saturday evenings of a rather more varied character.

The great assemblies on Saturday evenings and Sundays were, so to say, the façade of the Mission. Beyond that was much that provided intimate contact and fellowship for young and old. My own Bible Class was on Monday evening, and on the other nights the fellowship classes and clubs were in the hands of the deaconesses, my assistant, and voluntary workers. My wife had a splendid young women's class. In the Sheffield Mission there was a very large attendance of members regularly week by week in addition to the women's meetings and clubs. For many the hall provided the centre of their entire social life. Clubs and classes, parties at Christmas and other times, excursions and the like were not an attraction to the Mission primarily, but a necessary provision for the religious and social needs of the members.

The crowded services were not an end in themselves, or should not be so regarded. The day of these large congregations seems to have gone, but the point I want to make is true of any congregation. The question to be faced is: How can these people be brought right into an experience of God and the fellowship of the Church? Many will have travelled that way, but what of the others? The methods to be used will vary according to conditions. What I had to face was this critical question in relation to the congregation I was meeting every Sunday. The rather old-fashioned method of the ten days' mission was useless. These people were present on Sundays, but not a tenth of them could be brought to the hall on a succession of week-days. Sunday was the the one opportunity, and there were two principal ways we used it.

From time to time we invited a group of young people, up to a hundred or so, to spend a whole Sunday on our premises from 9 a.m. to 9 p.m. They worshipped with the congregation at the usual services morning and evening, but began the day with a devotional period. Then in the afternoon there were talks and group discussion. Before the evening service there was a serious talk on 'Decision', and after the service Holy Communion. The breaks for luncheon and tea provided happy relief from the more serious hours. We often arranged a special leader for the day, and W. Russell Shearer, years later President of the Conference, served splendidly on several such occasions. In a sense this was giving to these factory workers an experience which others were having at Swanwick and elsewhere. I am speaking, of course, of the decade immediately preceding the

Second World War. The value of this method in both decision and spiritual development was marked.

The other method was by way of a direct appeal to the large congregation. Three Sunday evenings were selected, generally in October or November, and special sermon topics announced, forming a unity and culminating on the third Sunday. The last page of our 'Order of Service' was used to sum up the main points of the message leading to the challenge of decision, with space for name and address. In the quiet at the end of this third sermon I asked all in the congregation who would to face this issue and sign the form. Those who signed were asked to remain after the service and join with the members in Holy Communion. Before they came to kneel at the Lord's Table, I explained what it meant. A formal act of commitment is necessary to complete such a decision, and what more suitable and impressive than participation in Holy Communion, which makes vivid both the acceptance of Christ and incorporation into the fellowship of the Church? The Table of the Lord is the place for repentant sinners, and thus to 'evangelize the Eucharist', as someone once put it, is to emphasize its true significance. I collected the signed papers and during the week following, each of the signatories received a duplicate of their decision form on card, with my signature. According to age and circumstance, they were brought together for training in Church membership. So we built up our membership year by year, and I am still moved by the remembrance of those occasions when upwards of a hundred people, young and old, made their decision.

There are, of course, other occasions of decision of a more spontaneous order. One Sunday evening in Sheffield comes to mind. I had an irresistible conviction as the service proceeded that I must bring it to a definite issue. An invitation to remain after the service and an appeal resulted in fourteen decisions. Several of these were of a particularly striking character. In any case, I should remember that night, for our daughter, Mary, was one of the fourteen. In her case it was not to mark the beginning of the Christian life, but to register a full commitment, even as in my own experience years before.

Associated with most of the central missions are other centres of social or evangelistic ministry within the inner belt of the city, each with its minister or deaconess in charge. In the Birmingham Mission we had a particularly efficient Working Girls' Hostel, with accommodation for 105. Then I saw the building of a modern girls' club-house in one of the poorest quarters of the city as well as a new hall and premises in still another area. Altogether we had five centres apart from the Hostel and Club, with a staff of five ministers, in addition to myself, five deaconesses, the Warden of the Hostel, and a secretary. In the Sheffield Mission we had six centres, beside the Victoria Hall, with three other ministers, three deaconesses, four lay evangelists, and a secretary. The colleagueship created by the regular staff meetings, where policy was freely discussed, were to me of great help and to the work of untold value in establishing unity and co-operation. I take a great deal of pleasure in recalling my various colleagues and following their subsequent careers, particularly the probationers, for whom I had a more intimate responsibility. Within the ten years in Birmingham I had ten probationer colleagues, always two and during several years three at one time. Eight have been or are successful superintendents of circuits and three have had charge of central mission work. The record includes two chairmen of districts and one district synod secretary. I should unduly flatter myself if I took any special credit for this, and yet I am sure that responsible association with a superintendent minister in the work of a central mission is as fine a practical training as any man could desire.

The other staff members, both in Birmingham and Sheffield, will understand if I mention four by name. Miss Hale, the Birmingham Secretary, was appointed by Dr Wiseman, served under Mr Benson, throughout my time, and for some years beyond. Her devotion, ability and incomparable knowledge of all the details was a great source of strength. Miss Hall, the Secretary in Sheffield, was appointed by my predecessor, and is still serving the Mission with wonderful skill and untiring spirit. Miss Brownhill was the Warden of the Birmingham Girls' Hostel long before my time and for years afterwards. Its striking success owed everything to her wise leadership, gracious spirit, and complete devotion. For five years we had on the Birmingham staff Sister Mary McCord. She is the widow of an Irish Methodist minister, and after the early death of her husband she gave herself to this work. Her dependability in all circumstances, her consecration, and her unfailing humour were a gift of God to us all.

My work in both Birmingham and Sheffield was in the period of acute unemployment between the two world wars. It is impossible to make a fair comparison with the work of the churches today against the background of an affluent society. The charge that the churches are losing touch with the industrial classes would not apply to the Central Mission activities in my time. Opportunities were seized in both cities. In Birmingham we had the regular open-air meeting in the Bull Ring on Fridays at 1 p.m. and all the cheap-jacks recognized this as the 'parson's hour'. I told the story of this meeting in a book, now out of print, entitled *With Christ in the Bull Ring*. The meeting became an institution noted and often reported by the Press. It was an audience composed almost entirely of men, many of them unemployed. While the major responsibility was mine and I spoke on most occasions, my colleagues assisted effectively. The second half-hour of questions was particularly exciting. The address, and especially the questions, provided a unique opportunity to declare and explain a Christian judgement in relation to the burning political, economic, and international issues of the day. From time to time we had acute opposition from rationalists, fundamentalists, and communists. But it was remarkable how the crowd itself would claim a fair hearing for the speaker even when they disagreed with what he was saying. When I am asked about the results of such a regular contact with a company of men like this outside the Church itself, I can give a very definite answer. Apart from other considerations, it is an invaluable experience for the preacher and for the Church that the Christian gospel should be proclaimed in its fullness where it can be challenged by the man in the street and where it has to be brought into intimate relationship with social justice. Prejudices having been broken, we were able to gather a group of the men to a men's class at the Hall, where a more intimate contact was possible. This is not all, for the individuals whose lives were changed through the Bull Ring meetings bore vivid testimony to the cumulative power of this regular presentation of the Christian message. To recall some of these: the rationalist opponent who became a Christian and rebuilt his broken home life; the intended suicide who was saved by the challenge of the meeting and whose revolver is now in my possession; the communist who found a richer fellowship and a new Master; the critic whose letter spoke of his discovery of something in Christianity he never knew before and his deep regret at the wasted years. That ten years' ministry in the Birmingham Bull Ring brought a rich reward.

In Sheffield I found at my disposal another sort of contact with the people we often call 'outsiders'. The setting was different, but it was in fact a similar crowd of the unemployed to those I had been meeting in Birmingham. My predecessor at the Sheffield Mission had started a Tuesday evening meeting for the unemployed in the large Hall itself. There was a wonderful response, and every week he was meeting upwards of five hundred men. From the first it was open for uninhibited comment and criticism. Visiting speakers were brought in on many of the evenings and I had spoken on several occasions before I found myself in charge of the meeting. Many of these men were violently opposed to Christianity, having swallowed the communist doctrine that religion is the opiate of the people. The mere fact that on the premises of the Church and face to face with a minister of the Church they could say exactly what they pleased was an argument in itself which they found difficult to rebut. These men had to be understood. In their hearts they seldom really meant what they said in the extravagance of an exciting discussion. On one occasion Hugh Redwood came to speak to them at my invitation. He wrote an article afterwards about the meeting, which he entitled 'The Men Who hate Christ'. He was really shocked by some of the things he heard and did not realize that they were baiting him as they did me when they got a chance. It is only when the barriers are down and they feel free to speak as they please that one has any opportunity of influencing them.

What hardships many of them were suffering at that time! I took a deputation to meet the Chairman and members of a City Council Committee on the Means Test which they deeply resented. Afterwards I took the four of them to a restaurant as my guests and suggested that they had a good meal. No, they would only have bread and butter with their tea. I protested, and one of them said, 'We appreciate your kindness, but we have been living so long on bread and scrape that we dare not touch any rich food; it would turn our stomachs.' And I had only suggested fish and chips to begin with. The man who spoke gave the whole of the dole to his wife to lay out as best she could for themselves and the children. He was neither a drinker nor a smoker, and all he kept for his own pocket was a shilling a week. We so easily forget the conditions of that pre-war period. In Birmingham a man looked me in the face one day and said, 'Look here, Mister. Could you be a Christian on fifteen bob a week?' That was the dole for a single man at that time. This is how it worked out. A shilling a night for a bed if he wanted a separate cubicle at the Rowton House. A shilling a day for food—and many were living on that. There was left a shilling a week for everything else—boots, clothes, stamps, a newspaper, cigarettes. If he was a drinker, well? Men found themselves walking with boots which had lost their soles, and nothing breaks a man's morale sooner than that. Why did we have to wait so long for the Welfare State to remedy some of these conditions? If we could not cure the unemployment we could have shared the available resources more adequately.

The most difficult and in many respects the most important part of one's work in such an appointment is dealing, not with the crowd, but with the individual. The personal needs and problems tax to the full one's mind and heart, but help given to a fellow creature perplexed and distressed from whatever cause is both the joy and the test of pastoral work. Hours for private interviews were announced and known to be confidential. This was not the Roman Catholic confessional, but in part of its use it served a similar purpose. Much is made in these later days of the value of psychiatry, but that alone is not sufficient. As I see it in the light of experience, it is most useful for the minister to know something of applied psychology, but it is his business to be a Christian pastor, not a clinical consultant. It is right and essential to link up with the medical doctor and the expert psychiatrist, but the duty and supreme privilege of the minister is to mediate the grace and power of God to sin-sick souls. Amongst the greatest joy I have in looking back over my years of mission work is the remembrance of the help I was enabled to give to some of God's children in their most grievous need.

One day a man staggered into my room, and it was only with the greatest difficulty that I learned the particulars of his sorry condition. He had worked in the silver-plate trade, where acids have to be siphoned. Taking the wrong but easier way to start a siphon, he seared his throat, and the permanent irritation produced continued insomnia and depression, which resulted in an attempt to end it all. He was rescued from the gas-oven just in time. Realizing what he had done, the fear of repeating it was added to the existing trouble. The doctors had done all they could for him; this condition required another remedy. I sought to give him assurance of the power of God as we prayed together. Then I arranged for him to come to see me every morning, as he did for some time. I had to share my faith with him and remove his fear by a partnership in confidence in God. I think a milestone in his progress was when, at my suggestion, he got his first sleep sitting and dozing in his chair by the fire. He knew then that he could sleep. There was no possibility of his being entirely cured of the irritation, but he became master of himself by the help of God. When our Birmingham Christian Social Council started occupation centres for the unemployed, he became one of the first managers.

It was very humbling to come into touch with the brave Christian loyalty of some of our people. A man who had started a typewriting and duplicating business was employed for a while by two racing tipsters. He did not realize at first the exact nature of this work he was doing. When he recognized the gambling and fraudulent nature of these racing tips, he threw it up immediately. That left him with so little business that he slept in his office chair for several months because he could not afford a bed. It was in the midst of his struggle that I came to know the situation and was able to put work in his way, so that gradually he was able to establish himself. He was told many times by those people who had employed him what a fool he was, and that it was really none of his concern. He was content to be a fool for Christ's sake.

An elderly woman with tears in her eyes came to tell me her troublesome problem. She had gone to claim her pension on reaching the appropriate age. When they had examined her papers at the pension office, they told her that as she was married in another name her marriage was invalid and there would be no pension. That was not her greatest trouble. If she was not legally married, her daughters were illegitimate. I promised to unravel it if I could, but what a tangled mess it was. The clue to the solution emerged when I discovered through legal friends that while use of a false name within the knowledge of both parties invalidates the marriage, that is not so if used by one party without the knowledge of the other. This was the truth in this case, but how was it to be adjusted. The Registrar-General sent the problem back to the Ministry of Pensions, who promptly returned it to Somerset House. Finally, I got it nailed down and the Registrar-General arranged for the people involved to see the official referee. We on our part arranged for a lawyer to accompany them. Some week or two later an interesting ceremony took place in my room. The Vicar of the parish brought the forty-year-old register with the entry. Marginal corrections were made and signed according to the instructions I had received. Then a new certificate was issued showing all the corrections. How happy they were as they went away, which was our repayment for handling a most complex situation and bearing quite an item of expense.

A man came to see me one evening to ask if I knew someone who would lend him £50. He was in frightful financial distress, behind with his petty-cash settlements at his work, and in the hands of four moneylenders. He was not only in danger of his home being sold up, but of conviction for embezzlement. His pitiable condition was chiefly due to misfortune. I had to tell him that lending money was one of the things I could not do. That night I could not get this man out of my mind, and I found that my secretary, to whom I had told the story, was equally worried, when I saw her the next morning. I decided to take the risk of getting him out of the sorry condition he was in. I advanced the money to clear his office account and then with a colleague, went round to settle with the moneylenders, demanding a reduction for the unexpired period of each loan. What an experience that was. The arrangement that I made with him was that he would repay to us the amount advanced at the rate of 12s. 6d. per week. He repaid the whole amount, but this is so exceptional that the rule against lending money remains unaltered.

These cases are all in the line of mission work and indicate the kind of personal help the Church should be ready and equipped to give. Not all by any means involve the time taken in these few instances, nor do they all present such complications. Of course, we met the charlatan from time to time and, fortunately, came to recognize him, so that we were not often imposed upon. But that risk must be taken. A telephone call one morning was said to be from Dr Brown at the General Hospital. He was sending a man to us in whom he was interested. Would we help him in any necessary way, and he would repay us. We should understand that he could not leave his medical duties. My secretary took the call and very wisely rang up the General Hospital to find that no Dr Brown was on the staff. It was the man himself ringing from a telephone-box and paving the way to what he anticipated might be substantial help. He failed to bring off his scheme that time. I recall a man boasting to me, as many did, of his wide knowledge of the Methodist ministry. I encouraged him to mention some of his supposed friends and he named the Rev. J. B. whom, he said, in answer to my question, he had seen some three months previously. I told him that he was a very clever man, for the Rev. J. B. had died four years earlier. He looked up into my face with a cheeky smile and said, 'That was a bad break, wasn't it?'

There is one story about a Sunday School girl at the Sheffield, Victoria Hall, which I tell with great joy. She was fifteen years old, and, as I knew, was eagerly seeking work. She had no father living, and her mother was only a cleaning woman so that the additional help that Rosie might bring was keenly anticipated. The dole of 5s. a week was very little. After many weeks of disappointment, the Labour Exchange sent her to take a place at a printers, and she went, greatly delighted. On arrival she found that this printer was engaged entirely in printing football pool coupons, which it would be her work to fold and despatch. Without hesitation, she told the manager that she could not take this job. Asked her reason, she said, 'I am a Christian, a member at the Victoria Hall, and I cannot have anything to do with gambling.' He swore at her and told her that he would report her to the Labour Exchange for having refused work, which would mean the loss of the dole. Serious as it was, that did not affect her decision, and she came to tell me what had happened. I went with her when she was called to meet the Court of Referees under the Ministry of Labour and I claimed that she was entitled to refuse work of this kind. One of the two assessors would not agree and we lost the case. However, as the sympathetic barrister in the chair pointed out, there could be an appeal to the Ministry of Labour. Rosie was ready to sign the appeal which I drew up on her behalf. The verdict from the Ministry was a complete justification of Rosie's refusal. The special interest was in the fact that this was the first time that that point had been challenged. The details of this case were sent to every Labour Exchange throughout the country to make it clear that any young person was entitled to refuse any work connected with gambling without being penalized. I like to quote this story to illustrate two most important points. The first, that a moral decision always has results beyond anything we can anticipate or measure. The second, that the positive teaching of the Church can and does establish the standards of Christian witness.

In 1931 the Wesleyan Methodist Conference, the last but one before Methodist Union, assembled in the Birmingham Central Hall. It has distinction for me, because at that Conference I was elected a member of the Legal Hundred. For a century and a half, from its appointment by John Wesley, that was the legal conference. It never acted in isolation, but only in confirming the decisions of the general conference. It was a coveted honour to be elected a member and the first step to any possible election to the Presidency. Methodist Union the following year brought this august body to an end. There are many today who think this to have been a mistake. It could not have continued in its original form, but modifications could have been introduced which would have enabled the continuity from the eighteenth century to have been preserved.

It was as a member of the Legal Hundred that I attended the great assembly of Methodist conferences in the Albert Hall on 20th September, 1932. Independent standing votes of the different conferences sanctioned the union of the three Methodist Churches. It was a great occasion and an inevitable development. It made no immediate difference to our work in Birmingham. Gradually, as the years passed, circuits and churches were united and the problem of redundancy progressively, if slowly, solved. An important step had been taken in the realization of Christian unity, and while we faced consequential difficulties we could rejoice in what the modern jargon calls the 'end product'.

The years 1931-3 found me with an additional task as a member of the Methodist Tune-Book Committee. The Hymn-Book Committee had completed its work, but hymns are made to be sung and the selection and arrangement of the tunes to nine hundred and eighty-five hymns was no small task. It was an exacting process, but full of interest to those with musical knowledge. The first Festival of Praise to introduce the new *Hymn and Tune Book* was held in the Birmingham Central Hall on 15th January, 1934. Dr F. Luke Wiseman, the chairman of the committee, was in charge of the Festival. Choirs from many of the Methodist churches joined in making a fine body of several hundred singers, which I had the pleasure and privilege of rehearsing and a share in conducting on this historic occasion. One permanent outcome of the work on the new Tune-Book was the establishment of the Methodist Church-Music Society. The annual conferences have been events of great interest and value, the importance of which is not always recognized by the non-musical members of the official bodies of the Church. In this connection we owe much to the work and influence of the late Dr Clifford W. Towlson and to the scholarship and ability of the Rev. Dr Francis B. Westbrook.

An experience of a very different kind fell to my lot in 1933. I was honoured by being nominated as the General Secretary of the Department which comprised the Wesley Guild and the Christian Endeavour. From the earliest days of my ministry I had been associated with the Wesley Guild and there was a great deal that was attractive about the appointment. My wife and I, however, after much prayerful thought, did not feel confident that this was the right move. We decided, quite deliberately, that, while we would, of course, accept the decision of the Conference, we would not express any opinion whatever of our own. In the Conference discussion strong opposition to my leaving Birmingham was expressed. Dr Lofthouse nominated the Rev. Alfred Robinson, who was then Superintendent Minister of the Leeds, Oxford Place, Mission, and was known to be interested. The ballot vote resulted in the closest division I have ever known in my long experience of the Conference. Alfred Robinson was elected by a majority of five. It was freely said that if I had expressed the slightest inclination for the appointment I should have received the majority vote. That may be so, but if we had been told that in advance it would not have altered the mind of my wife and myself. That is not quite the whole story. By an accidental oversight, the scrutineers were not given the opportunity to vote, and the omission was not discovered until too late. There was a rumour of another accident resulting in a basket of ballot papers being omitted altogether from the count. Philip Bailey the author of that long and little-known poem, 'Festus', has a line, 'What men call accident is God's own part'. I believe that and ultimate events demonstrated its truth. Alfred Robison made a splendid Secretary, and an opportunity for certain distinctive work along my own special line came my way some few years later. Sure as I was that we had acted rightly, it was a disturbing experience. This conference was held in the Westminster Central Hall. Across the way, in Westminster Abbey, there is a tiny devotional chapel opening off the south transept known as the Chapel of St Faith. I recall going for a few moments into that little chapel before and after the Conference discussion. The prayer was answered, for the outcome was unquestionably right for me, for the appointment and for the Church, as the following years made vividly clear.

When I went to Birmingham I registered the hope that I might complete ten years, feeling that by then I should have made my contribution and have reached the time for a change. It was at the end of exactly that period in 1935 that I received the invitation to the Sheffield Mission with the prospect of the chair of the Sheffield District. Like most of my moves, it was with little notice, owing to the sudden and unexpected removal of the minister who had been Superintendent for the previous eleven years. It was encouraging to have the assurance that no one in Birmingham desired the change, but it is always better to move when possessed of universal goodwill and at the peak, as far as one can tell, of one's work and influence. The move to Sheffield meant the continuance of similar work in another city which I knew well. This continuity of central mission responsibility in the two cities made it inevitable that in describing this work I should deal with experiences in both Birmingham and Sheffield.

The superintendent of a central mission of the Methodist Church carries a heavy financial responsibility, but not in isolation. The Conference-appointed committees of the Birmingham and Sheffield Missions were the courts of reference, and I pay a warm tribute to the splendid support I received from devoted laymen throughout the fourteen years. Though I cannot name them all I must record valued personal friendships with Councillor J. B. Field and Mr Shirley Smith in Birmingham and with Mr Maurice Cole and Mr Arthur Priestley in Sheffield who were splendid colleagues and whose service was typical of the interest and help of other stewards and members of the committees. Both my wife and I recall with gratitude our association with this fine body of laymen in the two cities. Then too I had the great advantage of the friendship of Methodist lawyers whose advice and guidance were always at my disposal —Mr Soutter Smith, following his distinguished father, in Birmingham and Sir Harold Jackson in Sheffield.

Birmingham in particular provided a unique opportunity for united action by the churches, and in the next chapter I turn to this story of real unity and in addition some of the experiences of social service which became possible.

CHAPTER VI

UNITY AND CITIZENSHIP

IF I thought that the change from the Temperance and Social Welfare Department to the Birmingham Mission meant the end for the time being of association with other churches and restricted action in social welfare I was never more mistaken. I soon found that the field of influence in the direction of Christian unity was definitely enlarged and opportunities for service along the line of citizenship extended. Against the background of central mission work, particularly in Birmingham, described in the previous chapter, I want to indicate the unique opportunity for the expression of unity and citizenship which opened out.

It so happened that five central figures in the Church life of Birmingham arrived in the city within eighteen months culminating in 1925. On the Anglican side these were the Bishop of Birmingham, the Right Rev. Dr E. W. Barnes, and the Rector of Birmingham, the Rev. Canon Guy Rogers. On the Free Church side there were the minister of Carrs Lane Congregational Church, the Rev. Leyton Richards, the minister of the Hampstead Road Baptist Church, the Rev. F. C. Spurr, and the new superintendent minister at the Methodist Central Hall. We became firm friends and remained in close association for ten years before there was any break in the group. In his autobiography, Canon Guy Rogers says of himself and the three Free Churchmen that we were spoken of as 'The Big Four'. That was evidently a journalist's quip, but it certainly did happen that we seemed to be able to speak and act for the churches of the city and carry their judgement with us.

In all our united action we had the fullest co-operation of the Bishop, and came to know him in a way not understood by those who were less close to him. He was attacked by the fundamentalists for his modernism and by the Anglo-Catholics for his liberal evangelicalism. Of course, he did seem to trail his coat and look for criticism. I cannot forget, however, an impromptu and private talk he gave when lunching with a group of Free Church ministers during a devotional retreat. Knowing that during the day we were considering the doctrines of grace, he talked to us about conversion, and revealed a deep personal experience not realized by the normal journalist nor by the official critic.

When I asked the Bishop to be the preacher at the midday service at the Central Hall connected with our Mission Anniversary he readily consented. Being always anxious to do the right thing, he asked, 'What shall I wear?' 'If you will,' I said, 'we should like you to wear your episcopal robes.' So he paid us the compliment of wearing his scarlet Convocation robes. He paid us a much greater compliment by his wonderful sermon on 'The Message of John Wesley'. I cannot forbear quoting a few sentences.

> 'Conversion was for John Wesley, and still is for those who have a true understanding of the things of the Spirit, the sudden, overwhelming recognition of God's presence within. With such recognition goes the knowledge that the life of the Spirit can be sustained by prayer and realization. That divinely strengthened life in all its fullness is independent of external accessories and needs no intermediary between God and man. . . . Wesley was supremely ready for his great missionary activity because he was certain of his faith. . . . I put this message before you today, not merely because it was the message of John Wesley, but because I am convinced that it is at the very centre of that reformation of faith, that restatement of the gospel which our age must make.'

The whole sermon, especially prepared for that occasion, is worth reading for its own value and also because it reveals the inner life and experience of a Bishop who was more deeply spiritual and personally greater than the controversy he so often provoked.

Quite early, Leyton Richards, F. C. Spurr, who had been President of the National Free Church Council, and I, found it necessary to undertake the reconstruction of the Birmingham Free Church Council. We three became a joint secretariat, and it proved to be an ideal arrangement. Representing as we did the three major denominations, we constituted a sort of inner executive, and were able to speak authoritatively and to act speedily. Our close association with the Rector and the Bishop fitted the Free Churches into the larger unity most effectively.

Our united group with the Provost, at that time Bishop Hamilton Baynes, were a major part of the Religious Advisory Committee of the Midland Region of the B.B.C. Those were the early days of broadcasting. We could none of us see the amazing development of forty years later, but we struggled hard, in co-operation with the other regional committees, in an endeavour to find the rightful place of religious broadcasting. Clearly, it needed to be in association with and not competition with the public worship of the churches. Several church buildings, including the Central Hall, were permanently wired, and we had the responsibility of being one of the main centres for both services and concerts. One year I was conducting the only Christmas morning service on the radio. Without previous notice, I was given permission to call for a collection for the relief of miners suffering through unemployment. By immediate post and from the congregation in the hall I received over £150. This may seem very small by comparison with the result of some of the good-cause appeals today, but it was spontaneous, at a time when such collections had not been established, and when the value of sterling was very much greater than it is at the present time. It was a pointer to the development of later years.

Perhaps the most constructive united action we took was the creation of the Birmingham Christian Social Council, a body representative of the Anglican and Free Churches of the city and able to act on social issues in the name of the churches. This was part of the outworking of COPEC. Canon Guy Rogers and I acted as joint chairmen and represented the Council on many occasions. When the Government Unemployment Bill was under discussion, we secured a meeting of the Birmingham Members of Parliament at the House of Commons, sponsored by the Right Hon. Austen Chamberlain, who presided. We were able to submit certain recommendations on behalf of the Christian Social Council arising out of our contact with unemployment in the city. As we learned afterwards, our suggestions were not without effect. Then we started occupation centres for the unemployed whereby their idle hours could be turned to constructive purpose for themselves and their families. As a Council we fought against the Sunday opening of cinemas, but when a limited opening was ultimately determined we secured restrictive conditions in the interest of the working staff as well as the public. What we were doing pre-dated the formation of the British Council of Churches, with associated local councils of churches, by nearly twenty years. Since returning to reside in Birmingham, I have discovered that the Christian Social Council has continued in activity through the succeeding years, and is now brought within the total responsibility of the Birmingham Council of Christian Churches. It is enheartening to know that we planned so well.

A particularly dramatic action in which we were involved, together with other specialist organizations, took place in the Brewster Sessions in February 1935. There was legislative permission for licensed premises to be open for an additional half-hour, to 10.30 p.m., under specified circumstances. The licensed trade regarded Birmingham as a key position, believing that if the extension could be secured here it would virtually assure its being obtained for most of the country. I have never seen such an array of barristers in a Licensing Court. Mr Norman Birkett, K.C., as he was then, led, with a junior counsel and seven other barristers representing various allied organizations. The Court were amused by the last of the group announcing himself as representing the Antediluvian Order of Buffaloes and the Loyal Caledonian Corks. We had three barristers on our side representing the Christian Social Council and certain temperance and other organizations. The case lasted two whole days, the first occupied by the application. The Mission staff co-operated splendidly in securing evidence from the canvassing of selected areas showing a large majority against any extension. I tested the large crowd of men in the Bull Ring to find that, though most of them patronized the public houses, they saw no reason for this extension. Knowing my association with the temperance movement, Norman Birkett used all his powers of sarcasm and subtle cross-examination to weaken my submissions. He did not realize how the evidence he had presented the previous day had made me feel indignant and determined to score if I could when in the witness-box. It is clear that we fully maintained the strength of our opposition, for the application was refused. One of the barristers whom I had met on other local cases paid me a compliment which perhaps I might quote. Speaking to one of our barristers after the case was over, he said, 'I told Birkett not to ask Perkins any questions, as it only enabled him to strengthen his case.' There is no doubt of the chagrin of the 'trade', for they had spent some thousands of pounds in anticipation of a favourable decision. I have no doubt in my mind that the most significant fact which impressed the Justices was the united opposition of Anglican and Free Churches through the Christian Social Council.

In the summer of 1930 we organized a united crusade throughout the city with the help of the Industrial Christian Fellowship of the Church of England. During two weeks meetings were held day by day all over the city. Many were in the open-air, others in factory canteens and workshops, with crowded central meetings in the Town Hall and the Central Hall. Unquestionably, the conscience of Birmingham was aroused at that time to a recognition of the social evils in our midst. The full significance of Christian citizenship was declared and the responsibility of the churches made clear. Two mighty processions from St Martin's Church and the Central Hall converged on the Town Hall for the final meeting. I remember that I was occupied with the overflow meeting outside. The actual conclusion of the crusade came later that evening in the Bull Ring. I am quoting part of the epilogue from my book *With Christ in the Bull Ring*:

'Nearly ten o'clock at night and a silent procession comes down New Street from the Town Hall into the Bull Ring. In the first rank are to be seen the Bishop and a Methodist minister walking with uncovered heads. Behind are 2,000 or more all walking in silence. They gather in the Bull Ring, other processions converging on the same spot. Soon it is crowded in every part and as far as the eye can see. A hymn is sung by the great assembly, led by the Salvation Army band. In prayer and thanksgiving, the voices are heard of the Rector of Birmingham and the Bull Ring preacher of this story. Then the Bishop mounts the Methodist platform and with clear voice asks for the blessing of God upon the work of all the churches and upon the life of the city. The many thousands go their several ways knowing that a new day is dawning, however slowly, and that the Kingdom of Christ is surely coming on the earth.'

I wrote that five years before the Second World War, as the conclusion of the book, now out of print. At that time we could not think another war to be possible; still less could we visualize what might follow the war—full employment with relative affluence for the workers and the Welfare State with its many material advantages. The primary poverty of those days has gone, the evil housing conditions have given place to new housing areas and new towns, and amenities of many kinds are within the reach of almost everyone. But is the Kingdom of Christ on earth nearer to realization or, on the contrary, have improved material circumstances and extended opportunity for comfort and enjoyment spelt spiritual decline? The question cannot rightly be ignored.

Our unity touched the inner life of the churches more closely than was possible through common action on social issues, though that had spiritual significance. In starting the midday services at St Martin's Church, for instance, the Rector was acting on behalf of us all. We ministers of the Free Churches preached from time to time and the visiting preachers were drawn from a truly catholic circle. An occasion like the Silver Jubilee of the Accession of King George V seemed to offer the opportunity for a demonstration of unity. A joint service in which the Parish Church and the Central Hall co-operated was arranged. Choirs, clergy and ministers, with a vast concourse of members of both congregations, assembled in the Central Hall for the opening act of worship with an Anglican speaker. Then, led by the choirs, the long procession moved down Corporation Street to the Bull Ring. At the West door of St Martin's Church stood the Bishop waiting to welcome the great company and lead them into the church. Following prayer and a brief address from a Methodist minister, this really wonderful joint service closed with the singing of the *Te Deum* and the blessing from the Bishop.

Could our unity go further than this? An invitation reached me from my friend, Canon Guy Rogers, to the communicant members of the Methodist Church at the Central Hall, asking that on the forthcoming Maundy Thursday evening they would join the members of the Parish Church in Holy Communion. It would be, of course, an Anglican celebration, but I was invited to sit with the clergy in the sanctuary and read the Gospel in the pre-Communion service. Several hundreds of our members joined in that service. Some time later, in accordance with the understanding, I had the joy of inviting the Rector with his assistant clergy and people to a Methodist celebration of Holy Communion in the Central Hall. Dr Lofthouse joined me as a celebrant, and the Rector sat with us within the Communion rail and read the Gospel, as I had done at St Martin's. The address was given by the Rev. R. Lee Cole of the Irish Methodist Church. Our Methodist Communion Service being almost identical with the Prayer Book Service, no communicants in either place suffered any embarrassment. This was truly inter-communion, but not, of course, inter-celebration, and took place long before the World Council of Churches had pointed the way. An occasional service of this kind does not lead us very far in the direction of union, nor does it in itself solve any of the critical problems. But it does demonstrate fellowship at the central point of the life of the Church—the Table of the Lord—and that surely is the one place where full unity is to be found.

The penalty of being reasonably well informed on particular issues is that one is open to be called upon for unexpected service. In view of my five years' experience in the Temperance and Social Welfare Department, and earlier work, I had supposed that I should find some opportunities of action against the drink evil and gambling. I soon found that rather more than that was involved.

The Temperance Council of the Christian Churches were anxious to have a survey of the contemporary drink problem in a modern city. Birmingham was ideal for the purpose and I was pressed to undertake the task. The results of the survey were given as a lecture at a Summer School of the Temperance Council and published under the title *The Ramifications of the Drink Evil in an English City*. When I started the research I stumbled upon a piece of very good fortune. The Chairman of the Licensing Justices, Mr Bryson, whom I had approached on other points, gave me access to the results of a statistical survey undertaken at the instance of the Justices. This showed the actual sales over a period of three years of beer, wine, and spirits in sixty-two licensed premises situated in an area constituting half the central ward. This part of St Mary's Ward consisted of the poorest artisan area of the city, with a population of 15,000 people. Those accustomed to research of this kind will know how valuable such a basis was for comparison with other areas. It was possible to relate to the actual drink consumption the vital statistics in comparison with other parts. Then the deplorable housing conditions in this special area were an important factor to be taken into account. The survey covered the whole city and examined the relation of alcoholic consumption to the main factors of social life. This survey was undertaken during the year 1928, so the conclusions no longer apply to the present scene. But they do stand as an accurate analysis of the drink problem at the end of the first quarter of the century, and they do show the effects of alcoholism under certain social conditions and as a result of a particular licensing policy. A few years later the number of licensed premises was reduced and still later as a result of war damage and replanning, the whole of the area was cleared of its outworn factories and its intolerable houses.

The following year the Government set up a Royal Commission on Liquor Licensing, of which my old chief, Henry Carter, was a member. I was claimed by the Temperance Council of the Churches as one of their witnesses. Mr Bryson, who was also a member, graciously allowed me to quote in my evidence the figures he placed at my disposal for the Birmingham survey. Prior to that I was under promise not to reveal their source. Of course, the conclusions I drew from the statistics were my own, as Mr Bryson explained to the Royal Commission. For months after my survey was published, and before the Royal Commission was in session, one of the legal officers of the liquor trade did his utmost to make me reveal how I had come to have those statistics. I must confess that I enjoyed that rather long correspondence, with my studied evasions and the lawyer's increasing annoyance.

One of the branches of the Birmingham Mission was known as 'The Sea Horse'. It had been a notorious public house, and when the licence was withdrawn the premises were made available for mission work. The old dance-hall was turned into an attractive assembly hall and a fine work was done through the years in this slum area. One of the things I did was to open the bar for the sale of cheap food and soft drinks. During the years of acute unemployment it was a boon, and enabled us to help many a man on the way. There is a story associated with the Sea Horse, which should be recorded, though it happened some years earlier than my time and when this branch was in charge of a splendid lay missioner named Ashmole. The Birmingham brewery companies had a popular May Day procession every year, consisting largely of the newly painted vehicles and the well-groomed cart-horses with plaited manes and polished brasses. One year Mr Ashmole secured a large open lorry and occupied it with a number of ragged, dirty children from the slums. They were pleased enough to have a free ride. Right along the length of the lorry a large sign was placed, with the words 'We are the Result'. When the procession began, this lorry followed on behind. I have been told that as the procession moved between the crowds lining the main streets the murmurs of applause which greeted the parade were suddenly turned into bursts of satirical laughter. That was indeed the end of the procession, for the brewery firms have never dared to risk a repetition.

On the gambling problem I found an opportunity of comparing the figures of its prevalence I had secured in Sheffield over twenty years earlier with a similar selective enquiry among the office and warehouse people of Birmingham. This included a large proportion of young people. The result showed just over 80 per cent. regularly participating in gambling of some form. This was almost identical with the Sheffield figures. About that time I was invited by the Methodist Church in the Isle of Man to present evidence to a Commission on Betting appointed by the Lieutenant-Governor and representing the House of Keys. The outcome of the Commission's findings was an effective Act prohibiting all gambling in connexion with outdoor sport. A greyhound racing company were laying out an elaborate track on Onchan Head. In spite of the frequent assertion that greyhound racing is a sport in its own right, they dropped the project at once when betting was prohibited. A change in the law allowing betting on outdoor sport in the island is an illustration of the change which has come over the prevailing attitude to gambling in these years since the end of the Second World War.

The group representing the Churches on the gambling issue which I had brought into being before I left London was now associated with the National Christian Social Council. When the Government appointed a Royal Commission on Lotteries and Betting in 1932 the machinery was ready for immediate action on behalf of the churches. A representative national conference was convened and the lines of action determined. I was appointed chairman of a small committee which was charged with the preparation and presentation of evidence. The main statement prepared by our committee was presented to the Commission by William Temple, then Archbishop of York. His own statement in addition was clear and uncompromising. In his cross-examination by members of the Commission he underlined, time after time, his positive view that gambling is wrong in principle, and therefore is wrong in the seemingly trifling instance as in the larger. I had the responsibility of submitting a supplementary statement with factual illustrations and the lines of suggested legislative reform. We presented seven other witnesses on detailed aspects of the problem. Largely because of work put into this by the small committee, I do not think that the mind of the Christian Churches on this problem has ever been more adequately submitted to a Government enquiry. This Royal Commission was undoubtedly the most judicious body which has examined this complicated problem, and its report is a well-balanced survey, with sound recommendations. The report was before Parliament in June 1933, and some of its legislative proposals were embodied in the Betting and Lotteries Act, 1934. My book, *Gambling in English Life*, written in 1950, gives an account of the report of the Royal Commission and of the Act of

Parliament. I refer in a later chapter to the most unfortunate report of a Royal Commission in 1951 and the disastrous Act of Parliament based on it passed in 1960, which opened the way to a great increase of legalized gambling.

There was a demand that this evidence committee which had prepared the statements presented to the Royal Commission in 1932 should be permanently constituted and take the place of the more informal group I had previously assembled. A Congregational minister, the Rev. H. Allen Job, became the most effective Secretary, and I was appointed Chairman, a position which I held for twenty years. This Churches Committee on Gambling ultimately became associated with the British Council of Churches. Considerable interest was aroused on the subject of gambling by the Royal Commission report, 1933, and the Act of Parliament the following year, and the National Sunday School Union asked me to write a book on the subject for the use of teachers, with an indication of educational method in dealing with so complicated a question and model lessons. This they published under the title, *Gambling and Youth*. As it deals with general principles, I believe it is still in use.

In these two chapters I have been giving some account of crowded and most interesting years of ministry in Birmingham and Sheffield. Birmingham appears more prominently, for the obvious reasons that I had ten years in that city and only four in Sheffield, and that the situation in Birmingham was unique in opening the way to united action of considerable influence. Near the end of my third year in Sheffield the conference designated me for appointment the following year as Secretary in the Department for Chapel Affairs—the traditional title for a most important department dealing with all aspects of Church buildings, including the extension in new areas and new towns. It was a surprising appointment, as I had no idea my name was likely to come up in that connexion, but it had very definite attraction. At the same time, I regretted leaving Sheffield after so short a ministry at the Victoria Hall and as Chairman of the Sheffield District.

It was during the earlier period of my work in Birmingham, on 26th December, 1928, that my father died in his seventy-fifth year, my mother living for another twenty years. He had retired from business and they were living in Leicester quite near to the church they had served for so long. He was a man of fine Christian character, with a reputation for unblemished rectitude in all business affairs. I could understand why he was so often asked to fill the office of treasurer, for his meticulous accuracy was well known. He sought no public position and found full opportunity for the exercise of his undoubted gifts in the quiet fellowship and service of the Methodist Church, rejoicing always in the work of his son and daughter.

When we arrived in Birmingham, Mary was just ready to move into the senior school, and the Edgbaston Girls' High School provided the right opportunity. She was very happy there and finished as a Prefect in the Sixth Form. During those years we had two German girls, both Methodists, in successive periods, each acting as *Haus Tochter*, as the Germans put it. The second of these, Elizabeth Straube, is a younger sister of Frau Wunderlich, the wife of the present Bishop of the German Methodist Church. Elizabeth and Mary became devoted friends, and still are, though both have changed their names and have responsibilities which prevent frequent meeting. Mary entered the Law Faculty of the Birmingham University and when we moved to Sheffield we left her behind for her final year. One of the extra things I was able to do was to form the Methodist Society in the Birmingham University. Mary became a member of the committee, and that was the beginning of a friendship with another member of the committee, the outcome of which belongs to another chapter. After all, that is the right kind of setting for such friendships.

In both cities the leave-taking was memorable. The great hall in Birmingham was crowded for the final service, when I tried to sum up the significance of the past ten years and conducted the choir for the last time. On the Monday evening another large crowd faced a platform which suggested the united activity in which I had participated. The speakers included the Bishop, Dr E. W. Barnes, the Rev. F. C. Spurr, Canon Morris, representing the Christian Social Council, Dr H. G. Wood, Dr W. F. Lofthouse, with my friend, Councillor J. B. Field, presiding. My wife and Mary were remembered in word and gift. It is a humbling experience to listen to tributes from such friends and to wonder whether they are really deserved, whether, indeed, one has done the best that was possible. But it is encouraging to be assured that some measure of success has been won. Following my last Sunday evening at the Victoria Hall, Sheffield, the Master Cutler —an important figure in the life of the city—presided over a meeting at which, with warm and generous words, we were assured of our place in the hearts of the people. At a more intimate gathering on the following evening, under the chairmanship of Mr Maurice Cole, we received a gift typical of Sheffield cutlery at its best, which we greatly value.

A week later war was declared.

CHAPTER VII

WIDENING HORIZONS

THE fourteen years of central mission work which ended with the outbreak of the Second World War gave us certain opportunities of travel abroad. Our chief holidays were spent in some of the countries of western Europe, and if sometimes I wondered whether we were inclined to be rather extravagant in this direction, though it took the place of other relaxation we might have had, I realize now that it paid extraordinary dividends in extended friendships and widening knowledge. After I had been at the Birmingham Mission for some years, the friends there provided us with our first motor car—a Morris Minor. This was a great help in my work, and also increased the facilities for overseas travel. I was very glad to have a car, and glad also that it was a small one. Apart from necessary economy, I could not have felt happy in meeting our poor people with a large and showy car. We never got beyond a Morris or Wolseley 8, and they served all our purposes in travel in such countries as the Austrian Tyrol and Switzerland, even ascending the famous Gross-Glockner glacier road in Austria and taking us over some of the Swiss mountain passes. In addition to this holiday travel, certain journeys abroad of an official type came my way, including a first visit to America. It would be easy to turn this chapter into a modified guide-book, a temptation which I must resist, but some of the facts and incidents arising from these overseas visits in that pre-war period had much to do with my work and its future development.

Two objectives took me to the French Riviera and Italy with my friend, Hobart Stacey, in 1927. One was to extend my study of gambling by visiting the notorious Casino at Monte Carlo and the other was to see Rome. This seemed to be a perfectly proper way of using some small royalties from one of my books on gambling. In addition to the main purpose, the journey itself was interesting. Travel has always fascinated me and is very much more than the shortest way of getting from A to B. My interest begins the moment I have crossed my own doorstep. Monte Carlo is one of the most beautiful places I have seen. Its background consists of the terraced heights rising to 3,000 feet above sea-level, with the old village of La Turbie at the top on the Grande Corniche Road and the tower erected by Caesar Augustus in 25 B.C. The view from there across to the blue Mediterranean Sea is unforgettable. The Casino is set in the midst of glorious gardens, and to enter it from this wealth of beauty is like entering another world. Here are within neither joy nor laughter, but only the signs of excitement, greed, and despair. The roulette tables were crowded, and so also were the rooms where that stupid game, *trente et quarante*, and other games were in process. The sunshine was shut out and the loveliness of the world outside forgotten.

We watched the roulette for some time and the crowd sitting or standing round the table and waiting for the voice of the croupier, '*Messieurs et mesdames, faites vos jeux.*' Then the hurried placing of stakes, the turn of the wheel, the announcement of the number, and whether red or black, the rapid payment of winnings and the gathering of losses, and the whole process, not taking many minutes, beginning again. So it goes on hour after hour. It seemed to us like the very punishment of Hell. We saw one man staking the maximum time after time and losing every time. One holiday couple lost 100 francs, but went on playing and regained their loss. But they did not stop, and we wondered what the end would be. An old lady staying in our *pension* told us that years before she lost 1,000,000 francs and so impoverished herself that she had to let her flat and live as meanly as she could.

On entering the Casino, the attendants supply cards with columns headed 'Rouge' or 'Noir'. They are for recording the run of red or black, the idea being that if one has had a long run the other is more likely to come up. It is entirely superstitious nonsense, yet many were following the runs. Actually, one turn of the wheel has no effect whatever on the next. The wheel contains thirty-seven pockets, eighteen red and eighteen black and one white zero which is in the interest of the Casino.

It is just less than an even chance every time whether red or black will result. There is a famous saying of Francois Blanc, the founder of the Casino and its proprietor for many years: '*C'est encore rouge qui perd, et encore noir, mais c'est toujours Blanc qui gagne.*'

The following day, being Sunday, we attended the English service at the American Episcopal Church in Nice. I can still recall the thrill with which I joined in the opening hymn with the vivid remembrance of the previous day's visit to a place 'of sin and woe':

> '*Pleasant are Thy courts above,*
> *In the land of light and love;*
> *Pleasant are Thy courts below,*
> *In this land of sin and woe.*'

During the week we spent in Rome we worked really hard, often under the guidance of my friend, the Rev. Giacomo Lardi, with whom we stayed. Of course, we saw the familiar features of the wonderful city—St Peter's and the Vatican, the other great basilicas, the Colosseum, the Via Appia, and the Forum, where we spent many hours. But I wonder how many visitors to Rome find their chief interest, as I did, in the houses of the early Christians. The Church of St Clement 'stratifies the history of the Church in a wonderful way', as one writer puts it. At street-level is the twelfth-century church, while at a lower level the fourth-century basilica has been revealed. This is one of the earliest churches to be built in Rome, for the early Christians were unable to erect their own churches until the end of the third century and the beginning of the fourth. About the year A.D. 600, Pope Gregory the Great delivered his famous sermons in this fourth-century basilica of St Clement. At a still lower level are rooms of the house of Clement, the friend of Paul. Here, where the very earliest Christian worship took place, pagan power has desecrated the hallowed spot by erecting an altar to Mithras. The Army must have taken possession of the house, for the Persian cult of Mithraism spread rapidly in the second century among the soldiers of the Roman Empire.

At the Church of Santa Pudenziana, the most ancient in Rome, I persuaded the old Curator to show me what had been discovered of the house of Senator Pudens. With our candles we groped our way to these long-buried remains. But what a story! Legend says that Pudens was the first person in Rome to be converted through St Peter. His name appears in 2 Timothy 4^{21}, with Claudia, his wife, of whom tradition says that she was the daughter of the captured British King, Caractacus. Her name was changed in honour of the Emperor Claudius. If this tradition is true she was the first of the British people to become a Christian and the only one to be named in the New Testament.

The house of Priscilla and Aquila is most significantly associated with 'the church in their house', as Paul puts it (Rom 16^5), but there is only a mere fragment remaining. On the Appian Way we went to meet Brother Damiano, an attendant at the Franciscan Church of St Sebastian. He told us his story. A year or two earlier he was digging the grave of a fellow Franciscan when he fell through the bottom into an unknown section of the Catacombs. This led to the discovery of the house of Hermes, another of the names mentioned by Paul in Romans 16. As the inscriptions indicate, this was the house of freedmen and slaves whom Hermes had liberated. It may very well have been the place where the bodies of Peter and Paul lay.

Under the Church of Santa Maria in Via Lata is the house where Paul is said to have had his lodging when under house arrest. He was chained, but able to meet his friends. On a column the words have been carved, 'But the Word of God is not bound'. Modern archaeologists have doubted this tradition, though unable to offer an alternative site. It is in these houses that we seem to come into touch with the first generation of the Christian Church, for many generations had to pass before they were able to move their worship from the houses and hired rooms to their own church buildings. During this visit I preached in our Methodist Church in the Via della Scrofa, which has been demolished since to make road widening possible. I shall refer later to our present Methodist churches in Rome.

On our homeward journey we stayed over in Florence long enough to see the famous Ponte Vecchio, the Duomo where Savonarola preached his powerful sermons, to look at a few selected pictures in the Pitti Gallery, and to see the Methodist church, which is a historic building attended by the family of Dante in the thirteenth century. We also spent some time in Milan to see the wonderful but much damaged refectory mural of 'The Last Supper' by Leonardo da Vinci, to visit the Gothic Cathedral, and to prowl about on the roof and discover the many tiny statuettes. So home by the Italian lakes and Switzerland.

In 1932 I was invited to be the guest preacher at the Metropolitan Church, Toronto, during the months of July and August. This was of particular interest, not only because it provided my first opportunity of seeing something of the American continent, but because it was primarily a visit to the United Church of Canada, a union which was achieved seven years earlier, in 1925. In order to obtain a glimpse of the United States, I decided to travel *via* New York. The outward journey was in the fine and comfortable *Berengaria*, a German ship handed over as part of the reparations after the First World War. The homeward voyage in the old *Mauretania* was not in the same class of comfort, though with a following wind, and during the days in the Gulf Stream we could bathe in the warm water of the swimming-pool and sit out on deck in little more than bathing costumes. In those two brief periods at the beginning and end of the Canadian visit I made acquaintance with New York from Riverside Drive to Greenwich Village, ascended the Empire State Building, and took a steamer trip to Coney Island. Travelling to Toronto by the night train, I experienced the now outdated sleeping cars, with their curtained bunks. Waiting for my turn to wash and shave the following morning, a typical Yankee, according to outward appearance, knowing by my speech that I was English, turned to me and asked, 'I say, what do your people put up with a king for, anyway?' Recalling some facts I had recently come across, I said, 'For one reason, because it is cheaper than your system.' It was not the sort of reply he had expected, and with, 'Oh, I guess not,' he turned away.

Toronto is a very attractive city and often described as very English. I began to think it would be more correct to describe it as very Irish when I saw the Orange procession on 12th July. It was more than five miles long, with all the traditional trappings—the banners of the various Orange lodges, the pipe bands, and King William on his white horse. As this indicates, it is strongly Protestant, in contrast to Montreal in the predominantly Catholic province of Quebec. The Metropolitan Church in Queen Street is in the central area of the city. Prior to Union it was the chief Methodist church. Some years before Union a fire destroyed the interior. In the restoration, what was left of the gallery was removed and the church made extremely beautiful, with a deep chancel, delightful panelling, and exquisite appointments. The finest organ in Canada was installed. The one defect was in the acoustic properties of what was now a very tall interior, unbroken, as previously, by the gallery. Microphones overcame the defect to some extent, but it was not an easy church for the preacher in that respect. While a large proportion of the regular congregation were away on holiday vacation, the visitors made up excellent assemblies. It was most interesting, after every service, to meet those visitors from almost every country, or so it seemed. One Sunday evening the Birmingham Society in Toronto came in a body with their badges and official regalia.

There was ample opportunity to see something of Eastern Canada, though I had not sufficient time to travel across to the West. The trip down the St Lawrence River by the Thousand Islands and on to Montreal and Quebec was delightful in the splendid boats. Then it included a change to the flat-bottomed boats to shoot the Lachine Rapids, an experience no longer possible since the opening of the new St Lawrence Seaway. Montreal is attractive because of the background of Mont Royale, from which a wonderful view is obtained. Quebec is the oldest city on the American continent and is a vivid reminder of the old French towns. On the way to the Roman Catholic shrine of St Anne de Beauprey one can see something of the more primitive conditions of the old settlers. On this particular trip I went on to Ottawa before returning to Toronto. The capital and seat of the Dominion Parliament is a most attractive city, with a very fine Parliament Building.

There were two short excursions which were full of interest. Mr Mason, one of the stalwart laymen of the Metropolitan Church, took me to spend some days at his fascinating summer residence on Lightwood Island in Lake Muskoka. He occupied, indeed, the whole island, with his garage on the mainland and a motor boat to connect with the tiny landing-stage. On another occasion Mr Hales, a Methodist lawyer, took his own minister, Dr Richard Roberts, Dr Martin Lloyd Jones, who was a summer preacher also in Toronto, and myself for several days up-country off the main roads and by the lumber trails in Haliburton County with its hundreds of lakes. When we arrived at Bancroft, which was little more than a main street of wooden buildings, we found that a meeting had been arranged in the wooden church at which the three of us were to speak. I was called upon first, and, after referring to my interest in the new United Church of Canada, I urged the congregation to look forward to the new leading of the Spirit. Martin Lloyd Jones put us all right by his strong affirmation that we had to look backward to the coming of Christ and it was the old, not the new, that mattered. To complete these particular remembrances I should include a reference to the few days I spent under canvas in the interesting Youth Camp on Beausoliel Island in Georgian Bay and, of course, several trips to the Niagara Falls.

The United Church of Canada is undoubtedly a great achievement, including, as it does, the Methodist, Presbyterian, and Congregational Churches. Neither the Anglican nor the Baptist Churches, both of whom were approached, would consider participating. The initiative was taken by the Methodist Church, which was distinctly the largest in membership and property, with the Presbyterian Church not far behind. The Congregational Church only represented about 2 per cent. of the total. The Methodist Church went to the utmost limit in concessions to meet the Presbyterian position, but rather more than a third of the Presbyterian churches refused to accept the basis of union and formed a continuing Presbyterian Church. On a visit to Canada a few years later an Anglican layman was taking several of us from England round Montreal. I asked him about the United Church. We were passing through a new development area and he pointed to a new United church and then within sight a new Presbyterian church on the same road. It is a tragedy that the union of the three Churches was not complete.

To a Methodist it is regrettable that in the concessions

ministers have ceased to be appointed by a central body. There are eleven annual conferences across Canada, but the big bi-annual General Council is the co-ordinating body. The Presbyterian system of the call of the minister by the local Church court, confirmed by the Presbytery, is maintained, and in a country like Canada, with the need for much pioneer frontier work, and with wide rural areas, there is a real problem. I attended a conference on rural work and found a measure of discontent. Ministers who are willing to spend a period in these difficult appointments wanted to be assured of a move to a city charge afterwards. With the policy of the local call, there is no assurance of this. I have learned in recent years that, through settlement committees, endeavour is made to overcome this difficulty, but at this point, as one of the Canadian leaders put it to me, the constitution 'grinds'. I am sure that very few, if any, of the ministers and people of the United Church of Canada would desire to return to pre-Union conditions. Much has been accomplished, and doubtless time and experience will make the instrument more perfect. In the meantime, it is interesting to discover that to the Presbyterians the hierarchy of the Stationing Committee in the Methodist Church is the denial of democracy. To such surprising and even amusing conclusions can those come who have no actual experience of the checks that limit a seeming autocracy.

This visit to America was at a time of a most serious economic slump. In New York I saw respectably-dressed men standing on the sidewalk and begging for 25 cents for a meal. In Toronto I saw many of the homeless living in tents and dreading what the harsh winter might mean for them. In these new countries with virgin land and untouched resources it was evidently assumed that unemployment and poverty were excluded until bitter experience proved the contrary. For those who suffered there was no such provision as unemployment insurance. There is a personal story arising out of these conditions and linked up with the Birmingham Mission.

A lady who had heard me preach in Toronto came to see me at the Birmingham Central Hall in great distress. Several years earlier she had married a Canadian and settled with her husband in Toronto. In the industrial slump her husband lost his position and as the weeks went by he tried in vain to secure other work. They saw their limited savings being sadly depleted and treasures of their home sold. Bitterness entered her soul, and, overwhelmed by the seeming hopelessness, she took what was left of the savings, bought a passage to England and returned to her parents. As time went on she began to see the seriousness of the wrong she had done. She wrote to her husband, but there was no reply. In deep distress, she told me her story, and then said, 'What shall I do?' It is a great responsibility to answer that kind of question but there are times when one becomes sure of the right answer, as in this case. Without hesitation I said, 'You must go back.' I tried to explain that she had done a great wrong and must take the only step that leads in the direction of possibly putting right the wrong. Of course, I said much more than that in a long interview, and we prayed together. She went back and I had a letter from her when she landed at Quebec. She told me that she had been sustained in that winter crossing of the Atlantic by something I had said as I tried to help her to see the right course. As she put it in her letter, it was this: 'God is not seeking to punish us for our sins: our sins work out their own punishment. God is seeking to save us from our sins if we will let Him.' At Quebec she faced the 600-mile railway journey to Toronto, and with no letter from her husband. In fact, her husband had received her letters, but only after a considerable time. They had followed him round as he had moved from place to place seeking work. When she reached the Union Station at Toronto she found that her husband had met every train for two days, lest he should miss her. The meal he had prepared to welcome her home even in his poor lodging completed the healing. As I heard from her later, she found work herself as a stenographer, which enabled them to carry on until her husband secured an established position. Eighteen years later I was visiting Canada and preaching one Sunday morning at the Metropolitan Church. Among the usual company who came to greet the visiting preacher was a smartly dressed lady with a beaming smile. She came to speak the thanks she had written at the time and to tell me that she and her husband had never looked back from the reunion those years before.

My interest in and association with Germany covers a

number of years and many visits. It began when I received an invitation from *The World Alliance for Promoting International Friendship through the Churches* to join a group representing the British churches on a visit of friendship to the German churches. This was in 1929, and was the first such visit since the ending of the first World War in 1918. The same body had arranged a visit of German churchmen to this country in 1928, and I had the pleasure of welcoming them to the Birmingham Central Hall. I explained to them something of the pattern and significance of central mission work, and my words were interpreted by Dr J. Ernst Sommer, later to become Bishop of the German Methodist Church. That was my introduction to one who became a great personal friend until his death twenty-four years later. This organization with the long name did a wonderful work and was one of the organizations that contributed to the founding of the World Council of Churches.

We had planned a holiday in Paris and I was preaching on one of the Sundays in our English Methodist Church in the Rue Roquepine. I went with my wife, her sister, and our daughter to the little French hotel in the Latin Quarter where we had arranged to stay. The rate of exchange greatly helped us that year. After spending nearly a week in Paris, I left to join the English church party in Hamburg. With the German visit over, I was able to return to Paris and conclude the holiday with my family.

This party of English clergy and ministers was under the leadership of the Bishop of Ripon, Dr Burroughs, and included five Anglicans, four Methodists, and representative Congregationalists, Baptists, Presbyterians, Quakers, and one Unitarian —twenty in all. At every centre we visited it seemed as though church dignitaries and people could not do enough to make the English visitors welcome after the tragedy of the war ten years earlier. The Senate of the Free City of Hamburg had arranged a reception and dinner in their Hall. They received us in their formal robes and ruffs and adorned the tables with their wonderful collection of gold plate. The gorgeous epergne opposite where I sat was a gift from King Edward VII. I stayed in the Methodist hospital, Bethanien, which was the only hospital left standing after the Second World War. During the train journey to Berlin I travelled with Dr Sommer and Professor

Karl Barth. After so long a passage of time, I have no intention of quoting from my rather elaborate notes of that conversation. It was not theological, but for me an opportunity to see the war from the standpoint of the conquered and to evaluate from that angle the significance of the Versailles Treaty with the Polish Corridor. We so seldom realize that our judgements can never rightly be a clear black or white.

In Berlin we were richly received by representatives of both the State Church and the Free Churches, with a special reception by the Theological Faculty of the Berlin University. If any of us had had no previous experience of German hospitality, we learned then what a formal dinner means, lasting several hours, with speeches between the courses. During the more general intercourse Leslie Weatherhead and I found ourselves in the company of Professor Adolph Deissmann. For nearly half an hour the distinguished author of *Light from the Ancient East* talked to us about his recent researches in Ephesus. Near the old eleventh-century church of Justinian they had uncovered the fourth-century church of St John the Divine, the church in which Cyril, Bishop of Alexandria, preached at the Council of Ephesus in A.D. 431. Below that they had found a room which might well be associated with the aged apostle John. Professor Deissmann explained to us his reasons for a strong feeling that the Pauline Epistles of the imprisonment were written from Ephesus rather than from Rome.

I carry vivid mental pictures of Berlin in contrast with the desolation I saw after the Second World War, but what we saw in some detail were some of the centres of work of the Innere Mission (Home Missions) of the State Church, which began at the Rauhe Haus at Hamburg, which we had already seen. This great organization comprised over 5,000 health centres—hospitals, homes, sanatoria, asylums—800 educational establishments, 2,000 labour colonies, with some 40,000 trained nursing deaconesses and an army of voluntary workers. Three of the centres we visited I shall never forget. A few miles from Berlin was Hoffnungstahl (Valley of Hope), a great area of forest and farmland being reclaimed by the labour of the unemployed, with a wonderful organization of redemptive ministry. In the Oberlin Haus at Potsdam for crippled and maimed children we saw five who were deaf and blind. They were being taught to speak and the older boy spoke to us in German. The whole five were talking to one another by the touch of their hands. The third centre at Bielefeld we visited during our last weekend. In this self-governing colony of Bethel, with houses, hospitals, schools and parks, there were the largest number of epileptics at any one place in the world. They live in the assurance of the help they need being always at hand. There were 1,500 in the church on Sunday morning, all but about 100 being epileptic. I had a long talk with one of the doctors who told me that it had become their verified conviction that a large percentage of the epileptics owe their condition to conception under the influence of alcoholism. I was very interested in one aged pastor who played to us on his *flügel* horn with its beautiful, smooth tone—an instrument not often heard in this country.

On our first Sunday I was invited to preach in Brandenburg, which is about thirty-six miles from Berlin. This delightful old town was celebrating the thousandth anniversary of its foundation, and people had come from the surrounding country wearing their national costumes. Some were from the Polish Corridor separated under the Versailles Treaty. Pastor Goehling met me and took me along to his Church of St John —an old monastic church of the eleventh century, but now a Reformed Church in the Prussian Union. An English preacher had been announced and the crowded church included the staff and pupils of the Oberlyzeum (High School). I was told that about half the congregation would be able to follow the English. The Pastor gave a précis of my sermon in German. My knowledge of German is distinctly limited, but at that time it was still more slender. However, after rehearsal by the Pastor, I managed the prayer before the sermon and the text in their own tongue. It was a particularly interesting experience, as also were the hospitality and conversation in the Parsonage afterwards.

We left Berlin for what amounted to a pilgrimage through the Luther country with official receptions at every centre. At Wittenberg we saw where the Papal Bull was burnt, the houses of Luther and Melanchthon, the church where Luther ministered for fifty years, the Castle Church on the doors of which Luther nailed the famous theses and where he is buried.

Though it was not in the programme, I could not pass through Halle without paying respect to George Frederick Handel, I saw both the reputed birthplace, with its plaster decoration of laurels, and the plainer house next door which Newman Flower affirms should have the honour. In the Market Place is the statue of Handel and across the square the Liebfrauenkirche, where young George was christened and where he had his first organ lessons from Zachow. There was another brief musical pilgrimage in which we all participated when we reached Eisenach. This was to the house where Johann Sebastian Bach was born, with its present wonderful collection of eighteenth-century musical instruments. I still recall the joy I had in playing the quaint old organ as we sang, *'Nun danket alle Gott'*—thankful indeed for the great gift of God in Johann Sebastian Bach.

It was with Martin Luther in our minds that we drove on to the Wartburg, an isolated hill standing some 600 feet above Eisenach at the north of the Thuringian Forest. The best preserved twelfth-century castle in Germany stands on the summit. It is the scene of the *Tannhauser* legends, and the hall where the contest of song took place may still be visited. The Elector George provided a retreat here for Luther after the Diet of Worms and gave him the opportunity to do his great work of translating the New Testament into German. There are some who say that we put John Wesley too much into the centre of our thought of Methodism, but it is not to be compared with the centrality of Luther in German Protestantism. The words we saw so often in many different forms were, *'Gottes Wort und Luthers Lehr Wird vergehen nimmemehr'* (God's Word and Luther's teaching can never pass away). As we walked through the archway to the hotel cleverly built on to the castle, choirboys from Eisenach welcomed us in song, and then sang most beautifully Mendelssohn's 'Lift thine eyes' and a rhythmically unfamiliar form of *'Ein feste Berg'*. When it was dark we saw the castle slowly illuminated until it was one glowing picture against the dark sky, and then a cross flashed out above the tower.

Two unforgettable occasions marked the climax of this official visit, though, in fact, the first was unofficial. During the second week-end we stayed all together in a villa in Bethel.

Bishop Burroughs called us to a celebration of Holy Communion early on the Sunday morning. The only place available was an unused kitchen and the only possible altar was the kitchen table. The Bishop arranged his travelling paten and chalice, several of different churches shared in the pre-Communion service, and we all communicated at the hands of the Bishop. It is impossible to describe the deep feeling created by this simple act of united Communion. It was indeed the Table of the Lord. Then, in Kassel in connexion with the annual German Council of the World Alliance, 4,000 people paid for admission to the City Hall to hear speeches on 'The Churches and World Peace'. We became acutely conscious of the tragic folly of the Versailles Treaty which sowed the seed of dangerous developments which we saw might follow and actually did follow only ten years after our visit and that amazing meeting. It is distressing today to realize that the whole of the Luther country we visited is now included in Eastern Germany under Soviet Control and beyond the Iron Curtain.

My friendship with Dr J. E. Sommer was established during those days and became ever closer in subsequent years. He was educated at Rydal School and took his degree at Cambridge and with his fine command of idiomatic English was of great service. When the Second World War broke out he was in Zürich, and before returning to Germany he wrote me the last letter I had from him for nearly eight years. In it he said: 'Nothing that has happened nor anything that can happen will disturb our friendship.'

On subsequent holiday visits, chiefly by car, we became increasingly familiar with much of the glorious scenery of Germany and with the German people. We travelled through other countries of western Europe, but always found more delight in Germany and Austria. There we found unfailing courtesy, cleanliness, and efficiency, even in the very ordinary hotel or hostel. We were never let down even when far off the ordinary tourist track. We soon discovered the mistake of one common idea; that it is necessary to drink the wine of the country. That is entirely false, even though it is wise to avoid ordinary water. We never failed to get natural mineral waters or palatable soft drinks in quite remote places. One evening we reached Trier, having overlooked the fact that it was the year of the exposition of the seamless robe of Christ, which is claimed to be one of the treasures of the Cathedral. The city was crowded with pilgrims, and every possible hostel fully occupied. The Manager of the hotel where we had hoped to stay saw our difficulty, and, after some telephoning, secured two bedrooms belonging to friends in nearby flats, so that with meals at the hotel we were admirably provided for, though we were complete strangers. That kind of couresty is not found everywhere. The Black Forest greatly appealed to us, and on several occasions we stayed at the German Methodist Kurhaus Teuchelwald in that most charming town, Freudenstadt. Is there a more delightful place in which to relax than Zell am See, in the heart of the Austrian mountains. Berchtesgaden is notorious as the place where Hitler built his mountain retreat but it is a very attractive old-world town, and a few kilometres away is the Königsee, one of the most exquisitely beautiful lakes I have ever seen. It was inevitable that these journeys should include two pilgrimages, one to the house where Wolfgang Amadeus Mozart was born in Salzburg and the other to the birthplace of Ludwig van Beethoven in Bonn. Each house incorporates a museum associated with the life and work of the great composers.

In 1934 there was arranged a special year for the Passion Play at Oberammergau to celebrate the 300th anniversary of the first performance in fulfilment of the communal vow which began it all. A Birmingham friend joined me, and we travelled out in my Morris Minor. Having stayed there before, at the boarding-house of Hugo Rutz, the *Schmiedmeister* who played the part of Caiaphas, I was able to make direct arrangements to stay for four nights, and thus we saw Oberammergau when the great company who had come only for the play had left it in quiet simplicity, as I had seen it before. There is something rather wonderful about this mountain village of just under 3,000 inhabitants. For one thing they have no crime and no police force. Many remark upon the exceptional beauty of the children. There is a marked contrast between the ordinary life and conditions of Oberammergau and other places in Bavaria of similar size. Is not the explanation that the whole culture of the village in the years between the performances of the Passion Play is based on the story of Jesus. The play is not a Roman Catholic production, though that is the faith of most of the villagers. There is a Lutheran church in the village and some Protestants take part in the play. One of the impressive facts is that they have resisted all efforts to exploit the Passion Play on the films, even though it would greatly relieve what is often a very restricted financial position. The situation is 2,700 feet above sea-level and surrounded by the high mountains of the Tyrol. Hanging over the village, as it seems, is a great conical rock rising right above the forest, which covers the lower slopes of the mountains. Having the extra time, we climbed the Köffel, as it is called, which very few visitors attempt. It takes just over two hours and the view over the mountains as one stands by the cross on its summit is very impressive.

In 1937 the Göttingen University celebrated the 200th anniversary of its foundation by King George II. It remains a memorial of the Royal House of Hanover and bears the English arms in its crest. I was able to render a service to a research scholar of Göttingen who was taking a course in the Birmingham University. He never forgot it, and as dean of one of the faculties he invited me to the celebration. I stayed with the Professor of Modern History, Dr. Kaehler. He and his charming lady were most kind. I can only think of Frau Kaeler as a true *Gnadigefrau*. This German word means literally 'gracious lady', but it has a rather more special significance in Germany. Through Professor Kaehler, I came to know his great friends, Professor Joachim Jeremias, and his wife. Prof. Jeremias is widely known for his great contribution to New Testament scholarship. They belonged to the Confessional Synod, the section of the State Church which was opposed to the Hitler control of the Church. It was a most critical time, and I was able to render them some slight help on returning to England. The University Service on the Sunday morning concluded with the singing by an enlarged choir of the 'Hallelujah Chorus' from Handel's *Messiah*. This was introduced owing to the Handel Festival, which was being held at the same time. What struck me was to hear those words 'The kingdom of this world is become the Kingdom of our Lord and of His Christ, and He shall reign for ever and ever' in the church and then two hours later to hear the same crowd shouting 'Heil Hitler!' I was privileged in having an opportunity to attend a performance of Handel's opera, *Scipio*, which was given with an orchestra and stage setting in exact reproduction of the eighteenth-century conditions. It began at 8 p.m. and concluded at 12.15 a.m. True, there were two long intervals. What a unique opportunity that was!

This incomplete account of travel during fourteen years is sufficient to indicate what an enriching experience it can be and what a valuable addition to one's life. It is not only the interest of it but the enlargement of one's background of personal knowledge. A coach-tour through these countries can be most enjoyable, but can only provide a very superficial understanding of the land and the people. It is when it is possible to meet people of all sorts through independent travel, establish friendships and enter the homes of the people, that one begins to understand their life and evaluate the characteristics of their country. Thus the travel becomes not a passing holiday, but a permanent possession. At the time I could not foresee how this background of experience in other countries would make a tremendous difference to the discharge of my responsibilities when I became a secretary of the World Methodist Council, which, at that time, had yet to come into being. So are we prepared for the duties of the future, as I have come to recognize time after time.

CHAPTER VIII

CHURCH BUILDINGS AND WAR DAMAGE

THE designation to responsibility for 'The Department for Chapel Affairs', to use the official title, was a surprise, as I have already indicated, and the wisdom of it was doubted by many of my trusted friends. I could see their point of view. The superintendency of a central mission extends one's powers to the full as preacher, pastor and administrator; to exchange that for an office desk seemed almost a personal disaster. Had that been a correct description of the change my friends would have been right. Having had the experience of one department I was fully aware of the danger of being imprisoned within administrative details, but I felt reasonably sure that I could avoid it. There were features about this new appointment which made a strong appeal to me. I knew from experience the valuable part played by the Department in relation to church extension. Then my continued interest in legal matters and a growing knowledge of church architecture were invaluable equipment for this new post. What none of us could forsee was the outbreak of war and the special responsibility which would rest upon the Department arising from the widespread damage to church buildings. The work in connexion with war damage became an outstanding part of my service in the Department and my once doubtful friends were the first to admit that I seemed to fit in to this unexpected task in a way that made perfectly clear the rightness of the appointment.

Less than a year after the spiritual experience which sent John Wesley forth on his great evangelistic work he found himself involved in building affairs. They proved exceedingly troublesome,[1] but, having obtained expert advice, his logical mind seized upon the right solution. This was the policy of the Model Trust Deed for all Methodist property, a policy

[1] See E. Benson Perkins, *Methodist Preaching Houses and the Law*, Epworth Press.

which was adopted and enjoined by the Conference in 1763 and is set out in the *Minutes* for that year. This important legal provision secured the unity of Methodism. The buildings were held for the use and purposes of Methodism, the preachers were to be appointed by the Conference after the death of the Wesleys, and the doctrinal standards were defined. In 1854 the various committees which had assisted building and exercised oversight were combined in one General Chapel Committee, with departmental offices in Manchester. The decentralization of departments was official Wesleyan policy for many years, and when the new Birmingham Central Hall was built in 1903 rooms were provided for the offices of the Home Mission Department. The more recent tendency to centralize in or near London is not likely to affect the Department for Chapel Affairs, which is too well established in Manchester to consider moving. With the rebuilt and enlarged offices, the necessary strong-room, and the experienced staff, a change of location would be extremely difficult. The arguments for any such change have never been convincing and departmental direction from Westminster and Manchester is to be preferred to concentration at one address.

When I entered the Department in 1939, my colleague, the General Secretary, was William C. Jackson, a man of quite exceptional ability and fine spirit. At Cambridge he secured a First Class in the Mathematical Tripos, obtaining a high place in the list of wranglers. He was the Chapel Secretary of the United Methodist Church prior to Union, and its last President. In 1935 he was appointed President of the united Church. On his retirement in 1942 I became General Secretary, and was joined by Albert Hearn, who was also a minister of the United Methodist Church before Union. At the time of his appointment to the Department he had charge of the well-known George Street Methodist Church, Burton-on-Trent, and was Chairman of the Derby District. The Department had secured a particularly able lay staff. I doubt whether many in the Methodist Church know all that the Church owes to the senior managing clerk, Mr William Shaw, who has been with the Department since 1925, and has an unrivalled knowledge of Methodist property throughout the country. The managing clerk in the legal office in my time and for some years afterwards was Mr A. M. Jewitt. At his death in 1962 he had brought to completion over a hundred years of service in the office rendered jointly by his uncle and himself. Mr Gordon Berresford returned to the office after war service and is the cashier in charge of the office of the Trustees for Methodist Church Purposes. The responsible Ministerial secretaries owe so much to the technical knowledge and ability of these senior members of the staff that I could not travel on with my story without paying a sincere tribute to these lay colleagues.

The Department has as its responsible and directing body one of the finest committees in the Methodist Church, consisting of lawyers, architects, surveyors, accountants, bankers, and business executives, with selected ministers of experience, including chairmen of districts and district chapel secretaries. It is able to give expert decisions on the many financial and technical questions which have constantly to be dealt with in such a department. This involves not only attendance at the quarterly meetings of the General Committee, but service on legal, architectural, and other sub-committees. It is a tribute to the Church that laymen of ability carrying their own considerable responsibilities are ready to give time and thought to the administrative work of the Church to which they belong. The senior treasurer throughout my period was Mr A. B. Hillis who became a personal friend. I found this committee to have a stimulating effect upon a secretary who must keep himself informed and knowledgeable on all these technical matters and be ready to guide the committee on questions of policy. The Committee recognized, what is my own deep conviction, that these technical and administrative responsibilities can only be rightly handled when they are intimately related to the spiritual life of the Church and, indeed, are part of the essential service of the Church for the Kingdom of God.

The routine and continuing work of the office—sales of property, building schemes, formation of new trusts, new sites, architectural plans, financial aid and the like, with interviews and deputations and endless correspondence—was soon interrupted as a result of the war, even during the year of relative quiet before the bombardment began. All over the country school buildings were requisitioned for Government purposes.

These purposes included rest centres, first-aid posts, Home Guard quarters, military headquarters, restaurants and other incidental uses. The total of such requisitions was over 4,000. Problems soon arose, one of the chief being the opening of wet canteens to supply alcoholic liquors on some of these school buildings. An appeal to Government headquarters became essential. My previous contact with Mr Hore Belisha was fortunate, for he was now Minister of War, and it was with the War Office that our chief difficulties were concerned. A direct appeal to him gave me immediate access to the Director of Quartering. With this introduction to the formidable building in Whitehall, I received that courtesy and consideration which one always found when dealing with high responsible officials. Our urgent problem was solved and we were assured of official orders which would exclude wet canteens from all our premises. I then took the opportunity of reminding the General of our responsibility as a department and I asked for authoritative access to buildings and areas which might be affected by war action. I obtained a document, still in my possession, with the War Office crest and the stamp of the Quartering Department stating that I was performing duties connected with Methodist Church buildings and asking that necessary facilities be given to me. I carried that document throughout the war and it was interesting to see how a sight of the War Office stamp turned the most dictatorial police officer into a helpful ally. After the interview I went across to our Westminster Central Buildings to find that a committee of the Social Welfare Department was in session considering what ought to be done about these wet canteens. It was, of course, an issue which that department would deal with if necessary. I am afraid, however, that I took an unholy delight in telling them that this particular battle had been fought and won. I often wished that other acute difficulties could be resolved with equal ease and courtesy.

Fortunately, an event of great importance to our family took place during that seemingly quiet year before Great Britain felt the impact of the war. During my service with the Chapel Department our home was in Wilmslow, that one-time village and now rapidly growing urban area in Cheshire some twelve miles south of Manchester. I had become a commuter once again. When we moved to Wilmslow we had in mind the wedding which was to take place in the summer of 1940. With her characteristic wisdom, my wife arranged that Mary should run our house for that ten months—under oversight, of course—in preparation for her own home. I wonder how many brides have that sort of training in these days when the mother of the house is so often engaged in a remunerative job elsewhere, even if the bride herself can arrange to take that time off from some post. The wedding took place on a glorious day in August and I had great joy in marrying our beloved daughter to George Stephen Lester, son of Mr and Mrs A. W. Lester of Walsall and the one-time University Methodist Society friend. Mary's husband is today a consultant surgeon, but at that time was assisting in general practice before being called up for war service. Some time after Stephen had left for overseas service, Mary came to us at Wilmslow with her little son, awaiting her husband's return from North Africa and Palestine.

When Mary left home, my wife's younger sister, Miss Hilda Bull, came to live with us, having retired, earlier than the appointed age, from her position as headmistress in a Leicester school. It has been a delight to have her with us during now more than twenty years, to the great enrichment of our home life. Her presence, by making possible my often long absences from home, has made a real difference to my work. I doubt whether otherwise I could have served Methodism and particularly World Methodism as I have tried to do.

The Battle of Britain was raging as my second year with the Department began. At the October meeting of the General Committee, 1940, we had to consider the first reports of damaged churches. This marked the commencement for me of a task which claimed priority in thought and service for years ahead. It is perhaps desirable that I should explain the secretarial method in our office. The two Secretaries shared completely the responsibility for policy and had full knowledge of each other's activities, so that no hiatus occurred in the absence of either secretary. At the same time there were sections of work we each had under our more immediate personal direction. It was clear that war damage would continue to be of paramount importance for a considerable period, and it was suggested from the first that I should take personal responsibility for this unprecedented task even after I became the General Secretary. No one could have anticipated how complex and extensive that responsibility would be.

While concentrating, as we were bound to do, upon the problems arising from the damaged and destroyed buildings of the Methodist Church, we never forgot the damage suffered by other churches, nor the more serious issues affecting homes and lives. It is worth while, I think, quoting from the first resolution passed by the Committee when war damage began:

> 'With our responsibility in respect of the property of the Methodist Church throughout the country we are constrained, as our first act . . . to have in deep and prayerful rememberance the disasters to other churches and the sad plight of all the suffering people . . . to record our sympathetic thought and prayer for our Methodist people who have been bereaved, have lost their homes and possessions, have had to leave familiar ground, and have seen their houses of prayer and worship shattered. . . . Amid this distress and anguish we thank God for the courage, endurance, and patience of our people and the devoted service and leadership of their ministers and deaconesses, and we commend all to the grace of God for tasks of the present emergency and the rebuilding in the days of peace.'

I felt it to be essential to see what was happening and to be in touch with our ministers where the damage was taking place. It is impossible to forget those experiences when, armed with the War Office document, I visited some of the scenes of destruction. During the daylight raid on Buckingham Palace I was in the basement of the shattered Stepney Central Hall, the headquarters of the East End Mission, where my brother-in-law, the Rev. Percy Ineson, Superintendent of the Mission, and my sister, had been living. Every shop and office in the area was closed down during the raid, but when we were badly needing some refreshment one of the deaconesses discovered that a fried-fish shop had a small chink open. She brought in the plebeian fish and chips, and could anything have been more delicious! I referred to this in an article, and shortly afterwards I received a letter from the fried-fish proprietor with a donation for the Mission. He said it was the first time the fried-fish business had received honourable mention in the pages of the *Methodist Recorder*. In Coventry it was the thirty thousand wrecked houses that presented such a picture of disaster, far more than the destruction of the Cathedral, though that, naturally, received great publicity. Visiting a northern city, less than twenty-four hours after a disastrous attack, to meet the ministers, was to find them all suffering, subconsciously, from delayed shock. They had passed through a very terrible night. The proposed meeting had to be postponed until they had recovered from their distressing experiences. With the variation of local circumstances, tragic and distressing scenes were to be found in city after city, but any attempt at a description would be futile.

One of the most amazing facts is the way in which the churches adjusted and sustained their activities during these terrible months. When trying to describe the situation in a speech to the Ecumenical Methodist Conference at Springfield, Massachusetts, U.S.A., in 1947, I said: 'Looking backward, it is difficult for those of us who have lived and worked through those years to realize how the churches maintained their work and their witness . . . to an extent beyond anything that could have been anticipated.'

The Goverment acted speedily in the consideration of the necessary legislation, and the War Damage Act was passed early in 1941. The Chancellor of the Exchequer, who had charge of the Bill, was Sir Kingsley Wood, who was the son of a Methodist minister and himself a member of the Methodist Church. The Secretary of the Conference, the Rev. Edwin Finch, and I saw the Chancellor in his room at the Treasury to put to him what we felt to be the needs of the churches arising in particular out of the experiences of the Methodist Church. The Chancellor not only listened to us with sympathetic interest and understanding, but discussed freely the proposals formulated in his own mind. While there had to be a contributory scheme for property generally, to which all property-owners would pay their proportionate amount and out of which the financial loss due to war damage would be met, he recognized that the churches were quite unable to contribute to such a fund on any appropriate scale. There must be, the Chancellor recognized, a special set of proposals under which the churches would be helped from other sources. No details were embodied in the Act of Parliament, but it was left for the War Damage Commission, under the chairmanship of Mr Malcolm Trustram Eve, K.C., as he was then, to work out and implement the intentions of the Act in consultation with the churches. It should be remembered that all the churches were involved in the compulsory Chattels (Furnishing) Insurance Scheme, and the total Methodist payment of those premiums was over £250,000.

With characteristic foresight, the then Bishop of London, Dr Geoffrey Fisher, called a meeting of representatives of the churches which set up what is still known as 'The Churches Main Committee', on which the Anglican Church, the Roman Catholic Church, and all the main Free Churches had members. From this body a small committee of twelve, equally divided between clerical and lay members, was appointed. The lay members were architects, surveyors, or lawyers. It was my privilege and responsibility to be on that small committee. Under the chairmanship of Dr Fisher, we met every two or three weeks to work out a policy for what was called 'church payment'. Stage by stage, we discussed our proposals with the Government Commission, taking the proposals back for further examination in the light of the joint discussion. It was only after three years of intensive work during the continuance of the war that agreement was reached and an acceptable policy declared in 1944. There was great value in this not being part of the War Damage Act itself, and therefore sufficiently flexible to meet the varied and often most complicated requirements of the situation.

For the purpose of this story, it is not necessary to go into all the technical details of a scheme of church payment which was a credit to the Government of our country and of inestimable value to the continued and extended life and work of the Christian Churches. The two vital points were: (*a*) that of equal treatment of all the churches, whether of the replacement of a destroyed church or the repair of a damaged church, and (*b*) that of the portability of the assessed payment to another site so as to avoid the restoration of redundant buildings. In my judgement, we owe very much, not only to the

CHURCH BUILDINGS AND WAR DAMAGE

insight of the Chancellor of the Exchequer, but to the wise guidance of Dr Fisher. He made us all his friends, and it was in those years that I came to know him with some intimacy. He retained the chair of the Committee until he became Archbishop of Canterbury, when the new Bishop of London, Dr J. W. C. Wand, took his place. The atmosphere of friendliness pervaded the whole group and we reached all our decisions by common consent.

In the working out of this agreed policy, the Government War Damage Commission sought to deal with the central authority of each of the denominations. No other denomination was so well equipped as our own to meet this requirement. I could give definite assurance that all the cases of Methodist war damage would be handled through our Department. There were endless complications, and my time was more than fully occpuied, not only in the functioning of our own office method in this particular field, but in frequent discussion with the principal permanent officials of the War Damage Commission and with the officers in charge of the regional sections of the administration. From the first, the Department for Chapel Affairs was recognized by the Government as dealing with all Methodist issues in this field, and we were able to guide the wise use of war damage payment and to take full advantage of the policy of portability. A lawyer acting for another denomination complained bitterly in my hearing of the relative failure to use the advantage of portability in his own Church. They had no authoritative central direction and the local committees or trustees had no vision beyond their limited local circle.

It is well known that the Churches Committee found itself serving the churches in matters far beyond those of war damage. For the first time there was a body representing all the churches and accepted by them as the instrument for negotiation with the Government. On the side of the Government, in its varied ministries, there was immediate acceptance of a Committee with which they could deal on matters of policy without having to face the complication of dealing with each separate denomination. Those of us who had something to do with the establishing of this Committee under the leadership of Lord Fisher of Lambeth, to use his present title, built better than we knew. So, as difficult issues emerged after the war—building licences, sites in the new housing areas and new towns, compulsory purchase, rating assessments, electricity and oil charges, charities, and many other issues—the machinery for consultation between the Churches and the Government was at hand. There are only two or three of the original members still active on the Committee. When it was reconstituted in 1962 I greatly appreciated being appointed by the Committee itself as a permanent member. The record of Mr J. A. Hinks goes back nearly as far as the beginning, for I nominated him as another Methodist member and a surveyor in the early months. He still serves as Chairman of the Technical Sub-committee. One of the early members whom I got to know rather well was the Roman Catholic Bishop William F. Browne. His titular bishopric was that of Pella, an early Christian see in Decapolis. What arguments we had, chiefly on education, before the Committee was called to order to begin its business! When I was in hospital at the end of 1943 for an appendix operation, he wrote me a delightful letter of remembrance as from one Christian to another. It was a pity that none of the Roman Catholic members could attend the service of thanksgiving arranged by the Archbishop of Canterbury in the restored chapel of Lambeth Palace. Now that the war was long past and many of the Churches were approaching restoration, he invited the members of the Committee he had inaugurated to give thanks to God for what had been accomplished by united action. There is great satisfaction in having taken part in this most valuable and constructive service by the churches unitedly. It is only the cynic who declares that the churches are only united when it is a case of getting something from the Government. There is far more to it than that.

A personal story which I have hesitated hitherto in making public can now be related. At one of the meetings of the Churches Committee in 1947 I referred to my interest in Methodist churches in Italy, where the Government were restoring the damaged Roman Catholic churches, but not the non-Catholic. Recalling that the Established Church in this country had sought no special privileges, but all had been treated alike, to the great assistance of the Roman Catholic and the

Free Churches, I inquired whether we could submit to the Cardinal Archibishop of Westminser, that he might suggest through the Vatican or in such other way as might be open that influence be brought to bear upon the Italian Government to adopt the same enlightened policy as had proved so advantageous. Dr Wand smiled, but thought it was not within the competence of the Committee. When we dispersed Father Anderson came across to me and strongly suggested that I should myself write to the Cardinal. A few days later I wrote a careful and, I hoped, diplomatic letter to Cardinal Griffin, and received within a few posts an astonishing reply in these words: 'Dear Mr Benson Perkins, I am very glad you have written to me about this matter. I will do everything within my power to secure similar treatment for the non-Catholic churches in Italy. Yours, etc.' Five months later, under date 31st May, 1948, I received a second letter from Cardinal Griffin with enclosures. This also was short and to the point: 'Dear Mr Benson Perkins, You may remember that you wrote to me on the 30th December apropos of help for bombed Methodist churches in Italy. I took immediate action and I am sure you will be glad to receive a copy of a letter and enclosure sent to me by the Italian Ambassador. With kindest wishes, etc.' This enclosed copy of a letter from the Ambassador conveyed the assurance he had received from his Government that 'non-Catholic religious establishments' would 'be granted a similar treatment to that accorded to Catholic establishments'. The second enclosure was a copy in Italian of the order issued by the appropriate department of the Italian Government. There was an important limitation that the 'similar treatment' would not extend beyond one non-Catholic establishment in each parish. Within that limit it was a notable achievement. To what extent this action of the Italian Government was due solely or in part to the intervention of Cardinal Griffin we shall never know, but that he did readily and immediately exert his influence is most significant. Something happened during that five months between the two letters of Cardinal Griffin.

There is a twofold sequel to this story. Just over a month after receiving that second letter from the Cardinal, my wife and I attended the Garden Party at Buckingham Palace, as I was then President-Designate. We saw three clergymen among the large concourse without taking particular notice until one of them came to speak to us. It was the Cardinal, who had recognized me from the days when he was Archibishop of Birmingham. He was most gracious and we had an interesting conversation. He spoke of being particularly glad that such a response had been forthcoming from the Italian Government and that he had been able to be of service to that end. Then on Sunday, 15th February, 1953, I had the great privilege and joy of dedicating a new Methodist church at La Spezia on the West coast of Italy. It is a particularly fine building, with a beautiful sanctuary, Guild and Fellowship rooms, accommodation for the minister, and a caretaker's flat. The Italian Government met the entire cost of this 'non-Catholic establishment', which replaced one destroyed during the war. I met Cardinal Griffin several times later at official functions and he impressed me as a great Christian. He died in 1956.

It is passing strange that the departmental office dealing with war damage should be the only one to suffer damage from enemy action. On Whit Monday, 2nd June, 1941, an isolated bomb attack set on fire the Central Buildings, Manchester, with the offices of the Department for Chapel Affairs and the War Damage Committee. We saw the terriffic blaze from our home in Wilmslow, twelve miles away, not knowing until a telephone call came through that it was our building. Fortunately, in a way, it was an incendiary bomb, so that the ground floor of the building was only slightly burnt, though much damaged by water. But the main hall, the other Mission premises, and our suite of offices presented a sorry spectacle when we were able to climb over the debris and see the amount of destruction. Our steel strong-room in the basement, constructed so as to stand against the collapse of the building, was not affected and all its valuable documentary contents were unharmed. How kind everyone was! The printers, for instance, had stocks of letter-paper printed and other office supplies ready before we had begun to think about such things. We secured temporary accommodation in the old Lever Street schoolroom. It was inconvenient enough, but we managed, and four months later preliminary repairs enabled us to return to the historic address.

We had set up a special and influential Methodist War

Damage Committee, and one of our immediate tasks was to secure a detailed test survey of war damage in a typical centre. Mr John Hinks, our advisory surveyor, carried out such a survey of all the varied items of war damage in Birmingham. The study of this and application of the conclusions to other areas made it clear to me that with generous Government payment we should need extra funds, which I estimated as, at least, £250,000. This was in order that we might take full advantage of the policy of portability of war damage payment and rebuild where the buildings were most needed. The total recorded cases of Methodist buildings destroyed or damaged was just over 3,000. About one-third of these cases were in the London area. When I submitted my conclusions to the War Damage Committee, there was much hesitation about raising so large a sum as a quarter of a million pounds, which seemed and was indeed a more considerable sum in 1942 than it was twenty years later. However, at a second meeting this was agreed, and at the Conference of 1942 the proposal to raise a building fund, which I presented, was approved. When, the following year, I submitted the figure of £250,000, the Rev. G. E. Hickman Johnson of the Mission House suggested the possibility of a joint fund for war damage at home and overseas where little or no Government aid was available. The Conference welcomed the suggestion, as I did, and we were instructed to meet and bring a specific proposal to the next Conference. I had the responsibility of proposing to the Conference of 1944 the raising of half a million pounds sterling, to be equally divided between the administration relating to war damage by the Committee centred in Manchester and the Mission House for war damage overseas. This proposal was adopted.

The Rev. William C. Jackson, even after his retirement, had been most helpful in respect of the Rebuilding Fund, but before the final resolution was approved by the Conference he died. In the division of responsibility within the office, which I have indicated, my colleague took over the secretarial direction of the raising of the Rebuilding Fund after the Conference in 1944 had given its approval. This the Rev. Albert Hearn carried through with great success, and when I was in the Chair of the Conference in 1948 he was able to report a final figure of £616,698. The exhibition, entitled

'How Great a Flame', brilliantly directed by the late Rev. F. Howell Everson, who was seconded to the Department for this purpose, made a wonderful contribution. Few financial efforts of this magnitude have provoked so generous and immediate a response in the whole history of Methodism.

The need to pass on detailed information on the many technical points arising from war damage and the situation generally for the use of ministers and district officials suggested a new use for the annual reports of the Department. The first such issue in 1943, entitled 'Answering your Questions', was welcomed with enthusiasm and led on to 'More Questions Answered', 'What does it Mean—a glossary of terms', 'Caring for the Churches' and 'Trusts and Trustees'. The sections of these five reports of permanent value were published in a small volume entitled *Serving the Church*. That was not the end, for the annual publication of such booklets has been continued and appreciated as a valued service to the Church. As building became possible, it was clearly desirable to give trustees and architects definite ideas concerning the requirements of Methodist Church buildings. The war had created a break with the past conditions and the new buildings required in the extensive housing areas and new towns presented a tremendous opportunity. A committee was appointed to examine the whole field of design and equipment for Methodist purposes. The services of three architects were secured to prepare model plans of the approved styles, and experts were consulted on other points. The results were embodied in a volume entitled *The Methodist Church Builds Again*, which my colleague and I edited from the committee and architects reports, writing ourselves the two introductory chapters. The book has, unquestionably, had a very wide influence. As it was published in 1946, the time has come for revision in the light of experience and fresh ideas. It is rather surprising that no other church has produced a comparable volume for its own specific purposes, though there are quite a few books dealing in general with church architecture.

Because of my knowledge and experience of church-building technique, I was asked to serve on the Coventry Cathedral Commission, which was set up in 1947 after the Royal Fine Arts Commission had rejected the first design. The proposed

CHURCH BUILDINGS AND WAR DAMAGE 119

Chapel of Unity and the Christian Service Centre had brought Free Church interest into the scheme. The Right Hon. the Lord Harlech was Chairman of the Commission, and the other five members were Sir Percy Thomas, ex-President of the R.I.B.A., Sir Philip Morris, Vice-Chancellor of Bristol University, the Bishop of Stafford, the Provost of Leicester, and myself. Our proposal for the Cathedral itself was a nave and choir suitable for diocesan purposes built on to the undamaged tower and spire on the site of the destroyed building. This could have been carried out within the war damage payment and extra appeals would then have been limited to the Chapel of Unity, the Christian Service Centre, and furnishings. This was rejected in favour of an architectural competition. Our recommendation in respect of the Chapel of Unity remained, and was stated as follows:

'The architect should be asked to design a chapel completely furnished for Christian worship which will, therefore, include a pulpit, lectern and Holy Table. Thus the chapel will be available for use by clergy and ministers of the various participating denominations for the celebration of Holy Communion according to their respective rites for those in communion with them. In addition, the Holy Table will stand as a symbol of the hope of complete unity.'

Thus far the regulations exclude Holy Communion altogether from the Chapel of Unity and there is no suitable provision for it in the circular chapel attached to the new Cathedral. Having worked as a member of the Commission, I am naturally prejudiced in favour of our agreed proposal, and I cannot avoid the conclusion that a great opportunity has been missed. The position and architectural form of the small circular Chapel of Unity as it has been built does not lend itself to what we as a Commission were satisfied should be the true function and use of a Chapel of Unity. On the cathedral itself I express no opinion beyond saying that the real test of its abiding value will come after a period, possibly seven to ten years, when the attraction of mere novelty has spent itself and the building can be rightly judged on its suitability as a House of God.

A section of the work which is distinct and yet has a definite association with the Department comes under the title, 'The

Trustees for Methodist Church Purposes'. This is an incorporated board established under The Methodist Church Act, 1939, which brought together two similar boards in the Wesleyan and United Methodist Churches as they were prior to the 1932 Union. The Board holds funds and real estate generally as custodian trustee. The extent of its operation is indicated by the fact that the index to the Annual Report, which is required by law, has over 6,000 entries. Through the Generosity of Mr Guy Chester, one of the members of the Board, it was decided to secure an authorized crest. I had the interesting and enjoyable experience of seeing this through with the College of Arms, an ancient body which dates from 1484. The old building in Queen Victoria Street known as Heralds' College was reconstructed by Sir Christopher Wren in 1666. As finally approved, the shield, based on one of the arms of a Wesley family in the fourteenth century, is described as, 'Argent a Cross between twelve Escallops Purpure over all a Castle of three Towers proper', which in modern language means a silver shield with a purple cross having three scallop shells in each quarter and a castelated keep in the centre. Dr Lofthouse supplied the motto, which was immediately accepted by the College of Heralds: *'Nobis Officium: Aliis Usus: Deo Gloria'* (To us the duty: to others the enjoyment: to God the glory).

With the war over, the Government came under pressure to deal with 'off the course' betting. Instead of accepting the judicious recommendations of the Royal Commission, 1933, a new Royal Commission was appointed. In November 1949 I accepted an invitation from a churches' group associated with the Churches Committee on Gambling to share in the presentation of evidence from the Christian point of view. It was at once evident that a serious change had taken place. Contrary to the approach of all previous official inquiries, this Royal Commission started with a tolerance for gambling and the idea of making suitable provision for it. I had a rather gruelling experience when giving evidence during some two hours, and found it very difficult to get the true Christian judgement across. The outcome was a most unsatisfactory report based on an *ex parte* judgement and containing errors of economic analysis and misleading factual statements. The

CHURCH BUILDINGS AND WAR DAMAGE

legislation which followed in 1960, providing for the licensing of cash betting offices and allowing the provision of gaming houses, was a most serious moral and social setback.

The Beckly Social Service Lecture Trust invited me to give the Social Service Lecture at the Bradford Conference in 1950. There was no difficulty in the choice of topic, as the subject of gambling, to which I had given close study during many years, had not been previously dealt with in this course of lectures. *Gambling in English Life* was the selected title, and I managed to get it written so that the book was on sale at the Conference bookstalls. This was doubly important. The book was not only available at the time of the delivery of the lecture but ready for circulation to the members of the Royal Commission then in session. The partiality of the Royal Commission is shown by the fact that they accepted a tendentious booklet presented to but not accepted by the Anglican Church Assembly, without indicating its lack of authority or referring to any other document setting forth an entirely different judgement. Of course, the lecture itself can only be a selected summary of a book of over 40,000 words. It is of interest that the first edition was exhausted after a few years and a revised edition, which was brought up to date regarding recent legislation, was published in 1958, with a further revision in 1960. It is still the only comprehensive study of gambling in its many phases with a considered Christian judgement. Mr John H. Beckly, the founder of this Lecture Trust, was a fine Christian layman of Plymouth whom I had the privilege of knowing forty years ago.

A further lecture invitation reached me from the Wesley Historical Society for the Preston Conference, 1952. The topic assigned to me was that of the development of the Model Trust Deed under which Methodist Church property is held. The subject was right along the line of much of my work in the Department for more than a decade. The title chosen was *Methodist Preaching Houses and the Law* and the publisher's 'blurb' on the jacket describes it as 'An account of an important, fascinating and little known feature of early Methodist history'. That is strictly correct, for this particular subject had not been the occasion of specific study before. I found great interest in the necessary research. With the help of Mr Jewitt of our legal office, a tabular comparison of the seven model deeds in use at the time of Methodist Union and the new one to which most trusts have been transferred was added as an appendix. It demonstrated the assertion in the Methodist Church Union Act, 1929, that the various trusts 'are similar in all essentials'. The actual lecture in the form of a précis of the book was given in the Springfield Road Church, Blackpool, and I was most agreeably surprised at the interest of the audience in what is usually thought to be a very dull subject.

A Standing Order of Conference provides that 'all departmental appointments shall terminate at the end of twelve years'. There is provision for extension if approved by a three-fourths majority of the Conference. In my case there was convenience in extending the term by one year, though if it is calculated from my appointment as General Secretary, as some would contend, I had only completed ten years. There is a good deal to be said in favour of a close adherence to this Standing Order. There are very few of us who have not made our full contribution, whether in a department, a mission, or any other appointment in ten or twelve years.

There was more significance for me in this decision than the end of a departmental appointment. It involved the conclusion of what is usually termed 'active ministry' after forty-six years. Everyone must regret reaching that point when health and vigour are still enjoyed. In my case there was less regret as it meant setting me free to give all necessary time to my new service as one of the two joint secretaries of the World Methodist Council, which is covered in a later chapter. I might be described in our official records as a 'supernumerary', but I was certainly not 'superannuated'—a distinction which has passed out of use, though in vogue in the Methodism of the last century. There is meaning in the distinction. It is one thing to be *beyond the number* (supernumerary) of those available for an ordinary appointment by the Conference, but quite another thing to be *beyond the years* (superannuated) of active service in other ways.

Strange as some may regard it, I had a measure of regret in leaving Manchester; I had acquired almost an affection for it. It has no claim to beauty, though few cities can rival the colour and charm of the Piccadilly Gardens right in the centre. The city has, however, a character and a dignity which is impressive when it is understood. I was quite glad to have the assurance of continued if only occasional contact as Honorary Secretary of the Department, Member of the Board of Trustees, and a Director of the Methodist Insurance Company.

Albert Hearn succeeded me as general secretary, and the new appointment was that of W. Oliver Phillipson, then chairman of the Stoke and Macclesfield District.

The question of residence had to be determined, though, in reality, it settled itself. The city of Birmingham, where we had many friends, was within two hours of London and as good a centre as any for my new secretarial work and the travel it would involve. Then Mary and Stephen, with the young people, were settled in Solihull, the new county borough which adjoins Birmingham, and we should be more than glad to be within a few miles of them. So we secured a suitable house in Moseley and have never regretted it.

CHAPTER IX

APPOINTMENTS EXTRAORDINARY

LET no one be misled by the use of 'extraordinary'. It simply means, as correctly used, 'in excess of the usual' or 'more than the normal' and does not imply at all anything unprecedented or of singular importance. Along the way there have been given to me quite a series of extra appointments. In so far as they afforded opportunities of distinctive service which I felt able to render I welcomed them, and I trust that any honour that may have been associated with them was carried without any false estimate or conceit. It seemed to me the right arrangement to bring them together in this separate chapter as being of interest in themselves and affording opportunity for comments outside the routine of one's basic appointments.

For twelve years in all I held the position known as 'Chairman of the District'. It is rather an awkward title, but it has proved impossible to discover or invent a suitable alternative. Some would prefer 'Moderator', as I should, but that does not exactly fit all the duties involved. Others would advocate 'Bishop', but that raises theological and other issues and provokes an entirely false comparison with the diocesan bishops of the Anglican Church. So we remain just 'Chairmen', and it works quite satisfactorily. The change from Birmingham to Sheffield was made during Conference and it was by Conference initiative that I was appointed Chairman of the Sheffield District. By the will of the District, I held the position for the four years, until I moved to Manchester. Two years later the Synod of the Manchester District nominated me to Conference as Chairman and it was eight years before I asked to be allowed to retire from that office through pressure of other work. At that time most of the chairmen carried that duty in addition to a pastoral or departmental appointment. Today the districts

APPOINTMENTS EXTRAORDINARY

of British Methodism have been enlarged in size and reduced in number, and the chairmen are free from any other appointment. There has been no change in the official duties, though the 'separated' chairmen are able to render other services in their districts. These official duties, as laid down in the Constitution, are: To preside over the District Synod, which meets twice each year and the various Synod committees: To exercise oversight of the 'character and fidelity' of all the ministers in the District: To secure the observance of Methodist Order and Discipline: To advise and guide ministerial appointments in the District as a member of the Stationing Committee of the Conference.

I did not find it an undue burden, partly for the reason that both in the office of the Sheffield Mission and in the office of the Department in Manchester I had the valuable assistance of a competent personal secretary. Then I found great satisfaction in taking counsel with both ministerial and lay brethren individually and in committee and thus helping to solve the problems that continually arise. Also I found great advantage in delegating some responsible and sectional duties to ex-chairmen or experienced superintendents in the District, more than most chairmen seem willing to do. This delegation I believe to be a wise procedure which might well be followed, especially in some of the large districts which have been created. It would be to the great convenience and advantage of the administrative work to have the arrangement of a deputy chairman to assist in the more remote sections of districts which cover a large geographical area. One of the old Sheffield ministers paid me a compliment recently. He had committed, inadvertently, a rather serious administrative mistake. As he recalled, I administered verbal reproof to him in private, but when I had to refer to it in the Quarterly Meeting of his circuit, I did so in such a way as to leave his reputation undimmed. That, of course is what a chairman should do. There are many personal issues where the chairman can exercise discretion to very great advantage. By holding a resignation in suspense and keeping an appointment open, I was able to save the career of one of our very able ministers. He was entirely conscientious in the step he had taken, but I felt sure that it was a mistake. The only way to prevent that mistake becoming a permanent disaster was to allow for a trial and keep the way of return open so that no hiatus would appear in his record. It is a privilege to have the opportunity and the authority to give that kind of help when necessary. Some of the most difficult duties are involved in directing the amalgamation of churches and circuits consequent upon Methodist Union and the still more difficult task of inspiring the closing of redundant buildings.

The more public duties of presiding over the sessions of the Synod can be full of interest. The two Synods over which I had to preside were typical of the larger districts and consisted of, approximately, a hundred ministers and rather more than two hundred lay representatives. They were both assemblies of distinct competence, fully capable of testing the knowledge and judgement of the chairman. The Methodist Church has a wonderful system of disciplinary courts entirely confidential and most effective. I doubt whether any church is able to deal with the occasional problems of this kind so effectively as within the privacy of the disciplinary practice of the Methodist Church. The ordered provision makes possible the preservation of the moral standards and at the same time the exercise of a redemptive ministry of healing and restoration. It is a most responsible part of a chairman's duties, which only seldom has to be put into operation, for which thanks be to God. Altogether I valued the opportunities of those years of District Chairmanship, and I cherish the remembrance of the confidence and appreciation shown by the members of the District Synods.

To my great surprise, I was nominated by the Royal Navy, Army, and Royal Air Force Board of the Methodist Church to pay an official visit to our chaplains and troops in Germany in January 1947. It was indeed thoroughly official, for I was gazetted 'Colonel' and travelled as a V.I.P. My wife insists that the proper description is 'Colonel for a fortnight'. After crossing the Channel, I travelled by train to Bad Oyenhausen, the Headquarters, to find Germany under snow and ice-bound. The Deputy Chaplain-General and our Methodist Chaplain, Gordon Brigg, met me, and after lunch and a discussion about my tour, I set off for the five-hour drive to Hamburg. I was provided with a Humber four-wheel-drive car and a soldier driver for the period. It was an uncomfortable brute of a car, but the only sort of vehicle to tackle the icy roads, the snow, and the hills. It could travel anywhere. My driver could certainly deal with the car, but seemed to know nothing beyond that. He knew no German and was not always sure of the road. We got completely lost one day in a snow-storm, but fortunately my knowledge of the country through previous visits and some acquaintance with the language eventually pulled us through.

Hamburg was an unforgettable sight by contrast with the city as I had seen it twenty years earlier. Only one small section had escaped destruction. For the rest one could look in every direction, and as far as the eye could reach, and see nothing but rubble. Here and there an iron pipe poked through the waste, with smoke coming through, indicating people living in the cellars underneath. Bishop J. E. Sommer had heard of my visit and, to my great joy, came to Hamburg to see me—our first meeting for nearly eight years. From him I learned something for the first time of the destruction of German Methodist churches and the desperate plight of many of our Methodist people and others in like state.

My duties in Hamburg and in all other centres where our garrisons were to be found were to confer with the chaplains, discuss our Methodist work with the commanding officers, and make contact with the men as far as possible. There were moral leadership courses where I spoke and lectured, and one morning I broadcast a message over the Forces Network. One course was held in the Schloss Düsterntaple, which had belonged to Baron von Cramm, the famous tennis-player. The electric power failed and we had to meet by candle-light and put up with cold water. Ordinary amenities were uncertain. Another visit was to the Church House at Iserlohn. I conducted service in the old Lutheran church which was used for garrison purposes. I do not think I have ever felt so cold, for there was no heating in the great stone building and all around were snow and ice. Hanover was another devastated city. Here the services were held in a splendidly equipped Nissen hut. Göttingen was included in the tour and I was able to meet again those friends I made ten years before—Professor and Frau Kaehler and Professor and Frau Jeremias. They made me most welcome, and I learned of the privations endured by these gracious people, and their suffering in seeking to maintain a truly Christian witness against the Nazi control of the Church.

My tour culminated in a visit to Berlin, and once again I saw the frightful contrast with the city as I had known it before. The snow seemed to make the sight of the heaps of rubble a little less depressing. In a short interval between official duties, I saw Hitler's Chancellory and went down into the concrete dug-out where he committed suicide. Consideration of difficulties in the Berlin arrangement of the Wesley House was one of the reasons for my visit to that city. The 'Wesley Houses', placed by our Board wherever possible, made a great contribution to our service for the troops.

The train journey from Berlin overnight permitted of a brief call at Bad Oyenhausen for lunch with Chaplain Gordon Brigg and his wife, who had been so helpful. On the second night on the train the electric light failed, but fortunately not the heat. Sharing a compartment with another Colonel (a real one) we managed to creep into our bunks by providing light for each other with matches. At the coast a rather long wait at a transit camp was followed by a fairly smooth crossing of the Channel in a transport vessel, and I was soon conscious of being demoted from my temporary rank. It was a valuable trip and I was assured that my detailed report to the Board gave guidance on several complicated issues.

The Seventh Ecumenical Methodist Conference was to be convened later in 1947 at Springfield, Massachusetts (see Chap. X) and, together with other members of the British delegation, I was invited to spend some time in the United States before the Conference opened. It was for me a unique opportunity to see the working of 'Church Extension' which is the equivalent of our Chapel Department. At that time the two central offices were in Philadelphia and Louisville, Kentucky. At both I received great kindness and help from the official secretaries. There is always something to learn and improvements to be made in administrative work but I was encouraged to find that in all essentials our organization stood up to comparison with the procedure in these American offices which covered a vastly larger area. Before travelling on to the Conference I spent a long week-end in the Duke University at

Durham, North Carolina, and saw many of the rural churches erected by the Duke Foundation.

At the Conference in Newcastle in July of that year, 1947, I was designated President for the Conference of 1948. As the designation is by ballot vote without previous nomination, the result is always uncertain, though the voting the previous year is some indication of what may happen. At the London Conference in 1946 Dr W. E. Sangster and I tied for second place, each of us receiving 100 votes. It was practically certain that one of us would be designated the following year and the choice came my way for the obvious reason that Dr Sangster was the younger and could come up later, as he did in 1949. The one designated must receive a majority of the total votes cast, and this often means a second or even a third ballot. It was a natural satisfaction to me that I received the necessary majority on the first ballot.

The Methodist Conference in 1948 opened in the Central Hall, Bristol, on Tuesday, 13th July. One of the unique features was that for the first time a woman was elected Vice-President. There is a certain anomaly about this office. All the legal responsibilities reside in the President or, if he cannot act, in the immediate Ex-President. The office of Vice-President does, however, provide the opportunity of honouring one of the laity, and the one so honoured does carry distinction throughout that year and is able to render special service to the Church. Mrs David Lewis, the first woman Vice-President, is a most gracious and gifted person. Her father was a well-loved minister, one time Chairman of the Nottingham and Derby District, and her late husband a layman of distinction. The ability and spiritual power of Mrs Lewis were revealed when she addressed the Conference and even more on the many occasions throughout the year when she spoke to the assemblies of Methodist people.

The induction of the President and Vice-President is always an occasion of great interest and the Bristol Central Hall, which seats 2,000, was crowded as usual. The Superintendent of the Bristol Mission at that time was an old colleague of mine, the Rev. E. W. Odell, and I received many kindnesses from him during those eleven days. My presidential robe was the gift of the Bristol District, and it was presented by the Chairman of the District, the Rev. W. Oliver Phillipson. The President receives from his predecessor the small Bible owned and used by John Wesley, often spoken of as the Field Bible, because it was printed by John Field. My predecessor in the Chair of the Conference was Dr W. E. Farndale, and with generous exaggeration he described what he alleged to be my services to the Church and my qualifications for this high office. It was my duty to express the thanks of the Church to him for his service during his year of office, and I did so with sincerity, knowing what he had done, particularly in connexion with the rural work of Methodism.

It was a deep regret to me that my mother was not present —a regret shared by those who knew her. She had thought much about this Conference and my induction as President. But she was in her ninety-sixth year and had finally concluded, under advice, that the emotional strain was likely to be more than she should undergo. The Conference sent its message of affectionate remembrance. When I visited Leicester soon after the Conference she was present at the Mayoral reception and the public meeting which followed.

I had made a compact with myself that even on this important occasion I would adhere to my practice of speaking without using either the full manuscript or notes. It is not surprising that as the hour approached I was nervous and greatly tempted to break faith with myself. However, I am glad to recall that I resisted the temptation, for it would have been a sorry reflection had it been otherwise. The photograph of the assembled Conference shows the reading-desk to have been placed on one side. I sent my typescript to the *Methodist Recorder* with the intimation that I was not reading it and the reporters must take note of any deviations. But they were very few, so that the reporters were not seriously troubled.

It is an exacting experience to preside for ten successive days over this assembly of 660 representatives. As I see it, the primary duties of the President when in the Chair of the Conference are to secure the proper order and flow of the business under the most efficient direction of the Secretary, to interpret rightly the rules of debate and to preserve the just privileges of all speakers. All but the most experienced speakers realize the difficulty of addressing this critical if sympathetic assembly, and regard the tribune as a somewhat frightening spot. The

Mrs Benson Perkins, 1948

(*above*) *After the service preceding the Labour Party Conference, October, 1955, at Margate.*
(Left to right) *The Rt. Hon. Earl Attlee, K.G., O.M., C.H., F.R.S., the Rt. Hon. James Griffiths, M.P., the Preacher.*

Washington, Wesley Day, 24th May, 1961. Dedication of Equestrian Statue of John Wesley, presented by the Rt. Hon. the Lord Rank.
(Left to right) *The Rev. Dr. E. Benson Perkins. Major-General G. K. Gailey (Washington Command), President Norman L. Trott (Wesley Theological Seminary).*

Conference can speedily show its impatience with any undue verbosity or irrelevance. While the relief of occasional laughter is welcomed, I do not think the President should indulge in wisecracks for their own sake, and most certainly not if they involve any embarrassment to a speaker or any other member of the Conference.

The major debate that year was on 'women in the ministry'. It ran through the whole of one morning and, regarded purely as a discussion of an important issue, it was first-class, showing the Conference at its best. There were seventeen participants in the debate and the speaking on both sides was excellent. To me it is an extraordinary fact that in the fifteen conferences since, we have not had another debate of that order and excellence. Possibly the discussion of the proposed scheme for union with the Church of England, which is looming ahead as I write, will provide the opportunity. We certainly must not lose the gift of genuine debate nor the effectiveness of spontaneous speech. A series of prepared addresses is not at all the same thing. The resolution asked for the admission of women to the itinerant ministry on exactly the same terms as men. I am satisfied in my own mind that if the proposal had sought the ordination of selected women to meet special needs at home and overseas, it would probably have been carried. There was little objection on principle, and a beginning in the way suggested could have led to the solving of the serious practical difficulties. It was these difficulties in the main which led to the rejection of the proposal by a majority of approximately two-thirds.

The official Conference service on the Sunday morning is the liturgical order of Morning Prayer as modified slightly by John Wesley. It is conducted by the Secretary of the Conference. At that time the Rev. Edwin Finch was in the full strength of his power, and his fine reading of the service was typical of all his work. That year the morning service was overshadowed by the Cathedral service in the afternoon, which was described by some as the official service of the Conference. The Cathedral authorities gave a particularly cordial welcome to the Conference representatives, visitors, and local Methodists who filled that fine old building. There have been similar services in other cities, and possibly the largest crowd of all in the

Liverpool Cathedral in 1960, but this Bristol Cathedral service seemed to me perfect in its way and for its purpose. The Order of Service was specially arranged, a unique feature being the 'Act of Faith, Hope and Love' in which I led the great congregation after the sermon which was, naturally, on 'The Unity of the Spirit'. The gracious attitude of the Bishop and Dean is shown by the fact that with their consent and by invitation of Sir Philip Morris, Vice-Chancellor of Bristol University, I preached again in the Cathedral at the Founders' Day service of the University in the following May.

The normal itinerary of the President begins almost immediately after the conclusion of the Conference sessions. He is expected to visit all the districts, fulfilling a programme of sermons and addresses, often lasting though several days in each district. In the five days of my visit to Cornwall, in which I had a special interest through my early ministry in the Helston Circuit, I gave fifteen sermons and addresses. In all the districts, as far as possible, I made a special point of meeting a conference of trustees. As far as I know, this had never been done before, and there was no doubt about the interest and appreciation of those present. So often the service of trustees is regarded as a rather dull necessity instead of a spiritual responsibility. It was time some official recognition was given to the work of this fine body of Methodist laymen.

As President of the Conference, I was leader of the delegation of our Church to the first assembly of the World Council of Churches in Amsterdam, which opened on 22nd August. I shall refer to this in the chapter on 'The Ecumenical Movement'.

For the first time in the history of British Methodism, the President of the Conference was authorized to visit the Central Conference of the German Methodist Church early in October, carrying a message of affectionate greeting and goodwill. The Conference met in the hall of the Methodist Seminary in Frankfurt-am-Main. Professor Gordon Rupp was my chosen and appointed companion, and I will quote his account of our initial difficulties:

'Travel in the American Zone of Germany was for the Englishman a highly skilled mystery, and in a situation where three kinds of currency are desirable if the visitor is to find bed and board, to say nothing of Coca-Cola, it is desperate to find oneself, as did the President and his companion on arrival, with only one currency, and that useless. The city was crowded for its industrial fair, and as the bus moved slowly through the jamming traffic once again did a servant of a Man of God, seeing the city compassed about with horses and chariots, cry, "Alas, my Master, how shall we do?" But, thanks to the prayers of many thousand Methodists, a series of particular providences, worthy of Wesley's *Journal*, supervened, and an anxious situation was relieved through the great courtesy of Colonel Rothwell of the British Command.'

Following Gordon Rupp's interview at the British Headquarters a staff officer rang through to me to apologize for the trouble and inconvenience, for which they were in no way responsible, and to inquire what time the car should call for us in the morning. The Seminary is in the suburb of Ginnheim, which is several miles from the centre of the city, but it had never occurred to me that a car would be available. But so it was. The generous thought of British Command placed an Austin saloon and driver at our disposal for the four days of the visit.

When I first saw the hall of the Prediger Seminar in Ginnheim, years before, the arch over the apse bore the words in gold letters, 'Einer ist euer Meister Christos ihr aber seid alle Brüder' (One is your Master Christ and you are all brethren). Before the end of the war an American shell smashed the arch. This was the first thing our German brethren restored. They put back the words in black letters, gold leaf being no longer available, as an expression of their faith even after the tragedy of the war. Under that restored arch with its message we stood— German, Swedish, American, British—and distributed the elements of the Eucharist to the members of the conference.

Bishop Sommer presided over the Conference, and the visitors included Bishop Arthur Moore from America, Bishop Arvidson of the Scandinavian Methodist Churches, and Dr Ferdinand Sigg, later to become Bishop of the South-central Conference of European Methodism. It was from British Methodism that our Church began work in Germany in 1831, and the war damage to German Methodist buildings included the destruction of a fine church in Sophienstrasse, Stuttgart, which was built originally by gifts from this country. It seemed to me that the most effective expression of our concern to heal the breaches caused by war would be a gift toward the rebuilding of this church. In my address I offered a gift of £10,000, which I anticipated could be made from the interest on our Rebuilding Fund. That announcement almost broke down the Conference. The members were most deeply affected, and with tears in their eyes they tried to speak their feelings of appreciation. It will be well to digress and complete this story of the gift. In due course, the church was rebuilt and given a new name—Auferstehungskirche (Church of the Resurrection). As I could not go out for the reopening, I recorded a speech in German and sent the record out for use during the ceremony of dedication. The unfortunate effect of this is that it creates a reputation for facility in the language which it is difficult to live up to. It is one thing to read a speech which has been checked over by more competent friends and quite another thing to acquire spontaneous fluency. However, the risk had to be taken and it was certainly a success. In 1952, when the European Methodist Conference was meeting in Frankfurt, I was able to visit Stuttgart and to preach and speak in the new church on the occasion of the unveiling of a bronze tablet which records the English gifts for the original building of the church and the participation of the British Conference in its restoration after war-time destruction.

Those who know our great friend, now Bishop Ferdinand Sigg, will appreciate one little incident which convulsed the conference. Dr Sigg, with his tall figure and emphatic, even on occasion boisterous, speech, had addressed the assembly in characteristic fashion. Then Professor Gordon Rupp, so striking a contrast in appearance and voice, followed and began in his fluent German, 'After the earthquake a still, small voice.' The whole of that conference was a rich opportunity of fellowship with our German brethren, ministers and laymen. Before leaving Frankfurt the Methodist bishops and ourselves were entertained at lunch by twenty American Methodist chaplains, with the Garrison Commander, General Duff, also a Methodist, as the guest of honour.

Every week, almost every day, had its interest and value. My wife was able to accompany me on some of my journeys, and we remember particularly the long week-end in Jersey, where I was first appointed, and the Irish Conference, when I was able to introduce her to air travel. The Welsh Assembly, over which the President presides during the English session, was held in Machynlleth in June 1949. There is a public meeting, generally crowded, when the President and other English visitors speak. In the Ordination Service the President uses the only English words in the ceremony. The Assembly that year was fully characteristic of what is an important event of which notice is taken by the local authority. At the luncheon, when greetings were presented from other churches, I was given an album of selected views of the town and district of Machynlleth from the local Council of the ancient borough, with an address signed and sealed by the Chairman, Vice-Chairman, and Clerk.

Immediately after the Welsh Assembly, I left by air for Italy on a visit to Italian Methodism. The journey to Rome was not without excitement. I have never suffered from airsickness, but I very nearly succumbed on that frightfully bumpy journey across France. It was a great relief when we crossed the Maritime Alps and the weather cleared. At Nice there was a long delay waiting for a party of Brazilian women on pilgrimage to Rome. The clatter on the plane was indescribable, and when we reached Rome there was further delay at the Airport, so that I did not reach the city terminus until well after midnight. The Rev. Giacomo Lardi describes the situation:

'A small deputation waited for three hours for the plane which was to bring the President of the Conference on an official visit to the Italian Church, only to be told that the plane had been delayed and would not arrive until 6 a.m. the next morning. Just before six the deputation met again and watched several arrivals . . . and we returned to our homes disappointed and somewhat perplexed. We found later that his plane reached Rome after midnight. The President, undaunted, picked up his bags and walked the streets of Rome (he had no Italian money to pay for a taxi), looking for a hotel—and we had arranged to give him a warm-hearted Methodist welcome to Roma Eterna.'

It sounds almost worse than it really was. I found a bed in a hotel that was open at that early-morning hour, and when I met Mr Lardi and the Italian friends later, and throughout the following days, they more than made up for the confused beginning.

The programme began on the Saturday evening with a reception and a truly ecumenical service inspired by 'Amsterdam', held in our beautiful church in Via Venti Settembre. Whit-Sunday followed, and, after the morning service and Holy Communion, we set off for a drive of some 100 kilometres, across the Appenines to Villa San Sebastiano, a large mountain village. The congregation, quite undisturbed by our rather late arrival, filled the lovely little church. I confess to being very much moved as I heard them sing in their own Italian, 'If ever I loved Thee, my Jesus, 'tis now'. There is a story connected with that church, which was built in 1930. Roman Catholic influence used official regulations to prevent the congregation assembling in their own church. They were allowed to worship in the basement, and every endeavour to secure freedom of use had failed. During the war a detachment of German soldiers with their officer came to the village seeking billets. They were told to use the disused church. The officer refused to quarter his men in a place of worship, and asked the Methodists to move into the church so that he could place his men in the basement. In this strange way the forces of oppression were defeated and our Methodist people secured and retained possession and use of their own church.

My programme included visits to Naples, Portici, Florence, Bologna, and Milan. I met groups of ministers and lay workers, and spoke at public services and meetings. I endeavoured to create a sense of the wide fellowship of the Methodist Church throughout the world. I also met leaders of the Waldensian Church, with whom our Methodist people have happy, fraternal relations. At Casa Materna, the wonderful Methodist Orphanage at Portici, a special reception had been arranged. Mr Lardi and I, having been presented with bouquets by two tiny tots, had to walk between a double line of nearly four hundred children, carrying those bouquets and attempting to do it gracefully. Mr Lardi managed it better than I did. The Rev. Ricardo Samti, the founder of the Orphanage, who has since died, was active at that time. His sons, the lawyer, the doctor, and the American Methodist minister were all actively concerned in the Orphanage. Fabio Santi, the lawyer and acting Mayor of Portici, was killed in a motor accident some years later. His death is a great loss to Italian Methodism. The Orphanage is now under the direction of the other two sons.

The Irish Methodist Conference, over which the British President presides, followed immediately after the visit to Italy. My wife and I greatly enjoyed our fellowship with the Irish people and our insight into their Methodist life and work. There was so much that was enjoyable during that week in Belfast, with the glorious sunshine which made the garden party one of the most perfect I have ever known.

It was during this conference that news reached me of the sudden death of my mother in her ninety-sixth year. Fortunately my sister was able to arrange for the cremation, so that the funeral service could be held in the King Richard's Road Church, our home church, in Leicester, immediately after the conclusion of the Irish Conference. Hers had been a wonderful life and her strength of character had left its impress on the Church of which she had been a member for just on seventy years. She retained a lively interest in the work right to the end.

I was very conscious of the privilege of conducting the first Methodist—indeed, the first Free Church—service of Holy Communion to be broadcast. It was held in our beautiful Harpenden Church, and I was assisted by the Minister, the Rev. J. Allen Fletcher, with the splendid co-operation of the Choir. Another Methodist minister, the Rev. Kenneth Grayston, then in the service of the BBC, gave the necessary introduction and explanation. I was told that it was the recording of this service which convinced representatives of the Church of Scotland that Holy Communion could, suitably and reverently, be broadcast on the radio.

Towards the end of my year of office I received an intimation from the Vice-Chancellor of the Manchester University that the Senate had decided to confer upon me the degree of Master of Arts (*honoris causa*). I had often wished that circumstances had enabled me to take a university degree. Now it had come to me by what the Chancellor of the Manchester University said was 'the hard way', in compliment to those of us who were receiving honorary degrees. The degree was conferred with all the usual ceremonial in the Whitworth Hall on the morning of what was actually the last day of my presidency. I was introduced by Professor T. W. Manson, whose death so soon after his retirement was a great loss to all the churches. I had been asked to speak for the honorary graduates at the luncheon which followed, but had to forgo that duty in order to reach Liverpool for the opening of Conference. My wife and I and other friends had just time to get through before the Conference session began, at which I had to introduce my successor in the Presidency, the Rev. Harold B. Rattenbury.

There are certain overseas conferences at which British Methodism is represented by fraternal delegates. I was privileged to serve on two such occasions, the first being the General Council of the United Church of Canada in 1950. It is most important to preserve close association with those united Churches in which the Methodist Church has participated, and the United Church of Canada is itself eager to continue these links. Before reaching Toronto, where the Council was assembling, I was able to fulfil appointments in the United States under the exchange scheme of the British Council of Churches. These engagements included a most interesting week as chaplain at Lakeside, Ohio, a summer vacation centre on Lake Erie, which was once a Methodist camp-meeting site. Then I preached at the beautiful church on Euclid Avenue, Cleveland, at that time in the charge of Dr Oscar Olson. Before the following Sunday I spent a few days at the summer residence of Mr and Mrs Charles C. Parlin on Lake George, in the northern part of New York State. Their house on a bank of Silver Bay is a sheer delight. I travelled to Washington to preach in the morning at the Foundery Church. In my experience, Washington, being practically at sea-level, can develop a degree of humidity more trying than any other American centre I have visited. On that particular Sunday the heat and humidity made almost any movement exhausting. Even with air-conditioning, preaching was a considerable effort. After a hurried journey of about a 100 miles, I preached in the evening at the church of my friend, Dr Carl Sanders, in Richmond, Virginia. Reaching Toronto, I made contact with Mr A. B. Hillis, the lay British delegate who was present with his wife. The General Council assembled in the Eaton Memorial Church. One assembly of this kind is very much like another, whatever its name. Even with some variations of procedure, I felt very much at home. My previous contact with the United Church of Canada enabled me to follow the business with understanding.

When we were approaching New York on the outward voyage of this journey I experienced one of the unusual hazards of sea travel. We were nearing the mouth of the Hudson river when the ship took a sudden turn out of its course and heeled over at an acute angle. In preparation for landing, a pile of cabin luggage had been assembled on the port side and as the deck sloped down with the turn dozens of suit cases and other baggage slipped off into the ocean. We none of us knew whether we had suffered a loss until we came to claim our luggage in the custom house. I was very thankful to be one of the fortunate ones with my various cases safe, and very sorry for those who suffered the inconvenience of luggage irretrievably lost. On a subsequent voyage an officer who was on the *Mauretania* at that time told me the explanation of the sudden alteration of course. Air target practice had got out of its rightful position and the ship had to suffer an immediate turn to avoid possible danger to the passengers and crew from the firing.

Two years later I was rather suddenly called to take a longer journey to attend the Quadrennial General Conference of the Methodist Church in the United States, which was to be convened in San Francisco. At almost the last moment Dr Farndale was unable to go, as appointed, through the illness of his wife. The whole journey was arranged by air, and I reached St Louis, Missouri, for Easter Sunday, preaching at the Grace Church for the first morning service and at St John's for the second. Very few of the churches in the United States have Sunday evening services, but the greater churches often have two Sunday morning Services to accommodate the large congregations. It was at St John's that Bishop Ivan Lee Holt had so successful a ministry before being appointed a Bishop. I was very glad to have the opportunity of visiting the home of

Judge Ivan Lee Holt, his son, and to meet the small son of the Judge, who once introduced himself to me by saying, 'I am Ivan Lee Holt the third.'

At St Louis I met Mr Lineham of Leeds, the lay delegate, with his wife, and we travelled on together to Los Angeles. It was unthinkable that we should miss the opportunity of making a detour at this point to visit the Grand Canyon of Arizona. Any attempt at a description is impossible. The lip or edge of the Canyon is 7,000 feet above sea level and the Canyon is 150 miles long, an average of ten miles across, and a mile deep. The fantastic shapes of the rocks, the coloured strata with the Colorado River, just discernible, and the vast space make a picture that is unforgettable. It seemed almost an impertinence to take coloured photographs of this unique work of nature through countless millenniums. In Los Angeles I preached to a crowded congregation in the Wilshire Avenue Church. Having heard of my interest in music, the Director arranged for the Choir to sing Vaughan Williams's festival setting of the *Te Deum*, accompanied by three trumpets as well as the organ. I was almost too thrilled by it to preach. Los Angeles covers a vast area, being really, as someone described it to me, fifty-two villages trying to be a city. It speaks of excessive wealth and while that wealth produces the almost artificial beauty of the gardens and the elaborate cemetery of Forest Lawn, there is the more natural beauty of the hills and the Pacific coast. Holywood, of course, speaks for itself.

San Francisco appeals to me almost more than any other American city I have seen. It is built on hills—rather more than the seven hills of Rome—overlooking the wonderful bay, with the Golden Gate Bridge spanning the link between the bay and the Pacific Ocean. It has a large foreign population, and Chinatown in particular attracted me. There are more Chinese here than in any other city outside Asia, and they have the reputation of being splendid citizens. I felt distinctly pleased that, having been coached in the right way of holding and using chopsticks, I went right through a Chinese meal with them. I asked the Chinese manager if I might buy them, and his reply was: 'We no sell.' I said what a pity that was, as I would have liked to take them to England. He smiled and said, 'Well, you have a pocket,' so I still have them. I paid a visit, of course, to the attractive Chinese Methodist Church in the heart of Chinatown.

The Conference assembled in the great auditorium, which seats 12,000. The number of appointed delegates is under 1,000, but it was when every seat was filled at some of the evening public assemblies that one seemed to get a picture of the largest unit by far of World Methodism. The bishops sit in a solid block on the platform, but they have no vote nor even right to speak unless asked to make a statement. That is an expression of American democracy. A different bishop is nominated from day to day to preside over the Conference. Visiting choirs from all over the United States are called upon to provide a musical interlude in the intervals of business. The singing of the whole Conference is not comparable with the singing of the British Conference, even with organ accompaniment—perhaps because of it. When I was received and spoke on the fourth day, I said that I hoped to sing a Wesley hymn with them before I returned home. We had not had one up to that point. The presiding Bishop responded by announcing 'And are we yet alive', which we sang to Ripon, to which it is set in their hymn-book, though under the name Dennis. But it is an amazing assembly, with its own way of handling the colossal amount of business.

American audiences are very quick to seize a point of humour, but it must be of the right order and in the correct language. I remember Dr Sangster, with his great gifts, telling a supposedly humorous story which fell absolutely flat, for the simple reason that he used the word 'angler', which they do not know, instead of the word 'fisherman', which they use. The late Dr Harry Holmes, who introduced Mr Lineham and myself to the Conference used the old crack about the sun never setting upon the British Commonwealth, and, having in mind the weather, added the explanation that it seldom rose. This gave me what I knew was a perfectly safe opportunity. I said that Dr Holmes was quite right about the sun never setting on the British Commonwealth, but he had the wrong explanation. The reason was that the Almighty could not trust the British in the dark. They rose to that all right and settled down for the rest of my speech. My souvenir of the Conference consists of the issues of the *Daily Christian Advocate*, giving a verbatim report of every word spoken and running to 650 large quarto pages in a prepared binding. It contains the full text of the Episcopal Address read by the late Bishop Kern on the evening of the opening day. This address occupies twenty-one pages, being over 20,000 words. The reading began at 8.10 p.m. and concluded at 10.55 p.m. This was a record which I understand is never to be repeated. As I sat through the whole two hours and three-quarters I can appreciate that decision. One of the highlights to me was a magnificent choral programme given one evening by a choir of over 500 to mark the publication of the *Interpreters' Bible*.

On returning I flew right through to London with a break of a few hours in New York. Air travel is comfortable, but there is an unrealized strain of which I knew nothing until after that long flight. For several days I had lost all energy and had to stay in bed until Nature had restored the balance. One becomes accustomed to air travel in these days as is necessary. If time allows, however, I much prefer the sea. Even then I would always choose the smaller boats rather than the 'Queens' with their class divisions. I have travelled in both of them but the Cunard ships sailing from Liverpool in which one has the run of the whole vessel appeal to me much more. The most enjoyable voyage I have had was in one of the City Line partly cargo boats sailing to South Africa with wonderful accommodation for just under a hundred passengers.

Leaving to a later reference my appointment as Vice-President of the British Council of Churches, there is one other office to which I should refer. In 1954 I was elected Moderator of the Free Church Federal Council. In these days of the Ecumenical Movement and the serious discussion of Christian unity, the question of the need for a Council of the Free Churches is often raised. In my address to the Congress at Worthing I admitted that the day might come when one body could represent all the churches, though it had not yet arrived, and said,—quoting my own words:

'The conditions of life in this ancient land, with its Established Church, require an effective unity of the Free Churches. As such we meet, but not with any idea of isolation or separation, such as seemed inevitable when the Free

APPOINTMENTS EXTRAORDINARY 143

Church Council was first called into being. We are today conscious of an intimate fellowship with the Church of England, and are prepared to do our thinking in terms of a world fellowship of the Christian Churches.'

Apart from presiding at the Congress, the Council, the Executive, and other committees, the duties of the Moderator fall into two groups. There are the visits to local and area councils throughout the country. No Moderator can cover them all, and it becomes a matter of arranging as full a programme of such visits as can be managed. These visits are most valuable, especially when associated with conferences of ministers and lay workers. The other group consists of official occasions which are more spectacular. They arise from the fact that the Government and other official bodies regard four dignitaries as representative of the Christian Churches in Great Britain. These are the Archbishop of Canterbury, the Roman Catholic Archbishop of Westminster, the Moderator of the Church of Scotland, and the Moderator of the Free Church Federal Council. This involved for me, as for other Moderators, a very interesting series of events. There was the Royal Luncheon at the Mansion House to welcome the Queen and the Duke of Edinburgh back from their Commonwealth tour. Similar occasions honoured the visit of the King and Queen of Sweden and the conferring of the Freedom of the City upon the Prime Minister of Canada. The Lord Mayor's Banquet in 1954 was held in Guildhall for the first time since the war. Considerable restoration after war damage was necessary. At that banquet I had the pleasure of sitting next to the late Sir Gilbert Scott, the architect who had directed the restoration of Guildhall. I recall with interest our conversation, for he was more than ready to talk about his work. There were other and rather different occasions, like the dinner of the Australia Society to the Prime Minister of that land, the dinner of the Anglo-German Society and the reception by the Foreign Office at Lancaster House in honour of the Prime Minister of Japan. There is no reason to exaggerate the importance of these occasions, but there is definite value in the Free Churches having an acknowledged place with the other churches in these official events. It was not always so.

Of course, there was the invitation to the Buckingham Palace Garden Party, so that my wife and I had a second experience of what is an interesting event. On this occasion we accompanied the President of the Conference, the Rev. W. Russell Shearer, and his wife.

Following a long correspondence and the ultimate recognition of the fact that the Free Churches should be represented at the great Albert Hall Festival preceding Remembrance Sunday, I had the privilege of being the first Moderator to participate in the service with which the British Legion Festival closes. The London correspondent of the *Yorkshire Post* took particular notice of this, and his comment is worth quoting:

> 'The Dean of Chichester, with some of the clergy and choir of his Cathedral, came into the Hall for the service, the Dean and Canons in copes, the Cross-bearers in tunicles, the Light-bearers in albs. This was the Church of England at its most dignified, and the Moderator of the Free Church Federal Council, black robed, did not seem out of place in such a procession.'

If I go on to mention another fact of interest it is because of its significance for the Free Churches. The Royal Family were present at the evening festival and Her Majesty the Queen asked to see me at the close to recognize the participation for the first time of the Moderator of the Free Church Federal Council.

During my year as Moderator, and since, I have been involved in the examination of the possibility of Free Church union. At present there would appear to be no likelihood of the overcoming of fundamental difficulties. Only the Methodist Church and the Presbyterian Church have a central body with authority to effect union if that is desired. The Congregational Churches and the Baptist Churches, being of the Independent Order, have no central body with adequate authority, and until that is secured consultation would have to be with each independent congregation. Then, in addition, there is the theological barrier created by the place which Believers' Baptism, invariably by immersion, holds in the thought and practice of the Baptist Churches. There are other difficulties in relation to some of the smaller Free Churches, such as differing views

APPOINTMENTS EXTRAORDINARY 145

on the nature of the ministry. Recognizing the evident advantages of the organic union of the Free Church denominations we have been compelled to the conclusion that no comprehensive scheme of union is possible, certainly not for the time being. This conclusion, unfortunate as it is, emphasizes the importance of maintaining the links of the Free Church Federal Council and cultivating close association within that limited union.

The continuous story must now be resumed with an account of my ten years of service as a secretary of the World Methodist Council, a decade which actually began in 1951, a year before my retirement from the Department for Chapel Affairs.

CHAPTER X

WORLD METHODISM

IT would be easier to write a book instead of a single chapter in order to give anything like an adequate account of the work of the World Methodist Council during the first decade since its formation in 1951. However, these selected highlights will, I hope, convey, not merely the story of the personal service in which I have been engaged, but a suggestive indication at least of Methodism as a World Church. First, certain preliminary facts.

The Methodist movement was worldwide in outlook and spirit from its very inception. As an American writer put it, with characteristic gift of phrase: 'Methodism has the global germ in its very blood stream.' Challenged by his friend, James Hervey, as to his catholic principles, John Wesley replied in a long letter which included the famous words: 'I look upon all the world as my parish, thus far, I mean that in whatever part of it I am I judge it meet, right and my bounden duty to declare unto all who are willing to hear the glad tidings of salvation.' This was written in March 1739, only ten months after his decisive Evangelical experience in Aldersgate Street. Writing in his *Journal* in 1785, Wesley says: 'I am now considering how strangely the grain of mustard seed planted about fifty years ago has grown up. It has spread through all Great Britain and Ireland . . . then to America from the Leeward Islands, through the whole continent into Canada and Newfoundland.' It should be noted that Methodism did not spread, as did several of the world denominations, by groups settling in another land and maintaining for themselves their religious faith and practices. The Methodist Movement advanced by indigenous evangelism, by declaring often through the lips and lives of laymen, 'unto all that are willing to hear, the glad tidings of salvation'.

The period from the death of Wesley in 1791 to the middle of the nineteenth century was one of Methodist division, both in this country and in America. Those divisions were never on questions of faith. The doctrinal emphasis and the basis of membership remained unaltered throughout the world. There were differences in Wesley's time—differences of order, for instance—but he could say in his last letter to America: 'Lose no opportunity of declaring to all men that the Methodists are one people in all the world and that it is their full determination so to continue.' During the latter half of the nineteenth century a new spirit was abroad, and in 1881 the first 'Œcumenical Methodist Conference' was held in Wesley's Chapel, City Road, London. Such *ad hoc* conferences were convened every ten years until 1931, alternating between Great Britain and America. After the break caused by the Second World War, an Ecumenical Methodist Conference was assembled in Springfield, Massachusetts, U.S.A. in 1947, under the joint presidency of Bishop Ivan Lee Holt and Dr Wilbert F. Howard. By then Methodist Union in Great Britain and the U.S.A. had healed the major divisions. There was the sense of a new beginning, and a revolutionary decision was reached, summed up in these words from the Message: 'The division which had existed for many years of Eastern and Western Sections was eliminated so that there might be one great World Federation of Methodists.' The world area was divided into twenty-four sections and a preliminary Council appointed. This proposal was taken over by the Eighth Ecumenical Methodist Conference assembled in Oxford in 1951. A draft consitution was adopted creating a World Methodist Council with representatives from all the sections to a total of 237. Bishop Ivan Lee Holt was appointed President and Dr Harold Roberts Vice-President. Dr Wilbert F. Howard was designated 'Hon. President'. For the first time there was to be a permanent secretariat of two joint secretaries resident in the United States and Great Britain, and Dr Elmer T. Clark and I were appointed to this joint office, with corresponding Treasurers—Edwin L. Jones in the United States and Duncan Coomer in Great Britain, followed on his death by L. A. Ellwood. The task that faced us as secretaries was to turn this paper constitution into living fact. As I go on to illustrate what has been done during the years 1951-61, I shall be drawing upon the record of my own personal work, together with incidents and experiences in which both secretaries participated. There is, of course, beyond that, the personal work Dr Elmer Clark, resident over 3,000 miles away, carried out in his own area. I held also, by appointment of the Conference, the post of Secretary of the British World Methodism Committee. It is of course impossible to give any account of the daily and increasing correspondence or of the details of organization.

The framework of the new organization consisted of meetings of the Council and generally the large conference every five years, with meetings of the Executive Committee, numbering about fifty, every year, thus far held in different centres in Europe or America. It was soon evident that occasional conferences with annual meetings of the Executive committee were too remote to deal with a world situation in any effective way. Something had to be done of a more intimate kind in smaller geographical regions. It was fortunate that in the year before the Oxford Conference I brought together on my own initiative a group of representative Methodists from Italy, Switzerland, Germany, Belgium, and the Scandinavian countries, with selected British Methodists. We met for three days in Southlands College, London. My friend, Bishop Sommer of Germany, greatly assisted in what was for all of us a new experience. This was the origin of what became, under the World Methodist Council, the European Methodist Consultative Conference, meeting every second or third year in different European countries.

The Rev. Wilfred Wade became convenor of this regional conference and of the European Relationship Committee in this country. What a revelation those European conferences were of the strength of these minority churches in countries predominantly Lutheran or Roman Catholic. We came to admire the scholarship and ability of their leaders and the loyalty and courage of the members in face of acute difficulty. How thrilled we were when the conference met in Bristol to have representatives from the other side of the Iron Curtain, who overcame most complicated regulations in getting through. They were able to tell us that Methodism in Eastern Germany had increased its membership by 50 per cent. since the end of the war. Some of the public occasions connected with these regional conferences will live in all our memories. There was the great assembly in the restored Pauls-Kirche in Frankfurt, where the first German Parliament met in 1848. The Blue Hall of the notable Town Hall in Stockholm was crowded, and honoured by the presence of the Lutheran Bishop of Stockholm and the President of the City Council. It was 1957, and the two hundred and fiftieth anniversary of the birth of Charles Wesley. A Methodist choir sang some of his hymns most beautifully. I had been asked to speak on 'Ecumenicity and Methodism', and it was indeed a privilege to do so in that place and to that company. In the Youth Rally at Forbach near Stuttgart in 1958 we were startled, not only by the audience of 2,000 and a choir of 200, but by a brass ensemble also numbering about 200. When I saw that long row of B flat bass and trombones I feared the worst. How entirely wrong I was! This was an assembly of instrumentalists from the many Methodist youth clubs in the district, and how wonderfully they played. With rich, melodious, and restrained tone they presented classical music with superb artistry, both on their own and in accompanying the choir. One could see at a glance what a true musician the conductor was. At Zürich in 1960 we enjoyed another great rally of this type. The background of these occasions is a fine Church life. The total Methodist community in Continental Europe is not less than a quarter of a million. In Oslo, for instance, there are four Methodist churches. When I visited the city to make arrangements for the World Methodist Conference in 1961 I suggested that the delegates would worship in those churches on the Conference Sunday. I was told that it was impossible, for those churches were filled to capacity every Sunday by their own congregations. Two European Youth conferences have been held in Stuttgart and London, with young people from most of the European countries. I have had so little responsibility for the detailed organization that I can say truly that Europe presents an example of what a regional conference can be and do, even when having to overcome the difficulties of travel and language. All this has been made possible by the enthusiastic co-operation of Bishop Odd Hagen of the Scandinavian churches, Bishop

Friedrich Wunderlich of Germany and Bishop Ferdinand Sigg of South-Central Europe.

Another preliminary step had been taken prior to the Oxford Conference in 1951. This was the setting up of a joint committee to arrange the exchange of preachers between Great Britain and the United States during the summer period. Dr Stanley Leyland became secretary of the British Committee and worked with American colleagues—Dr Karl Quimby until 1958 and then with Bishop Otto Nall. Something like a hundred ministers in both Great Britain and the United States have enjoyed the advantages of this system of ministerial exchanges.

The Oxford Conference suggested to all the sections of the World Methodist Council that the year 1953, which included the two hundred and fiftieth anniversary of the birth of John Wesley, should be a year of aggressive evangelism. In different ways, on a massive scale as in Australia or within the more normal organization of church life, this proposal was carried into effect. In the United States the culmination was a four days' convocation in the Convention Hall, Philadelphia. It was attended by many thousands of Methodists from every state in the Union. Four of us on this side—Dr Dorothy Farrar, Dr Harold Roberts, Dr Maldwyn Edwards, and myself—were invited to join the panel of speakers. We travelled by air, and in New York enjoyed a delightful evening with Dean and Mrs Lynn Harold Hough, whose gracious invitation was awaiting us. In spite of the heat, those days in Philadelphia were fully occupied with speeches and discussion on almost every aspect of evangelism. It fell to my lot to speak on the Saturday evening on 'The Abiding value of the Wesley Hymns'. Bishop Corson, who introduced me in his customary generous way, tells one of his successful stories about that evening. According to him he expected me to be wearing clerical attire, as is normal with British ministers, and he was disappointed, because he had come prepared to bear me company in that particular. Instead, he found me wearing a dark lightweight summer suit with a soft collar and tie. He tells how when I rose to speak I followed the example of most men in the audience and removed my coat 'to reveal to the astonished company brilliant scarlet suspenders.' Part of that is true. I had discarded the clerical collar for something more comfortable in the heat; I was wearing a lightweight suit, and I did in fact remove my coat when I rose to speak. For the rest, only those with as vivid an imagination as Bishop Corson would see the scarlet braces. But it would be a pity to spoil a good story.

After the Sunday morning service in Old St George's—the oldest Methodist Church building in America—a great open-air rally was arranged in the Franklin Field Stadium. Unfortunately, a heavy rainstorm spoilt the procession, but it was estimated that 35,000 people were present in the Stadium, brought from a wide area by 700 coaches. Before it closed, a number of young people who had made their decision bore witness to it as they gathered with their ministers in the central area. When the Convocation was over, we travelled to Lake Junaluska to take part in another Wesley commemoration for the great South-eastern area (or Jurisdiction, to use the correct word) and to see the estate where the next World Methodist Conference would be held in 1956.

Bishop Odd Hagen of the Scandinavian Methodist Churches invited me to give four lectures at the Methodist Seminary in Sweden in February, 1956. There are two Methodist colleges, or seminaries, in Continental Europe. The one at Ginnheim, a suburb of Frankfurt-am-Main, to which I have already referred, serves the churches of Germany and German-speaking Switzerland. The other which serves the four Scandinavian countries—Sweden, Norway, Finland, Denmark—is at Överoås, a suburb of Gothenburg. It was mid-winter, and as soon as I arrived in Stockholm for a preliminary week-end I bought one of those padded fur hats which we usually associate with Russia. What a comfort they are in the bitterly cold weather. The lectures given on four successive mornings were on the Ecumenical, Ethical, and Evangelical character and emphasis of Methodism, with a fourth lecture on Methodism in relation to Christian unity. All the students have to learn to read English, and most of them could follow the lectures as given. For the sake especially of visitors, my friend, Dr Anker Nilsen, at that time one of the tutors, acted as interpreter. These lectures followed familiar ground. If any apology were needed for taking this course, it is found in my conviction, shared by many, that in these days of probable change, with conversations about the union of the churches, it is of the first importance to be clear and definite about the positive points of emphasis which are the contribution of Methodism to the Universal Church. Other great confessions have their contribution to make, often of a doctrinal character. That of Methodism does not involve any basic difference from the historic creeds, but is concerned with priority of emphasis and practical application of the truth to life as a whole.

The lectures were to be followed by a tour round southern Norway—so ran Bishop Odd Hagen's invitation. Thus I visited Friedrikstad, Oslo, Arendal, Stavanger, Haugesund, and Bergen. It was a most interesting revelation of the simple evangelism of the Norwegian Methodists and the use made of the 'string bands'. This is a service largely of the young people, and freely used in the Sunday-evening worship as well as on other occasions. The 'string band', as they call it, consists of several violins, with guitars, and mandolines, used to accompany the voices. My last Sunday was spent in Bergen. The Central Methodist Church is a fine building with a church membership of about six hundred. For the evening service I was preaching at the older First Methodist Church, as it is known. Before the service I had been shown plans of a proposed new building on a new site nearer to the housing development, to replace the old church. With this in mind, I preached from the text (Rev. 21^5), 'Behold I make all things new', directing attention to the New Birth, the New Name, the New Heavens, and the New Earth. The minister who had splendidly interpreted the sermon then announced the concluding hymn. It was in Norwegian, of course, but to the familiar tune, 'Tell me the old, old story'.

In preparation for the Ninth World Methodist Conference, Dr Harold Roberts and I paid a hurried visit to New York to meet the American Committee and develop the detailed programme. It was a week before Christmas, 1955, and we are not likely to forget the bitter cold of New York contrasted with what to us was the overheating of the hotels and other buildings. We had the opportunity of seeing the amazing Christmas display of the shop-windows in Fifth Avenue and the giant Christmas tree and the skating in the Rockefeller Centre. A task given me by the Committee was the preparation of a small hymn-book with tunes for use at the Conference in

WORLD METHODISM 153

1956 and subsequently. There are marked differences between British and American traditions of congregational singing, as indicated by the contrast of the respective hymn-books. British Methodism and its associated churches, such as Ireland, South Africa, Australia, and New Zealand, have remained loyal to the Wesley tradition. The Hymn-book has 264 Wesley hymns out of a total of 984, more than a quarter. The American hymn-book has 51 Wesley hymns out of a total of 564, less than one-tenth. The Committee were desirous of encouraging a wider knowledge and use of the Wesley hymns. It was an exacting task to select a small representative number of Wesley hymns and to fit them to tunes known on both sides of the Atlantic. The collection, as published, contained 44 hymns, of which 29 were from the Wesleys. It was found desirable to include a few contemporary and modern hymns. I had the satisfaction of finding a general acceptance of this little hymn-book, which has now been used at two World conferences as well as at some of the smaller gatherings. For the Oslo Conference, I discovered Norwegian translations of six of the hymns, which were added as a supplement, so that on public occasions hymns could be sung in both languages.

The Ninth World Methodist Conference, in September, 1956, was held in the estate of Lake Junaluska, North Carolina, which is probably the most beautiful of the many such estates in different parts of the United States. Like these, it is used mainly for summer assemblies, though some people have their permanent residences there. Lake Junaluska is 2,600 feet above sea-level on the lower slopes of the Smoky Mountains in western North Carolina. In extent the estate covers four square miles. It is provided with hotels, boarding-houses, and apartments, a fine auditorium holding 2,000, a Memorial Chapel seating 300, and a Youth Centre. Dr Elmer Clark, who lives on the estate, carried through an ambitious scheme in erecting a World Methodist Building with library, reading-room and offices. It houses an almost unique collection of Wesley manuscripts, publications, portraits, busts, cameos, and other objects. The building was dedicated during the period of the Conference. The name of the estate is taken from a famous chief of the Cherokee Indians, who occupied this area and still live on a reserve in the Smoky Mountains. They are said to be the largest, proudest, and most cultured of all the Indian tribes. Methodism has its work amongst them.

During the days immediately preceding the assembly of the Conference in the large auditorium the Executive and Council had their first meetings. The President, Bishop Ivan Lee Holt, delivered his presidential address at the opening meeting of the Council in the course of which he recalled his many contacts with Methodism round the world and set out his hopes for the future. At the opening session of the Conference greetings were presented from President Eisenhower and Vice-President Nixon of the United States with other messages including one from the Queen of Tonga. The main theme was 'Methodism in the Contemporary World' which was expounded in its varied aspects by distinguished speakers from many parts of World Methodism. There were 1, 025 accredited delegates with official and other visitors to a similar total. Every continent and over thirty countries were represented.

The state of North Carolina is in what is known as the Deep South, and it had its discriminatory laws. This makes the more striking the resolution on the racial issue included in the Message of the Conference. I think this is worth quoting in full:

'The Conference composed of representatives from many nations and ethnic groups united in fellowship in Christ, deplores the embittered strife which bedevils human relations. The Conference is entirely convinced that the Church is committed by its very nature to the establishment of a human society in which discrimination based on race or colour will no longer exist. The Conference expresses its active concern for those of any colour or race who are suffering from political, economic, educational, social or religious discrimination or segregation, and the earnest desire that Methodists themselves will initiate, contend for and foster within their own societies a genuine all-inclusive fellowship.'

The *New York Times* called special attention to this resolution in an editorial, particularly emphasizing that this is essentially a moral and religious problem, which cannot be settled on grounds of legality and expediency. Prior to the Conference, Bishop Ivan Lee Holt, Dr Elmer Clark, and I visited a conference of bishops and leaders of the African Methodist Episcopal Zion Church, the second largest Negro Methodist church. This conference was meeting in Ashville, twenty-eight miles from Lake Junaluska, and our purpose was to explain the nature of the World Methodist Conference. The following morning the chief Ashville newspaper had a statement across two columns in the centre of its front page giving the surprising (?) news that at Lake Junaluska during the forthcoming two weeks white and coloured Methodists from all over the world, including American Negroes, would be living in the same hotels, and boarding-houses, eating at the same tables, and sitting together in the same conference as one people. This was in 1956.

There were many interesting experiences outside the formal programme, including the drive over the Smoky Mountains to the Indian reservation and the Cherokeee village of Oconaluftee, which is preserved in its original form. Dr Harold Roberts and I were made members of the Cherokees by solemn ceremony on different days. My Cherokee name is On-i-na-ski Un-e-li-we-sti Ou, which I am told means 'Builder of Churches', in recognition of my work in the church-building department of British Methodism. One most surprising event happened after the end of the Conference. The delegates included a vivacious lady missionary from Latin America. She was pastor of a Methodist church in a mountain village where no other religious work existed. She returned to find a Roman Catholic priest installed, presumably to save these people from the influence of the Methodists. However, the priest fell in love with the Methodist lady. Leaving his own Church, they were duly married in a Methodist church, and are now engaged together in Methodist work in another area.

At a picturesque session on the morning of the last day, preceded by a robed procession, officially delegated representatives of various Methodist universities and university colleges attended to confer honorary doctorates on fifteen recipients from eight different countries. I received the degree of Doctor of Laws (LL.D.) conferred by Bishop Paul E. Martin on behalf of the Senate of the Centenary College of Louisiana which was founded in 1825 and is one of the oldest of the Methodist university colleges.

There was a considerable amount of business dealt with by the Council at its several meetings and the Executive Committee, apart from the sessions of the large Conference. The Constitution drafted at the Oxford Conference in 1951 was completed and finally adopted. The World Federation of Methodist Women was accepted as an affiliated organization of the World Methodist Council. The many other questions considered included world statistics, evangelism, preacher exchanges, emigration, regional conferences, and relationship to the World Council of Churches. The secretaries and treasurers continued in office, and Dr Harold Roberts was appointed President for the next quinquennium, with grateful thanks to Bishop Ivan Lee Holt for his leadership as the first President of the World Methodist Council. The Covenant Service concluded this last day, and the following morning a group of about a hundred overseas delegates began the rich experience of a three days' tour by coach over the Blue Ridge Parkway and on to Washington, Philadelphia, and New York. In the White House gardens in Washington we were received by President Eisenhower. The last day of the tour was Sunday, and after a most interesting morning service in Old St George's in Philadelphia we had our evening service in the John Street Church, New York, which stands on the first site to be occupied by Methodism in America.[1]

The letter of appreciation for the wonderful hospitality at Lake Junaluska and all associated with it was endorsed by the plenary session and addressed to Bishop Ivan Lee Holt, Dr Oscar T. Olson, Dr Elmer T. Clark and Mr Edwin L. Jones who were responsible. Grateful thanks were extended through them to a host of helpers.

The preservation and use as far as possible of historic Methodist shrines is one of the concerns of the International Methodist Historical Society, which is associated with the World Methodist Council. My responsibility included the settlement of two important shrines in this country. The old Epworth Rectory was built in 1709 on the site of the previous rectory, which was destroyed by fire in February of that year. For 245 years it was the residence of the rectors of that parish, and

[1] For full report see, 'Proceedings of the Ninth World Methodist Conference', edited by Elmer T. Clark and E. Benson Perkins (Methodist Publishing House, U.S.A.).

the Anglican decision to build a new Rectory opened the way for the boyhood home of the Wesleys to become Methodist property. It is today owned by the World Methodist Council. Contributions from British Methodists covered the purchase price of the estate of some two acres, and generous gifts from American Methodists through the great interest of Edwin L. Jones met the heavy cost of restoration and furnishing. On a glorious summer day, 29th June, 1957, the old Rectory was reopened and dedicated as Methodist property by the President and officers of the World Methodist Council, with the Bishop of Lincoln taking part in the proceedings. There were many visitors representative of Methodism in Great Britain and overseas. At the suggestion of the Bishop of Lincoln, a joint Methodist and Anglican service was held in the Parish Church on the Sunday morning following. The Bishop, the Rector, and Methodist ministers participated in the service, the sermon being preached by Bishop Ivan Lee Holt. It was the first time that the followers of John Wesley had worshipped, as such, in the Epworth Parish Church. Increasingly, the Old Rectory attracts a great number of visitors, and is used for small residential conferences and retreats.

On the outskirts of West Bromwich, about five miles from the centre of Birmingham is the tiny four-roomed cottage which was the boyhood home of Francis Asbury, whom John Wesley sent to America in 1771, and who became the first bishop of the Methodist Episcopal Church, as it was called at the Conference in 1784. The property belongs to the West Bromwich County Borough Council, who secured its registration as a historic building. The World Methodist Council shared with the borough the cost of further restoration and furnishing in period style. On Friday, 27th November, 1959, Sir Roger Makins, who had served as British Ambassador in Washington, unveiled the bronze plaque and Dr Harold Roberts offered the dedicatory prayer. The American visitors present and the large crowd of British Methodists will remember the brilliant and understanding speech of Sir Roger Makins at the assembly afterwards in the old Manor House.

At the meeting of the Executive held at Freudenstadt in Germany in 1958, Dr J. B. Webb of Johannesburg submitted a specific proposal for a regional conference on the European pattern to be held in Salisbury, Southern Rhodesia. This was the outcome of a suggestion made by Bishop Ivan Lee Holt when visiting South Africa, and arising also in correspondence I had with Dr Webb. I went out to represent the World Methodist Council at the conference, which was finally fixed for April 1959. The South African Methodist Church invited me to spend a week or two in their country before travelling north to Southern Rhodesia. This is the second largest church in the Union of South Africa, now an independent republic, and has the largest African membership of any of the churches. It was a privilege to preach to the fine congregations in Cape Town, Port Elizabeth, Durban, and Johannesburg. Early on Easter Sunday morning I preached to the Indian Mission in Durban and was decorated with a beautiful garland of carnations by a charming little Indian girl.

I was particularly concerned to visit the African locations, which no white person is allowed to do without official permission. In the company of some of our ministers, I came into direct touch with the effects of the intolerable and un-Christian policy of *Apartheid*, which seems all the more unjust and inhuman when one is face to face with some of the fine African people. In Evaton, an African Reserve, twenty miles or so from Johannesburg, I attended a session of the Southern Transvaal 'Manyano' Conference. This is an association of Methodist African women throughout South Africa and numbers over 100,000 members. At the Sunday morning service associated with the conference I preached to an African congregation which crowded the large church inside and around the doors and windows outside—1,000 or more. Two Africans interpreted the sermon with amazing rapidity into Xhosa and Sesutu. There was a splendid choir, and the singing, as in all the African churches in South Africa, was unaccompanied. Beside the African lyrics, the choir sang in perfect English and splendid artistry the familiar setting of 'O taste and see how gracious the Lord is'. In the procession before and after the service the choir swayed to the rhythm of the hymn and those of us who followed could do no other than join in the dance. There are bad Africans, just as there are bad Europeans, but here were a fine people with whom it was a joy to worship.

At Kilnerton, near Pretoria, I visited the boarding school and teacher-training college, with its most attractive buildings and beautiful chapel, in which I spoke to the whole company. Under the Bantu Education Act, this splendid work, carried on by the Methodist Church for more than fifty years, is being taken over by the South African Government, and because the buildings are on Methodist property outside the African location the Church will be left with the Kilnerton buildings, but no boarders or teacher trainees. So in another way the South African Government have taken over control of the 1,400 African schools owned and maintained by the Methodist Church. This is only one aspect of the terrible situation. It includes the crowding of four-fifths of the population into less than one-fifth of the territory, the denial to the Africans of the right to own property, the inferior standard of education for the Africans, the far lower rate for African labour compared with the standard rate for the same work by others, the infringement of human rights by the Group Areas Act, the oppressive Pass Laws, the imposing of regulations against which the Africans have no right of appeal, and other restrictive conditions. I would like to quote at length from a factual study of civil liberty undertaken by two trained political scientists on the initiative of the South African Institute of Race Relations, a study which is free from all polemics.[1] These two quotations must suffice: 'Almost completely in the Reserves and to an increasing extent outside them, he [the African] has no rights against the Government and no real civil liberty. The Native administration of South Africa is to an increasing extent legalized despotism. It is sometimes benevolent despotism, but always despotism.' 'Freedom', even of the whites, 'is being sacrificed in order to maintain the barriers against racial equality ... and to ensure the political supremacy of the larger of the two white groups.' The South African Methodist Church has declared its condemnation of this policy of *Apartheid* strongly and definitely on Christian grounds. Most disastrously, the Afrikaans of the Dutch Reformed Church support their own white supremacy on a religious basis. The subsequent sad happenings at Sharpeville, near Evaton, have

---

[1] Edgar H. Brookes, J. B. Macauley, *Civil Liberty in South Africa* (Oxford University Press).

intensified the distressing situation, and the political changes still later will undoubtedly have their effect.

Because of the difficulty of arranging such a multi-racial meeting in South Africa the regional conference met in Salisbury, Southern Rhodesia. It included representatives of the South African Methodist Church (both European and African), the African Methodist Episcopal Church (U.S.A.), the Southern and Northern Rhodesian Synods (U.K.), the Methodist Church, U.S.A., in its work in Mozambique and Angola and the work in Northern Rhodesia of the United Church of Canada. No such meeting of the representatives of these different units of Methodist work had ever been held previously. Dr J. B. Webb, who is a Vice-President of the World Methodist Council, and has been President of the South African Methodist Conference several times, presided. During the five days of the conference, Methodist activity in the whole of that vast area of southern Africa was surveyed and the acute problems frankly discussed. The conference released to the Press its unanimous judgements which included these two claims: '(*a*) Equal opportunity to all children at all levels of education, irrespective of race, wealth or creed. (*b*) The right and responsibility of the Church to declare a Christian judgement whenever basic principles are involved in regard to questions of race relationships, social welfare, and other political issues.' Those who are familiar with the conditions in southern Africa will know how radical and far-reaching are these affirmations. The decision of the conference to convene further assemblies to include also Kenya and the Congo, thus covering Africa south of the Equator, was prevented from early fulfilment by events in South Africa. More recently steps have been taken toward the carrying out of this intention.

The Conference met in the splendid English Methodist church (Trinity), and a most successful public meeting was held in the Presbyterian Hall, over which I presided. The conference also paid a visit to 'Epworth', the training college for African ministers, which is a few miles from Salisbury. I discovered that, including myself, there were five Handsworth College men present at the conference, one of them being an African tutor at Epworth. The Chairman of the Southern Rhodesia District, the Rev. Jesse Lawrence, who had been most helpful in the arrangement of the conference, the Rev. Douglas Thompson of the Mission house, and the Rev. Frank Edmonds, Secretary of the South African Methodist Conference, were the others. The five of us spent a very delightful evening at the Chairman's manse, which Mrs Lawrence was so good as to arrange. Being multi-racial there was no hotel or restaurant in Salisbury where it could have been held, at that time.

I had travelled out to Cape Town by sea, but subsequent travel was by air. As a first stage on my return journey after the Conference I flew from Salisbury to Kenya to make a short stay with the Chairman and his wife in Nairobi, the Rev. and Mrs R. E. Kendall. This gave me the opportunity of reporting to a Methodist gathering the work and results of the Salisbury conference. I must break away from the more serious record to tell my only lion story. Mr and Mrs Kendall added to their kindness by taking me to the game reserve. We certainly saw a variety of wild animals—wildebeest, gnu, giraffe, herds of zebras, baboons climbing over the car, eland, hartebeest, impala, wart-hog, dik-dik and the graceful gazelles. We turned off the dirt track on to the coarse grass and bumped along towards where we understood the lions would be found. Eventually we came in sight of a fine lioness and four young lions playing together. At that point, some twenty yards away from the lions we rode over a great tuft of grass and the front axle slipped over a concealed stone and we were stuck. It is an offence, as well as being dangerous, to open the car door in the reserve, but what else could be done? Mrs Kendall and I kept our eyes on the lions, ready to shout if they looked our way, while Mr Kendall got out and tried every manoeuvre to free the car, but without effect. Another car, whose occupants were watching the lions, moved alongside, seeing that something was wrong. The driver, a massive African, consulted with Mr Kendall and then went to the front of the car, while Mr Kendall got into the driving seat. With the engine in reverse, the African lifted the front axle over the stone, and we were free, fortunately without any damage to the car. When I tell this story to the children I explain that it is not really a lion story at all, but a story of what is possible when black and white work together.

There were many experiences of interest associated with the

annual meetings of the Executive Committee. The three meetings prior to the Junaluska Conference were held in Birmingham, England, linked up with a great open session of the British Methodist Conference: in Evanston, U.S.A., in conjunction with the Assembly there of the World Council of Churches, and in Belfast, Ireland. At the London meeting in 1957 dinner was arranged one evening at the House of Commons through the courtesy of Mr George Thomas, M.P., at which the principal guests were the Right Hon. Selwyn Lloyd, M.P., then Foreign Secretary, and Mr Frank Salisbury the artist. The following year Bishop Friedrich Wunderlich invited the committee to meet in the attractive Kurhaus Teuchelwald of the German Methodist Church at Freudenstadt in the heart of the Black Forest. Through the kindness of Bishop Arthur Moore the 1959 meeting was held in the Methodist estate known as 'Epworth by the Sea' which is part of St Simon's Island, Georgia, where the settlement of Frederica was situated to which John and Charles Wesley went out in 1736. The last meeting of the Executive prior to the Oslo Conference was held in Zürich by invitation of Bishop Ferdinnand Sigg. At that meeting an artist friend of Bishop Sigg presented a simple triangular design which was so obviously right for its purpose that I used it for the badges and printing for the forthcoming Conference in Oslo. The Executive meeting in Oslo had no hesitation in adopting it as the official mark of the World Methodist Council.

The journey to the Executive Committee meeting in Georgia in 1959 gave me an opportunity before the meeting to visit Nashville, Tennessee, as invited by Dr J. Manning Potts and Dr Emory S. Bucke. Nashville has some claim to be regarded as the headquarters of the Methodist Church, U.S.A., seeing that three great departments—Evangelism, Education and Publications—are located there. The Board of Evangelism, whose secretary is that great evangelist, Harry Denman, is housed in a magnificent building which includes the unique Chapel of the Upper Room with an almost life-size *bas relief* reproduction of the famous mural of the Last Supper by Leonardo da Vinci. Manning Potts, the editor of the 'Upper Room' world-wide daily devotional publication is Dean of the Chapel and at his invitation I preached at the Wednesday

8.0 a.m. service for the staff of the Board of Evangelism which filled the chapel. The Board of Education has an impressive concrete building with an interior arrangement most cleverly designed. Emory Bucke who is the Book Editor took me round the immense printing and publication buildings with their great modern machines for colour printing on a large scale.

When the Executive meeting concluded we had the opportunity of visiting that fascinating old-fashioned city of Savannah where John Wesley was Anglican pastor for not quite two years. My journey took me on to the new Wesley Theological Seminary in Washington with its most interesting and attractive modern buildings. I had the privilege of conveying to President Norman Trott the most generous offer of Lord Rank concerning the equestrian statue of John Wesley which was fulfilled rather more than eighteen months later. Leaving Washington I flew on to Toronto to consult with friends in the United Church of Canada and to visit their fine new headquarters.

There had been some hope that the Executive Committee might meet in Rome and, indeed, an invitation to do so had been received. There being difficulties in the way the President and I paid a short visit to Italy in 1957. We met a group of Italian Methodist ministers in Bologna, who were serving in the northern area of Italy. In this city of half a million the Methodist church is the only Protestant place of worship. We met other ministers in Rome and also the Moderator and leaders of the Waldensian Church. On the Sunday morning Harold Roberts preached in the church I have previously referred to in Via Venti Settembre while I conducted one of the series of English services in the attractive, though smaller, church on the ground floor of the Methodist building at Ponte S. Angelo (opposite Hadrian's Tomb). We stayed with the Rev. and Mrs Reginald Kissack who were living in the flat above, from the roof of which there is a wonderful view of St Peter's and the Vatican with the River Tiber in the foreground. During the three days of travel Mr Kissack made it possible for us to cover some 500 miles seeing various centres of Methodist work and paying a passing visit to Assissi which of all the places I have visited in Italy seems to have a spiritual rather than an ecclesiastical atmosphere.

The President and I were again together on a second weekend

visit to New York in November 1960, to meet our American colleagues and complete preparations for the Oslo Conference, ten months later. I stayed on an extra day so as to accept an invitation to attend the banquet in Philadelphia of the Society associated with Old St George's Methodist Church, to which I have made several references. Our American Methodist friends have their own way of recognizing those to whom they wish to pay particular honour, and to my surprise I was presented with a 'Certificate of Merit' on behalf of the St George's Society in recognition of 'work with the World Methodist Council'. It was certainly a most interesting occasion and splendidly arranged.

Three significant events occurred in my final year as Secretary, culminating in the Tenth World Methodist Conference in Oslo. The first was in Washington on Wesley Day, 24th May, 1961, and came at the end of a long process of negotiation. At the Junaluska Conference in 1956 President Norman Trott of the Wesley Theological Seminary in Washington showed me the plans of their new buildings adjoining the American University, which is a Methodist foundation. He was wondering whether it was at all likely that a duplicate of the bronze equestrian statue of John Wesley, which stands in the forecourt of the Wesley Chapel (New Room) Bristol, could in some way be secured for a wonderful site on the campus of the new Seminary fronting Massachusetts Avenue. There followed for me a long correspondence, with necessary consultation of legal opinion on the question of copyright and the possibility of making a duplicate, seeing that all the drawings and models were destroyed during the war. These points were ultimately resolved and a definite quotation secured for making a duplicate from the expert Morris Singer Company in South Lambeth. Then Lord Rank graciously offered to present the statue to the seminary. As he could not travel to America for the dedication on Wesley Day, I had the duty of representing him and British Methodism at a most colourful ceremony held on the open campus in the brilliant sunshine of a glorious summer day. The beautiful reproduction on its prepared plinth has been greatly admired. Curiously enough, the Seminary is in the area known as Wesley Heights, and fronting the statue on Massachusetts Avenue is Wesley Circle, previously so named.

At the end of July that year the Inaugural Conference of the independent Methodist Church, Ghana, was held at Cape Coast, and I was invited to attend and take part in the Conference as a representative of the World Methodist Council. I spent just over two weeks in Ghana, and came to know something of that really wonderful people. After my experience in South Africa, it was more than interesting to enter a West African country and to be conscious from the first of the entire absence of a colour bar. There is the desire of the new Government to make the country as completely African as possible, but that is not based on any sense of human difference between white and black. I stayed for some days with an African barrister and his doctor wife in Accra, and it was a delightful experience to enjoy their gracious hospitality. Through their interest I was able to attend an evening reception by Sir Arthur Snelling, the High Commissioner, where I had most interesting conversations with the Speaker of the House of Parliament and a paramount Chief who sat in state wearing robes and crown and receiving the guests introduced to him. When I reached Takoradi by air from Accra I was met by the Rev. and Mrs H. W. Dennis, an old colleague and friend, with whom I was staying for a while in the Mission House, and by the singing band from the church with their reiteration of *'Aquabah!'* (Welcome!).

The opening session of the inaugural conference was crowded, enthusiastic and impressive. I shall not forget the entrance of the robed choirs as they came up the aisles in procession singing, 'Omnipotent Redeemer, our ransomed souls adore Thee', particularly the men's voices, providing a bass like deep pedal notes. In some ways the most impressive occasion of those days was the procession and open-air assembly the following morning. We stood on the balcony in front of the Wesley Church, Cape Coast. Behind us was the church, with its pulpit, which stands over the graves of the early missionaries of 125 years ago who sacrificed their lives in what was then known as the 'white man's grave'. The procession came along, turning the corner and crossing the front of the church, where the Rev. Francis C. F. Grant, President of the new Ghana Methodist Conference, the Rev. Dr Maldwyn Edwards, President of the British Methodist Conference, and the other visitors were standing. Each section took its place in the large open space in front. The Boys' Brigade led the way, and then came the Wesley Guilds, the choirs in their robes, the young people from the high schools, the Women's Fellowship, the Singing Bands, the Men's organizations, and other groups, with the ministers in their white suits and clerical collars completing the wonderful procession. The space in front of the church was ultimately crowded with thousands of Africans making a wonderful coloured picture of Christian Africa happy and joyous on this glad day. They had been singing as they came along and were now ready to join in the brief service which followed. Several of the experienced missionaries to whom I spoke could hardly restrain their emotion as they faced this great scene, with all it implied of toil and triumph and prospect for the days to come.

The church at Takoradi is large, but the interior as I saw it was mean and ugly, only relieved somewhat when filled with people. They knew something had to be done about it, and Mr Dennis asked me to meet the Building Committee and tell them what was required. This I did, and submitted a scheme which I had worked out after examining the whole structure. When I got back to England I prepared a detailed report and an architect friend drew some coloured perspective drawings of the proposal. They accepted it and set to work, under the guidance of my old colleague. They have already re-floored the building, secured a new pulpit, Communion table and rail, panelled the east end, installed a gallery, and placed in position the organ I was able to secure as a gift from England. When the new pews are ready and some other details of the scheme completed the African committee want me to go out again and dedicate the restored church building.

Barely a fortnight after returning from Ghana the Tenth World Methodist Conference opened its sessions in Oslo, Norway. This was the first time that the Conference had assembled outside the English-speaking countries. Oslo is as interesting a city as Norway is a country, and state, city, and Church (the established Lutheran Church) united in giving a real welcome to this representative conference of World Methodism. The Central Methodist Church in Oslo had just been rebuilt as part of a fine modern building which includes office accommodation for church and other organizations. Almost adjoining is the Filadelfia Hall, seating over 2,000, which admirably accommodated the conference and its principal public assemblies. There were 1,289 accredited delegates, and with visitors from many countries and the interested Norwegian people the hall was full to capacity on all the public occasions. In the Conference itself forty countries were represented, and more than half of these provided speakers or other participants on the programme.

The main theme was 'New Life in the Spirit' and it was impressive how a succession of able speakers from various parts of World Methodism created a sense of unity in their exposition of different aspects of what is of primary emphasis in Methodist theology. In the second half of each morning the conference divided into three sections, (1) for continuous Bible study, (2) for group discussions on questions arising from the main theme, (3) for talks on Methodism in Action by speakers from different countries, mainly for visitors. The evenings were occupied by the public assemblies, an interesting feature being the singing by Norwegian choirs and the Mount Union College choir from America.

During the morning of the opening day King Olav V received the officers of the World Methodist Council at the Royal Palace—introduced by Bishop Odd Hagen. The King, Ambassadors and other dignitaries attended the first session of the Conference that evening. The official heads of the independent Methodist Churches round the world were personally received and greeted by the President, Dr Harold Roberts, who delivered his Presidential Address. Another outstanding occasion was the Ecumenical Service in the Cathedral by courtesy of the State Church, the Bishop of Oslo welcoming the Conference and the address being given by Dr Visser 't Hooft, Secretary-General of the World Council of Churches. The Sunday services were held in the large new Sports Hall on the outskirts of Oslo, the Methodist churches in Oslo being closed for that day so that the Norwegian Methodists could join with the great company from many lands. The result was indeed impressive, for the congregation at each service numbered approximately 4,000. The unofficial assemblies included a reception by the city in the wonderful City Hall and dinner in honour of the retiring secretaries who were presented with the silver medal awarded by 'World Outlook' of America.

The World Federation of Methodist Women, with its associated groups in every continent, held their conference and meetings under the presidency of Mrs Ernst Scholz of Berlin during the three days in Oslo before the World Conference opened. The Federation comprises fifty-two units in forty-seven countries, with approximately 6,000,000 members. The Council and Executive held their meetings during the afternoons of the Conference period to deal with the routine business and receive reports, giving the chief time to a revision of the Constitution. The statistics presented, obtained and revised by the secretaries, showed a recorded adult membership throughout the world of 19,029,000, with a world community, including youth organizations and adherents, of 42,170,000. In the final business session Dr Elmer Clark and I handed over our positions as joint secretaries to Dr Lee F. Tuttle of the United States and the Rev. Max W. Woodward of Great Britain. We were given positions on the Executive Committee as Secretaries Emeritus. Bishop Fred P. Corson was appointed the new President in succession to Dr Harold Roberts. In accordance with American custom, Bishop Ivan Lee Holt had prepared citations which acknowledged in most generous terms the services of both the retiring and the continuing officers and a form of recognition of the appointment of Bishop Corson, with the presentation to him of the President's badge. In the last business meeting of the Executive Committee, Bishop Odd Hagen, on behalf of the Scandinavian Churches, presented gold medals to Bishop Corson, the new President, Dr Harold Roberts, now a Past-President, Dr Elmer T. Clark, and myself. In the final plenary sessions we did not fail to acknowledge our most grateful thanks to the Norwegian Methodists, and especially to Bishop Odd Hagen and to Mr Ragnar Horn, the Chairman of the Hospitality Committee, for their quite amazingly efficient arrangements for the Conference. Dr Harold Roberts will be especially remembered for his guidance through the five years, his brilliant addresses at the meetings of the Executive, and his illuminating opening address at this Conference. Bishop Fred P. Corson had the good wishes of the whole conference as he assumed the Presidency and widespread appreciation of his address, which preceded the Methodist Covenant Service with which the Conference closed.[1]

In this account of outstanding events in the development of the World Methodist Council the names of many colleagues have been mentioned with whom it has been a joy and privilege to work in various countries. In this country there is a group without whose splendid service my work as a general secretary would have been impossible. Ministerial colleagues include Eric W. Baker, the secretary of the British Conference and now a Vice-President of the World Methodist Council. He has been an invaluable ally and in association with A. Kingsley Lloyd particularly helpful on financial matters. Rupert E. Davies has been a most reliable assistant secretary with special interest in educational affairs. A. Stanley Leyland has had the arduous task of arranging with his American colleague the annual exchange of preachers. A. Raymond George has carried responsibility in this country for the Methodist Theological Institute meeting from time to time in Lincoln College, Oxford. Wilfred Wade has had secretarial responsibility for the European region. Harold Roberts is of course included in this group. Among valued lay colleagues are L. A. Ellwood, Treasurer, his associate treasurer John Mills, Dr Dorothy Farrar, Vice-President of the World Federation of Methodist Women and Sister Lillian Topping in connection with the Theological Institute. The mention of this group of close friends and responsible colleagues is itself an indication of the far-reaching character of the work of the World Methodist Council.

I should find great personal satisfaction if I could go on to add the names of a host of other friends and colleagues with whom it has been a delight to serve. It would include distinguished laity like Charles C. Parlin and Dorothy McConnell, outstanding ministers such as Ernst Scholz and Karl K. Quimby, well known bishops like Paul E. Martin and Bertram W. Doyle and officials in the churches, to name, Ernest E. Long, Secretary of the United Church of Canada, Frank W. Hambly, President General of the Australasian Methodist Conference, and Francis C. F. Grant, President, The Methodist Church,

[1] For full Report see 'Proceedings of the Tenth World Methodist Conference', edited by E. Benson Perkins and Elmer T. Clark (Epworth Press, London).

Ghana, West Africa. These are typical and representative of many whose friendship I cherish and whose service has been creative in the growing influence of the World Methodist Council.

It would be ungracious not to refer to the happy occasion within the last year before the Oslo Conference, when my colleagues and friends associated with the British Committee of the World Methodist Council invited my wife and me to a complimentary dinner to mark the completion of fifty years since my ordination and our golden wedding anniversary. There were some sixty present, and we remember with intense gratitude the kind and generous things said formally at the dinner table and privately to us afterwards by everyone present. No words can express the value of the friendships thus so wonderfully demonstrated. It is a rich blessing in life to have friends who see in a golden light what has been done, and it warms the heart even though one realizes how much the assessment owes to generous thought which reaches beyond the actual achievement.

CHAPTER XI

THE ECUMENICAL MOVEMENT

THIS autobiography would be incomplete without some account of my participation through the years in the Ecumenical Movement, especially as it was expressed in the international conferences in Stockholm, Amsterdam, and Evanston. As I have indicated in the previous chapter, Methodism is itself a world Church, and in that sense truly ecumenical. But it does not and cannot in itself exhaust the content of that word. The decision to substitute the word 'World' in its title was deliberate in order to set free the word 'Ecumenical' —*OIKOUMENE* in the original Greek,—as the distinctive mark of the new movement which finds its expression in the World Council of Churches. In so far as I have worked for World Methodism in building up the World Methodist Council, it is not for Methodism in any narrow or exclusive sense, but for the Methodist Church throughout the world as part of the Universal Church of our Lord. The World Council of Churches is not that Church, nor indeed a church at all. It is, however, the most complete expression thus far realized of the God-given spirit of unity through which we may come to know the One, Holy, Catholic and Apostolic Church beyond all the differences of our earthly organizations.

My first vivid experience of the fact and significance of the Ecumenical Movement was as a member of the Universal Christian Conference on Life and Work in Stockholm in 1925. The place of the Stockholm Conference in the movement tends to be overlooked, yet I am satisfied that it was as creative in its own field as the Edinburgh International Missionary Conference of 1910 was in another area of thought and action. The Stockholm Conference was the culmination of a long process, particularly in this country. I have referred to the Wesleyan Methodist Union for Social Service, which was started in 1905. Years later I became its Secretary until it was absorbed in the Christian Citizenship Department. From 1912 there were important interdenominational conferences of the social service unions in the different churches. It was these discussions which led on ultimately to the Conference on Christian Politics, Economics and Citizenship (COPEC) which met in the Birmingham Central Hall in 1924.[1] COPEC had formative relationship to the Stockholm Conference the following year and thus played an influential part in the early days of the modern ecumenical movement. The twelve COPEC reports were basic material, in fact the only basic material, for the international 'Life and Work' conference. The authoritative history of the Ecumenical Movement from 1517 to 1948, edited by Ruth Rouse and Stephen Charles Neill,[2] has this significant statement:

> 'COPEC was the most considerable effort made up to that date anywhere in the world to focus Christian thought and action on the urgent problems of the day. All the subjects scheduled for discussion at Stockholm, 1925, and a good many others as well, were handled in the twelve volumes of the COPEC reports, on the basis of wide and intensive preparation, in which Roman Catholics had participated.... Dr Temple said succinctly at the opening session of the conference: "Our conference is itself the British preparation for the Universal Conference on the Life and Work of the Church." The COPEC reports were in fact submitted in abridged form as the British contribution to Stockholm, 1925: no preparation of equal thoroughness had been carried out anywhere else in the world.'

The Stockholm Conference, the first international assembly on the social life of mankind, consisted of approximately 500 representatives from forty different countries. It was the first time that the Orthodox Churches had been personally represented at an international church assembly. It was also the first time that German and French representatives had sat down together since the ending of the First World War. Of the sixteen delegates from the then three British Methodist

---

[1] See *supra*, Chapter IV, pp. 55f.
[2] *A History of the Ecumenical Movement*, S.P.C.K., pp. 540f.

Churches, Henry Carter and I were the only ones present at the Amsterdam Assembly in 1948, twenty-three years later, and I was the only one of that Stockholm group who attended the Evanston Assembly in 1954.

No city could have been more delightful in setting and hospitality than Stockholm. My friend and I were entertained in the home of Professor and Mrs Fries. He was Professor of Botany in the University, and they lived in a house most beautifully placed in the heart of the Botanical Gardens. When we arrived at the station and were handed the address of our hosts, we wondered what it meant, not knowing any Swedish —Bergianska Trägården. We were to discover how very fortunate we were. One afternoon the Patriarch and Pope of Alexandria, Photios by name, the Archbishop of Nubia, and other Orthodox delegates came to have tea with our hosts and to see the gardens. The Patriarch, a delightful old man whose signed portrait hangs in my study, died on the return journey after the Conference.

The great opening service was held in the Storkyrkan (Cathedral). I can still recall how the Bishop of Winchester, Dr F. T. Woods, having announced his text, 'Repent ye, for the Kingdom of Heaven is at hand', sent his fine voice ringing through the building: 'Change your minds! Adopt a new outlook! Get a fresh point of view! That was Christ's challenge to His own generation. That is the challenge which in His Name we make to the men and women of these modern days.' So he went on to plead for the sovereignty of Christ through the whole range of human affairs. The service closed with Martin Luther's great Reformation hymn, *'Ein' feste Burg ist unser Gott'*, and for the first time, often repeated in following years, I heard the hymn being sung simultaneously in various languages—German, English, French, Swedish. There followed a reception in the Royal Palace by Their Majesties King Gustav and Queen Victoria of Sweden.

At the regular sessions of the Conference progress was rather slow. While advance translations of the principal addresses were available, all the speeches in discussion were followed by a précis in each of the other two of the three languages used—English, German, French. The modern system of immediate translation through short-wave radio transmission was not available at that time. These translated summaries were generally rather dull and this made an experience of mine rather striking. I had participated in the discussion, by arrangement, on the gambling issue, and had dealt with its international aspect. To the surprise of everyone, including myself, the précis in German was greeted with loud applause by the German delegation. They were moved, I discovered, by the fact of an Englishman condemning the gambling speculation from which they had suffered so grievously since the war. One of the most exciting debates was on methods of dealing with the drink problem, Lord Salveson, a Scottish law lord, and the Rev. Henry Carter being the chief protagonists. That was the last time the problems of alcoholism and gambling were discussed in any of the international church assemblies. The only other reference I know is in the report of the Youth Delegation at Amsterdam, which said: 'We believe that the constant drink habit, gambling, and sexual immorality have played a large part in the depersonalization of our time.' Why is it, I wonder, that these social evils have been passed over in the more recent assemblies? At one point the whole conference was deeply stirred when Bishop C. H. Brent of New York, after a brief analysis of the injustice, brutality, and stupidity of war, said: 'I reaffirm my belief that the Christian Church, if it be so minded, can in the Name of Christ, rule out war and rule in peace within a generation. I may be a fool, but if so I am God's fool.'

The main theme of the Stockholm Conference was 'The Purpose of God for Humanity and the Task of the Church'. At the opening session we were faced with the same kind of theological conflict which came out so prominently at the second World Council Assembly at Evanston. Bishop Ihmels of Saxony declared: 'The Kingdom of God . . . is something quite different from the natural and social order with which it is surrounded. . . . Christianity is religion and nothing but religion. . . . The transformation of society can only be achieved by the conversion of the individuals who constitute society.' He was followed by Pasteur Wilfred Monod of Paris, who said: 'It is not enough to state that individual souls are called to salvation; we must contemplate in all its extent, in its cosmic frame, the plan of a collective salvation.' Most effectively he went on to point out that the prayer given to us is not addressed to *my* Father, but to *our* Father, and we ask, not for *my* bread, but for *our* bread. The conference closed with a service in the Cathedral at Uppsala, the preacher being the Archbishop Dr Nathan Soderblom, one of the greatest and most gifted figures in those early days of the ecumenical movement. As we left Stockholm, conscious of a great experience, we could not foresee the wonderful development which was to come nearly a quarter of a century later.

There are various links between Stockholm and Amsterdam. There was a further conference on 'Life and Work' in Oxford in 1937. Developments in theological thought led to a conference on 'Faith and Order' at Lausanne in 1927 and another in Edinburgh in 1937. The outbreak of the Second World War in 1939 hindered the projects which had already emerged from the conferences in 1937. But under the leadership of that great man, William Temple, who became Archbishop of Canterbury in 1942, the main features of a World Council of Churches were being determined. It was at his enthronement in Canterbury Cathedral that William Temple used those oft-quoted words, 'the great new fact of our era' as a description of the new Christian world fellowship. To our sorrow, he did not live to see the culmination of his work at Amsterdam in 1948.

There was something profoundly moving and distinctive about being a member of the Amsterdam Assembly of the World Council of Churches. There would be other assemblies, but there could not be another 'first'. There had been earlier conferences, to some of which I have referred, but here was the creation of a permanent ecumenical fact, a fellowship which had come together in order to stay together. It was not an excessively large assembly. The delegates numbered 351, with 238 alternates. In addition there were about 150 consultants, 100 in the Youth Delegation, and a number of accredited visitors. The most significant fact is that this total company represented 137 separately organized churches in forty-four different countries. The principal omissions were the Roman Catholic Church, the Russian section of the Orthodox Churches, the Southern Baptists of America and the Missouri Synod of the Lutheran Churches. Practically all races were represented, and both sides of the Iron Curtain. Never before had so widely representative an assembly of Christendom been brought together, or certainly not since the Council of Nicea in the fourth century, if then. How we differed in race, colour, language, dress, church order, and theology! It was not surprising that some observers declared that unity could never be achieved in such a conference. But it was. The striking message of the Amsterdam Assembly was adopted by a standing vote without a single dissentient. The point of our unity was that with all our differences we all believed in our Lord Jesus Christ. We found unity in His presence.

The sessions of the conference were held in the admirable Concertgebouw, but the two special acts of worship took place in the Nieuwe Kerk (New Church) built in 1414, and only new in that it was built a few years after what is known as the Old Church. On the first Sunday the service included two addresses, both, as it happened, by Methodists, the aged Dr John R. Mott of the United States and Dr Daniel T. Niles of Ceylon. On the second Sunday morning history was made by the great service of Holy Communion according to the rite of the Netherlands Reformed Church, with some 1,200 communicants. The invitation was to all communicant members of the participating churches. Six ministers from other churches assisted in the celebration, and I count it to have been a very great privilege to have been one of the six. The form of celebration was strange to many of us. The communicants came forward in successive companies of about 100 and sat down at both sides of a long, white-covered table. Each of the officiating ministers in turn consecrated and began the distribution of the bread and then of the wine, which were passed from hand to hand down the table. If it was strange, it was impressive, and the details beautifully arranged. This was a new beginning in church relationships, for we cannot go back from this sharing together of Holy Communion across the frontiers of church divisions. I recall how deeply moved Bishop Sommer was as he sat at the table where I officiated and for the first time joined in the fellowship of the Lord's Table with ministers and laymen of the German Lutheran Church. So in like manner it was a new and wonderful experience for the great company who shared that fellowship.

The main theme was 'Man's Disorder and God's Design'. There were four chief study sections, and my place was in Section III, 'The Church and the Disorder of Society'. One of the interesting features was the frequent clash of debate between Professor Emil Brunner, the Swiss theologian, and Professor Reinhold Niebuhr of the Union Theological Seminary, New York. At one point Professor Brunner remarked in his quiet way that communism was the climax of capitalism, which aroused Professor Niebuhr to wrathful indignation. I found myself having dinner one evening in a group which included Professor Brunner. He admitted with a smile that his comment which had provoked such indignant repudiation was a 'slight exaggeration'. Speaking beautiful, idiomatic English, he told us about his visits to America. After one lecture an American said to him, 'Professor Brunner, you speak very fine American, but with an English accent.'

To my thinking, the Message of the Amsterdam Assembly is one of the most impressive documents that has come out of the ecumenical movement. There are some of the sentences which I find pregnant with meaning. I have, for instance, often quoted these words: 'It is not in man's power to banish sin and death from the earth, to create the unity of the Holy Catholic Church, to conquer the hosts of Satan. But it is within the power of God. . . . By our acts of obedience and faith we can on earth set up signs which point to the coming victory.' The hymn sung most frequently, and since then associated in many of our minds with the Amsterdam Assembly, was the Swiss hymn translated from the French, 'Thine be the glory, Risen, Conquering Son', sung to the tune taken from an oratorio by Handel, who was born a German and became a naturalized Englishman—surely an ecumenical fact in itself. Together with some visitors, there were about 150 members of the Methodist Church round the world who were present at Amsterdam, and we had two meetings to greet one another and consider our place as Methodists in this great ecumenical movement.

The second assembly of the World Council of Churches at Evanston, near Chicago, U.S.A., in 1954 brought into prominence some of those tensions which were latent at Amsterdam six years earlier. The first assembly was creative, and that gave Amsterdam distinction. The second assembly at Evanston was testing, and that seemed to create a tense atmosphere. The assembly opened in the North-Western University on Sunday, 15th August, 1954. I was present as a fraternal delegate representing the World Methodist Council. The setting was less restful than at Amsterdam. After morning devotions in the First Methodist Church, Evanston, we travelled in coaches three miles or more to the McGaw Hall, which is a sports arena, excellent for its primary purpose, but not as comfortable nor as convenient for the Assembly as was the Concertgebouw at Amsterdam. The main theme was 'Christ the Hope of the World', and it was expounded first of all at the afternoon session on that hot opening Sunday. I was vividly reminded of the opening session at Stockholm twenty-nine years earlier. There were two addresses, the first by Professor Edmund Schlink of Heidelberg University. Speaking in German, he declared: 'Wherever the coming of Christ is spoken of as the Hope of the World the end of the world is always spoken of too. . . . The Name of Christ is taken in vain if it is used as a slogan in this world's struggle for its own preservation.' The second speaker was Professor Robert L. Calhoun of Yale. In striking contrast, he said: 'God is our Hope because in Jesus Christ He has come down in the midst of earthly history . . . and filled the human scene with a vast new light. . . . In Jesus Christ He came down to share our lot and break the tyranny of sin and death.'

That different interpretation and emphasis remained throughout the Conference, and was never fully resolved. That there is a synthesis between *now* and *then* cannot be doubted. The Kingdom of God is both a present fact and a final reality. What did emerge in the discussions, both in the sectional studies and the plenary sessions, was that difference in theological statement or in church order is no sin so long as it does not issue in division. The emphasis upon that truth and its illustration in the fellowship of the Assembly was to me the permanent value of Evanston. These differences in the field of theology and also in the field of sociology are not simple of solution. This was very marked in the study section of social questions to which I belonged. The call to responsible social action can be variously interpreted with equal sincerity.

The point of first importance which is stressed in the Message is that 'God had gathered us together to be His Family'. So the Evanston Assembly, with difference of thought and statement brought into the open, strengthened the fact of the unity achieved in the World Council of Churches and gave fresh impetus to the extension of the ecumenical movement throughout the Christian churches of the world.

As at Amsterdam, on the second Sunday morning there was a united service of Holy Communion, held in the First Methodist Church according to the usual Methodist rite. Bishop Ivan Lee Holt was the presiding celebrant, with other ministers assisting. There was a feeling that the communicants were not as representative a company as at Amsterdam, but it was difficult to tell. The following Sunday there was a celebration according to the rite of the Church of South India. That afternoon the Methodist delegation met together in the beautiful Methodist Church at Wilmette, some miles north of Evanston. Thought was given to the World Methodist Conference to be held in North Carolina two years later.

The full number of participants in the Evanston Assembly was half as large again as at Amsterdam. I had the feeling that it was too large. The numbers attending the Third Assembly at New Delhi, India, in 1961 were smaller, and if that was due to its location in India it was none the less, in my judgement, a wise decision. I was not present at New Delihi, but I was a consultant member of the Central Committee, and thus able to follow the quite amazing growth in extent and influence of the World Council of Churches. It is worthwhile recording that the three significant developments at New Delhi were: (*a*) the uniting of the three strands of thought which made possible the World Council of Churches—Life and Work, Faith and Order, and Missions—by the integration of the International Missionary Council with the World Council; (*b*) the association in membership of the Russian section of the Orthodox Church through the Patriarch of Moscow; (*c*) the presence of official Roman Catholic observers. The New Delhi Assembly adopted the new basis of the World Council which we had recommended after a long discussion at the Central Committee at St Andrews, Scotland, in 1960. It now reads: 'The World Council of Churches is a fellowship of churches which confess the Lord Jesus Christ as God and Saviour according to the Scriptures and therefore seek to fulfil together their common calling to the glory of the one God, Father, Son and Holy Spirit.' The two additions are the reference to the Scriptures which was a Lutheran point and the inclusion of the Trinity which was pressed by the Orthodox delegates.

When I was in South Africa, I had the opportunity of a long talk with the Archbishop of Cape Town, Dr Joost de Blank. As we discussed the tragic situation, I reminded the Archbishop that two ministers of the Dutch Reformed Church in South Africa were members of the World Council of Churches. 'Yes, I know,' he said. 'And I have pointed out to them that it is easy to be ecumenical everywhere except in your own country.' That is the critical point. The World Council of Churches is based on the direct membership of the churches, but the ecumenical movement will largely fail unless the churches come together in their own country. Here in Britain this has been achieved in the formation of the British Council of Churches, which anticipated the World Council by being formed in 1942. It took over the Christian Social Council, which was the direct outcome of COPEC. I counted it a signal honour to be appointed one of the two Vice-Presidents of the British Council of Churches for the years 1952-4. The Archbishop of Canterbury has been the President from the beginning, Dr William Temple being the first. Dr Geoffrey Fisher followed in 1945, and gave great and distinguished service until his retirement in 1961. The two Vice-Presidents are usually chosen to represent the Church of Scotland and the British Free Churches. It was a pleasure as well as a privilege to work with the Archbishop. I have continued on the Executive Committee, and could speak of the developing work of its various departments—International, Social Responsibility, Education, Youth, Faith and Order, Inter-Church Aid and Refugee Service. This is the ecumenical movement finding active expression in our midst and calling for the co-operative interest of every Christian church and congregation.

It was in 1953, ten years ago, that, when returning from Italy after dedicating the new Methodist church at La Spezia, I stayed over in Geneva for an interview with Dr Visser 't

Hooft, the Secretary-General of the World Council of Churches. One of the points I raised in that hour has proved to be of more importance than I realized at the time. I could see then that if the World confessional organizations, like the World Methodist Council, were isolated from the World Council of Churches it would be unfortunate, and could be disastrous. My suggestion was that a conference of the executive officers of these world organizations with the officers of the World Council of Churches, should be convened to examine this situation. Dr Visser 't Hooft was entirely favourable to the idea, but, with the Evanston Assembly less than eighteen months away, felt unable to do anything about it for the time being. Later I discussed the proposal with Dr Lund-Quist, then Secretary of the Lutheran World Federation, who was most helpful, and with others. Eventually I was able to share in the summoning of such a conference in Geneva in the autumn of 1957. This included the representatives of the Baptist World Alliance, the Friends World Council, the International Congregational Council, the Lutheran World Federation, the World Convention of the Churches of Christ (Disciples), the World Methodist Council, the World Presbyterian Alliance, and the Church of England in its world relationships. There was no desire or intention to establish yet another organization, but the first conference indicated how valuable would be the meeting together from time to time of the officers of the world denominational organizations. A second conference was convened in 1959, and a third in 1962. Meeting at the Headquarters of the World Council of Churches in Geneva, an invaluable link is forged which may prevent possible conflict, and instead establish a most helpful alliance. This is the practical answer to certain quite sincere criticisms of the confessional organizations which were voiced at New Delhi.

In the course of his Presidential Address at the opening of the World Methodist Conference in Oslo, Dr Harold Roberts said: 'There are two movements towards unity of momentous concern for our time. One is what may be described as the world confessional movement, in which the World Methodist Council shares.... Then there is the union of the communions of different traditions in the World Council of Churches....

These two movements need each other, and we must at present seek to hold both together within the divine purpose for the Church and the world.' With that I am in complete agreement and I am profoundly thankful that toward the fulfilment of that purpose I was able to intervene to secure this consultative conference of confessional excutive officers, not meeting for their own ends, but with the officers of the World Council of Churches for that larger purpose which has yet to be achieved.

If this chapter has taken more the form of argument than the telling of a story I can only plead that it does portray an essential part of that story. Thought and action are intimately related, or should be, and to know something of the principles which have been finally accepted after thought and discussion is to have the key to the interpretation of the life itself.

CHAPTER XII

'THINKING BACKWARD AND LIVING FORWARD'

THE title of this final chapter is a quotation which I found in a book over fifty years ago written by F. S. Marvin, an Oxford historian, entitled *The Living Past*. He puts it within quotation marks without indicating its source, and, as I have not been able to discover its origin, I can only do the same. The sub-title of the book is 'A Sketch of Western Progress' and this is his conclusion:

> 'We know that the stream which bears us on from the infinite behind us will not slack its course, and we begin to recognize a regular movement and a certain goal. The stream is unbroken and the past lives on. But while we look back with reverence, the heart goes out to those who are to travel further and see the fuller light.'

That was written before the First World War, but we could certainly have guessed that without needing to be told. The belief in the 'regular movement' and the 'unbroken stream' was characteristic of the Victorian and the Edwardian days. But any complacent belief in the inevitability of progress has been rudely shaken. What the First World War and the years of disillusionment that followed failed to do has been most disastrously accomplished by a Second World War and the moral decadence which followed. The unbroken stream has lost its way in a bog which lacks movement and has neither boundary nor direction. True, the past lives on, but it is easy to lose confidence in the 'certain goal' and the 'fuller light'. Yet the implications of the title of this final chapter remain true. We must think clearly and courageously through the experiences behind us in order to have confidence in the life ahead. In these final words, I am not proposing to do more than recall some features of my story and relate them to certain conclusions that in my own mind govern the tasks that await us.

Then, first of all, let me record my deep thankfulness to God that my life has been spent in the service of the Methodist Church. I would gladly choose that way again if I had the opportunity. In Methodism there is an overwhelming sense of being a member of a vast family. As a minister one belongs to the whole and one is never left unattached. I was travelling one day with an Anglican naval chaplain who was leaving the service and intending to return to parish work. But he was feeling depressed. The Bishop of the diocese from which he came had no post to offer him, and the only suggestion which had reached him from another source was a church and vicarage which for him was financially impossible. Knowing that I was a Methodist, he burst out, 'I wish we had your system or that I was in your Church.' Naturally, in such a conversation, I began to point out all the disadvantages, but he would have none of it. He went on, 'Look at the Methodist chaplains I know. Not one of them is in my fix. They know there will be an appointment and a manse when they leave the service. It may not always be just the appointment they would have chosen, but they can move later. Not one of them is left stranded, as I am at present.' Methodism offers no large stipends, but is not the basic sense of an approximate equality, whether stationed in town or country, the right arrangement for a church? Our allowances call for frugality and personal discipline, but is that not exactly the sort of character that should be associated with the Christian Church? On the other hand no one has a finer opportunity for the fullest possible service than has the Methodist minister. He has a large area of freedom within the authority of the Church and many channels of leadership in the life of the community. There are difficulties, and from time to time in this or that situation a sense of frustration which can be hard to bear. But the dedicated servant of the Lord has no reason to be defeated by circumstances, and in the Methodist Church he is not left alone to carry his burdens.

What stand out most vividly for me as I think backward over my varied experiences as a minister are not the great public occasions. I suppose I may have had a larger share of them than I had any right to expect. They have their interest and I am not undervaluing them. But, as I said in an earlier chapter, it is the more intimate personal things that live. My remembrances become heart-warming when I think of some I have assisted on the way. There is the girl whose decision for Christ was made on one of those Sunday evenings at the Birmingham Central Hall and in recent days has been Vice-President of the Wesley Deaconess Order. There is the youth in the boys' club who today is one of the most influential laymen in a suburban church. There is the young local preacher whom I brought on the plan and is now a nationally known business executive, still a local preacher and a member of the Methodist Conference. There are those whom I was privileged to help on the way to the Methodist ministry. That farm lad of limited education who became a most devoted superintendent, serving especially in rural circuits. That one, most brilliant of them all, whose life was cut short in the First World War. That older candidate who, after splendid service in English circuits, is doing a magnificent piece of work in Africa. I suppose the list would be quite a long one if I attempted to set it out in full. There are few joys greater than to meet some of these in more mature life and to rejoice with them over one's share in the beginning of things. This kind of service lives on, and no changes of modern life make this out of date.

It is probable that, through a combination of circumstances, I have as extensive an experience of the Methodist Conference as any of my contemporaries. But then I always found the Conference fascinating, and was glad to make the effort to be present even when I was not a member. There is no other church court quite like it. An Anglican whose judgement I value was attending our Conference for the first time, discharging an official commission. After he had experienced four or five days of it, I took him on one side for a frank talk about his impressions. There were just two things he wanted to say, and they were both said in genuine admiration. One was the splendid control and direction of the business. That was a tribute to the Rev. Edwin Finch. Other secretaries would have provoked the same comment. The other impression was the way in which all the speakers, laymen no less than ministers, related whatever they had to say, even on business details, to vital spiritual principles. I believe that to be a sound judgement, and I would like to add to it another. The Conference has built up through the long years the desire and intention to be true to early Methodism in preserving a high standard of Christian living and a clear enunciation of the moral disciplines of the Christian life. There was never greater need for this and I feel strongly that whatever changes may come in the course of union developments the Methodist Conference, with the character it has acquired, must be preserved.

It has always been with me a conviction that membership of the Conference carried with it the responsibility of sharing in its business. By that I mean not only voting, but speaking if one has anything constructive, or even on occasion destructive, to say. That conviction, upon which I have acted evidently accounts for a comment I heard from a brother minister recently. He had been hearing me preach, as he said, for the first time, and later in the day made public reference to it. Then he went on: 'Of course, I have heard him speak many times, for when we go to Conference we always expect to hear Benson Perkins.' Was that intended to be a compliment? I think he meant it to be so regarded, or otherwise he would hardly have said it publicly, and I am prepared to receive it in that sense. At any rate, if it were possible to relive the past, I do not think I should make any change in that particular.

To think backward over the prevailing conditions and character of community life during the years of this century is a sorry experience if one honestly faces the facts. In external circumstances there has been a wonderful improvement. If only because I came into intimate contact with the living conditions of a vast number of people fifty years ago, I am the last person to under-value the provisions of the Welfare State. A BBC critic surprisingly complimented me for what he called my 'rapid survey of the astonishing improvement in social conditions which has come over this country'. It was made in a speech which was broadcast in 1954, and this was the passage referred to: 'Primary poverty has been largely banished, full employment has been secured to a considerable extent, universal provision for the treatment of sickness in hospital or home has been established, unemployment insurance and retirement pensions provided, together with the collective direction of basic industries and services.' The critic called this 'a most heartening exhibit', and that is what it was intended to be. But this is only one part of the picture. It is in the external conditions of life that such marked improvement has been secured. Fifty years ago many of us believed that if we could secure better wages, better houses, better provision for illness and for unemployment, life itself would become better. It has not worked out like that, and we have had to learn by sorry experience that to lift up the physical conditions of life does not mean that the moral conditions are also lifted up.

The repeated references to gambling, due to my personal involvement in that particular problem, will have revealed, I hope, the growing seriousness of the situation. The nation has suffered a moral defeat, of which gambling is one, but only one, of the disastrous effects. Before the second World War there was an underlying assumption that, while gambling was widespread, it should be restricted as far as possible. The Royal Commission, 1951, on the contrary started with the preconception that gambling was to be accepted as one of the features of social life and provision made for it accordingly, with some safeguards against possible abuse. The result is that today Great Britain is possibly the greatest gambling country in the world, a distinction once held by China. Many thousands of licensed betting shops have been allowed, in spite of their being closed by law in 1853 because of the harm they did. Millions of people spend hours every week at the childish game of bingo because of the money involved. Eighteenth-century gaming clubs are being reopened, with roulette, baccarat, chemin de fer, and the rest. We are promised casinos at all the holiday resorts. Football pools take the place once occupied by the public lotteries, and they are actually lotteries, for there is no skill involved. Then there is a seemingly respectable national lottery in Premium Bonds. Horse-racing and dog-racing persist, with the totalisator competing with the bookmakers. Why is it wrong? people still ask. Because it has no economic justification, being an exchange of money without any increase or even recognition of value. Because its only ultimate attraction is selfish gain through the loss of others. Because it cultivates the irrational and superstitious belief in luck. In a word, because it is opposed to the Christian standard of life, which involves honesty, unselfishness and love. Is it surprising that the Methodist

Church appeals to all members to accept the duty of abstaining from every form of gambling?

Another factor in the general depressing situation is alcoholic indulgence, which is also a subject with which I have had to do. Much the most distressing feature is the presence in the churches of those who deny the existence of a 'drink' evil, and recognize only the evil of 'intemperance'. I wish the word of St Thomas Aquinas were remembered: 'There are things contrary to a good condition of life and the temperate man does not use them in any manner, for this would be a sin against temperance.' The scientific evidence available today makes it absolutely clear that alcoholic beverages are 'contrary to a good condition of life' even in what is called moderate use. The smallest indulgence has an appreciable effect in blunting mental reaction and impairing judgement. This is the fact which is intimately related to a large proportion of the road accidents. Yet public opinion resists action by the Government to compel scientific tests of drivers involved in accidents. Social custom and personal indulgence loom larger and more important than the killing and crippling of thousands of our people. Here is another moral defeat. The Methodist Conference appeals to all members to abstain habitually from the use of intoxicating liquors for Christ's sake and the common good, but one wonders how many Methodists are to be included in the greatly increased section of the community who regard alcoholic indulgence as an essential part of social life.

While I have made very little reference to the question of sexual standards, it was part of my special responsibility when I was a secretary of what was then called the Temperance and Social Welfare Department. There has always been such a problem, but as it then existed it was not to be compared with this issue in the life of today. Looseness of sexual behaviour is openly advocated and publicly justified as a necessary expression of life. Pre-marital intercourse and even the more casual intercourse of teenagers are coming to be regarded as normal. It would be a mistake to exaggerate this or to ignore the fact that we still have in many directions a fine body of young people who have adopted a true standard of life. But the tendencies are so marked that one fears for the future. The flood of a certain type of miscalled literature is one of the causes of this moral decay. The trial and the verdict in the case of *Lady Chatterley's Lover* were a disgrace to this country. It would appear that the prosecution was not intended to succeed, for not a single witness was called. As strong and influential a body of people might have appeared against the publication as were presented by the defence in its favour, but no opportunity was given. The result, and seemingly the intended result, is an open field for other books of a similar type. The reviewer of one such book in *The Times* quotes the publisher's statement that it is 'a foremost classic of twentieth-century literature' and says truly: 'If that be so, the world is even more sick than one thought.' Who can measure the devastating effect upon youth of this deliberate attempt to disguise pornography under a cloak of literary style? Perhaps the saddest feature of this whole situation is that from some pulpits of the Christian Church come declarations that the traditional moral code is out of date, that fornication is no serious matter, and the claim that homosexuality is the delight of a new relationship. Who was it first gave currency to that unfortunate contrast between 'Charity' and 'Chastity'? Those who have intimate knowledge are saying that from the standpoint of decency, not to say purity, the English stage is worse than anything in Europe. Even Television has carried plays of this kind into the homes of the people to the embarrassment of parents and the soiling of the minds of children. As I write we have been startled and dismayed by the revelation of sexual depravity in so-called high circles of political and social life. Some of these things are still exceptional, but the drift and the tendency are unmistakable, and we are guilty of spiritual cowardice if we turn aside and refuse to face these unpleasant facts.

The situation has been most accurately and graphically described by Sir Richard Livingstone, the great educationalist and one-time Vice-Chancellor of Oxford University, in this way: 'When we were young there were moral fences along the road of life. We did not always keep to them, but we knew when we had crossed them. Today all the moral fences are down, and look at the world. Your job is to build those fences anew.' That surely describes our task. It would be bad enough if the moral fences were ignored, but the tragedy is that they are no longer there. The moral principles themselves are challenged. I was impressed by the exact analysis of the present position by Dr Harold Roberts in the booklet he wrote in preparation for the Oslo World Methodist Conference. In consideration of 'New Life in the Spirit', which was the main theme, there was a sub-title 'The Holy Spirit and Moral Standards'. Under this he says:

'Truth and right as realities existing independently of our own wishes and inclinations seem to have no meaning for a considerable number of our contemporaries. Words like obligation, responsibility, guilt, shame represent experiences which to many are becoming increasingly unfamiliar. . . . The consequence of this retreat from absolutes of any kind is perhaps most patent in sexual morality and in the violation of the marriage bond. . . . It should not be forgotten that the decline in the regard for moral standards is no accident. . . . Where the eternal dimension of life is ignored, people cast off restraint. . . . Hence our campaign for a revival of Christian morality must be grounded in a revival of faith in God.'

This use of the words 'absolutes' and 'moral standards' suggests at once a movement which is seeking, with considerable success, to persuade people to accept the absolute moral standards under the leadership and power of God. I have become interested in Moral Re-Armament (MRA for short) because I have seen what it has done in meeting this moral decay, and have come to see how desirable it is that the Christian Church should accept this movement as an ally or, more truly, as part of the activity of the Christian Church. It is not another church or sect or society, nor even an organization in the ordinary sense. There is no recorded membership, nor any such thing as joining it in any formal way. It is simply a movement proclaiming for acceptance certain principles of life. It is Christian in its incepton and stands for three practical features of the Christian life. These are CHANGE— the change of heart and life in turning from self to God; GUIDANCE—the influence of God if we will give Him the opportunity to direct our lives; ABSOLUTE MORAL STANDARDS —these are made specific under four requirements, Absolute

Honesty, Absolute Purity, Absolute Unselfishness, and Absolute Love. This is a high level of moral life, and such a revival of Christian morality must be grounded on faith in God, which means the change of heart and life.

In a very remarkable way MRA has brought into use the media of the film and the stage on the highest professional level to a degree beyond the normal possibility of the Church. This has been a wonderful missionary service, bringing under its influence many thousands of people who were right outside ordinary church circles, for the movement is itself free from dogma or ecclesiasticism. Roman Catholic co-operation has been increasingly noted. I have seen the value of this movement amongst members of the Methodist Church in giving a richer vitality to the expression of their faith and providing a protective armour for young people placed in situations of acute temptation. It is easy to criticize some of its marginal expressions, as indeed any movement, like the criticism of Methodism in the eighteenth century. The thing to be noted is its positive value in this struggle against the present moral decline, and its desire to be a gateway into the fuller worship and the sacramental devotion of the Christian Church.

We do well to recognize all our allies in this unavoidable struggle for the true standards of both personal and social life, such as the Public Morality Council, the Marriage Guidance Council and the guidance on a wide field of the Methodist Christian Citizenship Department. There is an intimate relationship between the different facets of moral decay which should be understood. Alcoholic indulgence ministers to sexual perversion and addiction to gambling is followed by personal degeneration. However the modern prophets evade the truth; the cause of the whole mischief is sin and the only cure comes by faith in God.

Thus when thinking backward over half a century and more I am greatly distressed by the decline in the community sense of moral values and see in this direction a major task of the Christian Church if modern civilization is to be saved from itself.

It has already been made clear that a large part of my life has been closely associated with other churches in common action. The Temperance Council of the Christian Churches and the Churches Main Committee on War Damage included Roman Catholic representatives. The Roman Catholic Church also had its participants on the preliminary commissions of COPEC. Then there was Free Church association through the Free Church Federal Council and the wider representation in the British Council of Churches. Most distinctive were the great ecumenical assemblies in Stockholm, Amsterdam, and Evanston, with the formation of the World Council of Churches. This whole development broadly covers rather more than the first half of this century, and must lead on to changes in the extension of ecumenicity and to actual church unions which are not clearly foreseen at this stage. This is not the opportunity to discuss the details of proposals which are beginning to take shape and will be under serious examination during these coming years. But I want to point out certain general conclusions or issues which emerge out of the past experiences and have formulated in my own mind. They are related to our forward duties and responsibilities, even though they do not represent final judgements.

One of the first and important things impressed upon me is the necessity of distinguishing between unity and union. Unity is a spiritual fact. 'The Unity of the Spirit' is given by God, and can and does exist across human divisions. Years ago I had a close friendship with a Roman Catholic priest. The Rev. Father Hays was an outstanding temperance worker, and at one period I frequently spoke at meetings with him. I can still recall some of his Irish stories. We had many long talks, and he did not hesitate to join with me in prayer. The ecclesiastical division between us was seemingly unbreakable, but that did not prevent an experience of spiritual unity. That is personal and may be regarded as an extreme instance, so let me refer to the deep and effective unity we knew across the divisions of the churches, which was so rich an experience in Birmingham. Unity may lead to union, but not necessarily. Union is the creation of a common organism, and is of little value unless pervaded and inspired by the fact of unity. Our responsibility is to accept God's gift of the unity in His Spirit and express it as perfectly as we can. While organic union of churches is to be desired in various directions, it should be recognized that

that is not always the case. Unity can be received and practised where organic union may not be the right outcome. That is most especially true in the realm of ethical and social witness. Is it not in that field we should be seeking to realize our unity more completely?

A word which I find difficult to use is 'r*e*union'. Are we to go back to create a union that once existed? There was surely unity in the early Church, though in New Testament times it was broken by party claims. But was there union as we understand union in that Church of the first century? 'Never have all those who have professed themselves to be followers of Christ been one. From the first generation of Christians divisions have existed.' So Professor K. S. Latourette has declared. In any case, we are not living in the conditions of the first century, and if there had been union then, nothing that we might achieve would be after that pattern. Surely we should be living forward, however much we may and should reverence the past. We seek for union as the expression of the unity of the Spirit, and the Spirit 'bloweth where it listeth'. We should be looking forward to be guided by the Spirit, not looking backward to reproduce something which probably never existed.

There is no more difficult point of discussion when union is the aim than episcopacy. As a form of church government, there may be much to be said for it. The American Methodists took that view from the beginning, but without creating thereby a separate order of the ministry. As their constitution points out, the term 'bishop' is the equivalent of 'general superintendent'. He is an elder, like his brethren, but charged with special duties and responsibilities—in fact, a presiding elder. There is little need for discussion about this form of functional episcopacy. It is the claim of the 'historic episcopacy' that provides the problem. If this term implied no more than the antiquity of the office of bishop in the Church, it would arouse little or no controversy. It would then state merely a historic fact. The problem arises from the claim of unbroken succession from the Apostles, with the spiritual authority that that implies. It is admitted by its advocates that the historic succession cannot be proved historically, but it is assumed as a spiritual necessity. It is nearly a hundred years since the first publication of Bishop Lightfoot's commentary on St Paul's Epistle to the Philippians in which he stated, 'It is a fact now generally recognised by theologians of all shades of opinion that in the language of the New Testament the same officer in the Church is called indifferently "bishop" (ἐπίσκοπος) and "elder" or "presbyter" (πρεσβύτερος). As far as I am aware modern New Testament scholarship has not modified this opinion on the identity of these two terms. In the famous dissertation on 'The Christian Ministry', Bishop Lightfoot declares emphatically that the opinion 'that the same officers of the Church who were first called "apostles" came afterwards to be designated "bishops" is baseless'.

Moving about among the European Churches, one meets strange anomalies. The Anglican Church accepts the historic succession of the bishops of the Lutheran Church of Sweden, but not the bishops of any other Lutheran Churches. The Bishop of Stockholm is therefore in the succession, but not the Bishop of Oslo nor Bishop Dibelius of Germany. The Swedish bishops, I am assured, know no distinction whatever in their relationship with the bishops of the Lutheran Churches in other countries. Then neither the Roman Catholic Church nor the Orthodox Churches acknowledge the orders of the Anglican Church or recognize their bishops as being within the historic succession. One of the great difficulties in the way of union would be removed if episcopacy could be set free from this concept of succession which cannot be proved, while preserving the true spiritual continuity of the living Church. We should then no longer hear the sort of statement made by one speaker in the plenary session of the World Council of Churches Assembly at Evanston. I will not identify him further than by saying that he was an Anglican Bishop. He said that when he came to discuss the World Council of Churches with his clergy he would have to point out that some of the participating churches in the World Council were really not churches at all, but only sects.

It is not without significance that among the churches of the Reformation the Anglican World Communion, which is smaller than several, is the only one which claims to have the historic episcopate and ministerial orders derived therefrom. The Swedish Church does not claim it for itself. Thus in the total world community of the Reformed or Protestant churches approaching 265 millions only one ninth, roughly, pay regard to the historic episcopate. The Lutherans, the American Methodists and some smaller churches have bishops but with no thought of a historic and in that sense an apostolic succession. John Wesley was emphatic, but surely right, when he wrote in a letter to his brother in reference to the episcopate, 'The uninterrupted succession I know to be a fable which no man ever did or can prove.' But, that apart, the episcopal form of church government has values which should be recognized while the continuity of Apostolic teaching and doctrine is secured in and through the living church.

One of the particular facts demonstrated by the World Council of Churches is that of unity amid diversity. It surely leads to the conclusion, not only that unity does not imply uniformity, but that union need not of necessity claim uniformity as its basis. There is much talk about 'the coming great Church'. I am still waiting to know whether any content can be put into that phrase. It cannot possibly mean one vast organized and uniform Church. The very idea fills me with dismay. The diversity of church order and worship are surely essential in a world like this. The great service of Holy Communion at Amsterdam was not less significant nor less spiritually satisfying because its liturgy and form were so entirely different from anything many of us had previously experienced. Is it unthinkable that true spiritual unity may call for a church union in the future which will comprise within itself diversity in forms of worship, in expressions of fellowship, and even of organization and administration?

Another important point of demonstration by the World Council of Churches is that of a unity which is beyond the divisions of nationalism. In the *Minutes of the Methodist Conference for 1747* the following question and answer appear, the answer presumably by John Wesley,

> 'What instance or ground is there in the New Testament for a National Church?
> 'We know none at all, we apprehend it to be a merely political institution.'

It is disturbing that in this scientific age, when the means of contact and communication between the nations would seem to make internationalism more possible than ever before, there should have developed an intense nationalism with all its divisive elements. This fact is forcing geographical limits upon the churches when, in fact, the Christian Church is the one truly international reality in the modern world. It is a point to be considered in every proposed scheme of union. It may well be also a major task of the World Council of Churches to preserve the freedom of the Christian Church from the restrictive limits of nationalism, a task in which the World confessional organizations, such as the World Methodist Council, must co-operate.

There is one other reflection which raises in my mind a very serious query. One of the distinctive qualities of World Methodism is that the basis of membership, when put into its simplest form, is faith in the Lord Jesus Christ. The unity of Methodism is found in the Person of our Lord. That too is the point of unity in the World Council of Churches. The most vivid outward expression of that unity is found when we gather round the Table of the Lord. It is indeed a tragic fact that through the centuries of the history of the Church so much that is unreal, un-Scriptural and divisive has become associated with the Lord's Supper. Do we not find its essential truth in its simplicities? Two occasions to which I have referred I look back upon with special significance. One is set in a kitchen where the only altar was a kitchen table and an Anglican Bishop distributed the bread and wine to members of many churches. All the essentials were there, and Christ was present to the faith of the communicants. The other was the vast company at Amsterdam, where there was no altar, but a long table set for a meal and the broken bread and the chalice were passed from hand to hand. None could mistake either the Unity or the Presence. Is it impossible for us as simple followers of Christ to leave our differences of creed and orders behind and come to the Table of the Lord wherever the Sacrament is observed in truth and sincerity? That is my query, and while I can anticipate the answer I still put the question. I do not undervalue the importance of theologies and ministries and liturgies which have their place, but surely that place is not that of a barrier against full admission to the Table, which is His, not ours? There, welcomed as His guests, we might come to know more fully the Unity of the Spirit and see more clearly the form of the union which would be a true expression of that Unity. So, thinking backward, runs the query in my mind.

Before concluding this chapter of reflections and writing *finis* to this book I must refer to two great world issues which have primacy in the thought of all nations. These issues of War and Race are universal in extent, appalling in their possible consequences and seem almost to defy solution. As I look backward I see the frightful devastation in Hamburg, Hanover and Berlin, so much vaster in extent and greater in intensity than we have experienced in Plymouth, Coventry and London. There are for me intimate personal remembrances. In Germany in January, 1947, I handed to the wife of a university professor some bars of English chocolate for their children. Her amazed and tearful welcome for something the children had not seen for years was such that I handed over all I had. A trifling matter?—but was it? I saw in Germany after the First World War some of the tragic consequences of the so-called peace treaties which precipitated the second world conflict. Years later I saw the tragedy of the supposed peace settlements which create the possibility of a third world war with all the horror of nuclear power and threatened annihilation. The Stockholm Conference in 1925 passed by an overwhelming vote this statement, 'We summon the churches to share with us our sense of the horror of war and of its futility as a means of settling international disputes'. The Amsterdam Assembly in 1948 unanimously commended this declaration, 'The part which war plays in our present international life is a sin against God and a degradation of man'. With all the subsequent discussion we still await the clear and united witness of the Christian Church that war is wrong with all that that implies of judgement and action both nationally and internationally.

I have seen something of the problem of Race in the United States and the frightening situation in South Africa. It is of interest that one of the most influential speeches at the first Ecumenical Methodist Conference in Wesley's Chapel, London, in 1881 was made by a young negro minister, Joseph Charles Price. The sums he collected in England were the first contributions to the founding of Livingstone College of the African

Methodist Episcopal Zion Church. An African friend of mine, a keen politician, came to accept through MRA the policy of love without violence as the way of life and of political action. He is a Methodist and at the mixed Synod he apologized publicly to the white chairman for the trouble he had previously caused. It takes a big man to do that. Yet the South African Government denies the position and rights of citizenship to a man of that character. The rising to adult status of the African people, east and west, is rapidly outdating every policy of segregation and the negation of human equality whether in this country or elsewhere.

As we look forward it becomes increasingly clear that the Christian Church is being tested, most of all, as to the clarity of its judgements and the courage of its actions in the whole field of Christian ethics. The realized unity of the Church should mean united influence and action:—A) to overcome moral decadence: B) to secure social justice: C) to claim racial integration: D) to outlaw internecine strife. This is an impossible programme apart from the power of God, but, as the Amsterdam message declared, 'By our acts of faith and obedience we can on earth set up signs which point to the coming victory'. Are we willing and ready for the commitment of such faith and the sacrifice of such obedience?

In its time sequence this autobiography comes to its conclusion with the Oslo World Methodist Conference in 1961, almost exactly eighty years after my entrance into the world and when I retired from my official appointment in the general secretariat of the World Methodist Council. While this has enabled me to hand over many secretarial duties it seems to have made surprisingly little difference to the total extent of my work in various directions. I would not have it otherwise so long as I enjoy strength of mind and body. Through these many years I have recognized, humbly, the guiding Hand of God and I hope still to travel on

QUO MONSTRAT DOMINUS.

INDEX

Aquinas, St Thomas, 188
African Methodist Episcopal Church, 160
African Methodist Episcopal Zion Church, 155
Air travel, 142
Aldersgate Street, 146
Allen, Rev. Dr Thomas, 16
Amsterdam, 132, 171, 175ff
Apartheid, 158f
Arvidson, Bishop Theodor, 133
Asbury Cottage, Bishop, 157
Auferstehungskirche, Stuttgart, 134
Australia, 143, 150
Austria, 88, 101

Bach, Johann Sebastian, 100
Baker, Rev. Dr Eric W., 169
Baptist Churches, 94, 175
Barnes, Right Rev. E. W., Bishop of Birmingham, 75f, 86
Barrow-Clough, Rev. J. A., 13
Basis of World Council of Churches, 179f
Beckley Social Service Lecture, 121
Beethoven House, 102
Belfast, 162
Belisha, Right Hon. Leslie Hore, M.P., 60f, 108
Benson, Rev. F. H., 56
Berchtesgaden, 102
Bergen, 152
Berlin, 98, 128
Berresford, Gordon, 107
Betting Facts, 54
Bielefeld, 99
Birkett, Right Hon. Lord, 78f
Birmingham, 15-21, 55ff, 59-86, 123
Birmingham University, 86, 103
Black Forest, 102
Bologna, 163
Boughey, F. J., 41
Bourne, Cardinal, Archbishop of Westminster, 49
Brandenburg, 99
Brent, Bishop C. H., 174

Brewster Sessions, 78f
Bristol, 129, 131
Bristol Cathedral, 131f
British Broadcasting Corporation, 77, 186
British Council of Churches, 57, 142, 180
Browne, Bishop Wm. F. (R.C.), 114
Brownhill, Miss M., 64
Bucke, Dr Emory, 162
Buckingham Palace, 110, 115, 144
Bull, Miss Hilda J., 97, 109

Cadman, Commissioner Elijah, 3
Calhoun, Professor Robert L., 178
Canada, 92ff, 163
Cape Coast, Ghana, 165
Carter, Rev. Henry, 45f, 47f, 55f, 173f
Casa Materna, Italy, 136
Cecil, Right Rev. Lord William, Bishop of Exeter, 51
Centenary College, Lousiana, U.S.A., 155
Central Hall, Birmingham, 20, 56f, 59ff, 106
Chadwick, Rev. Samuel, 9
Chairman of District, 124ff
Chamberlain, Right Hon. Austen, M.P., 77f
Chancellor of the Exchequer, 111
Channel Islands, 13f
Chapel of the Upper Room, 162
Chapel of Unity, 119
Cherokee Indians, 153ff
Christian Citizenship Department, xii, 17, 45, 108, 172, 191
Christian Social Council, 77f, 84, 86
Churches Committee on Gambling, 54, 85
Churches Main Committee, 112ff
Circuit system, 24
Clark, Dr Elmer T., 147f, 153f, 156, 168
Coal Strike, 1912, 33
Cole, Maurice, 74
Cole, Rev. R. Lee, 81

Collier, Rev. Samuel, 9
Coomer, Duncan, 147
Conference, Methodist, 9, 12, 129ff, 185f
Confessional Organizations, 181
Cooper, Thomas, 2, 11
COPEC, 17, 55f, 77, 172
Cornwall, 21-8, 32
Corson, Bishop Fred P., 150, 168
Coventry Cathedral Commission, 118f
Cumbers, Rev. Dr Frank, xiv

Davidson, Most Rev. Randall, Archbishop of Canterbury, 49
Davies, Rev. Rupert E., 169
Decision, 7, 63
Deissmann, Professor Adolph, 98
Denman, Dr Harry, 162
Dennis, Rev. H. W. and Mrs, 165f
Department for Chapel Affairs, 85, 113, 116
Departments, Methodist, 45
Doyle, Bishop Bertram W., 169
Drink problem, 47ff, 81f, 174, 188
Duke University, Durham, U.S.A., 128
Durham, U.S.A., 128

Ecumenical Methodist Conferences, 111, 128, 147
Edinburgh Conferences, 171, 175
Edmonds, Rev. Frank H., 161
Edwards, Rev. Dr Maldwyn L., 150, 165
Eisenhower, President, 154, 156
Ellwood, L. A., 147, 169
Episcopacy, 193ff
Episcopal Address, U.S.A., 142
Epworth Old Rectory, 156f
European Consultative Conference, 148ff
Evangelism, 62f, 146, 150
Evanston, 162, 171, 177, 194
Everson, Rev. F. Howell, 118
Exchange of preachers, 150

Faith and Order, 175
Farndale, Rev. Dr W. E., 130, 139
Farrar, Dr Dorothy, 150, 169
Fellowship of Freedom and Reform, 48, 50f
Festival of Remembrance, 144
Field, Counsellor J. B., 74, 86
Finch, Rev. Edwin, 16, 111, 131, 185

Findlay, Rev. Dr J. Alexander, 17
Fisher of Lambeth, Lord (Most Rev. Geoffrey F. Fisher), 112, 180
Fletcher, Rev. J. Allen, 137
Florence, 91, 136
Forward Movement, 9, 59
France, 15, 97
Free Church (Federal) Council, 8, 41, 77, 142ff
Free Church Union, 144f
Freudenstadt, 102, 157, 162
Fries, Professor and Mrs, 173

Gambling, 34ff, 41ff, 47, 70f, 83ff, 88ff, 174, 187
Gambling and Youth, 85
Gambling in English Life, 84, 121
Gambling, The Problem of, 40f
Game Reserve, 161
Geneva Conference, 181
George, Rev. A. Raymond, 169
German Central Conference, 132ff
Ghana, 165f
Göttingen University, 103, 127
Grand Canyon, 140
Grant, Rev. Francis C. F., 165, 169
Grayton, Rev. Kenneth, 137
Griffin, Cardinal, Archbishop of Westminster, 115f
Griffiths, Rev. Vavasor, 16

Hagen, Bishop Odd, 149, 151, 168
Hale, Miss, 64
Hall, Miss E., 64
Halle, 100
Hambly, Rev. Dr Frank W., 169
Hamburg, 97, 127
Handel, George Frederick, 27, 100, 104, 177
Handsworth College, 15-21
Harbottle, Rev. George, 10
Hearn, Rev. Albert, 106, 117, 123
Helston, 21-8, 132
Henderson, Right Hon. Arthur, M.P., 48, 52
Henson, Right Rev. Hensley, Bishop of Durham, 48
Hillis, A. B., 107, 139
Hinks, J. A., 114, 117
Historical Society, International Methodist, 156
Historic Episcopacy, 193
Holdsworth, Rev. W. West, 17

INDEX

Holt, Bishop Ivan Lee, 139, 147, 154, 156, 158, 179
Holt, Judge Ivan Lee, 139f
Holy Communion, 63, 81, 101, 119, 137, 176, 179, 196
Horn, Ragnar, 168
Hornabrook, Rev. John, 29, 32
Horses, 28f
Hough, Dean Lynn Harold, 150
Howard, Rev. Dr Wilbert F., 18, 147
Hudson, James, M.P., 52
Hughes, Rev. Hugh Price, 9
Hughes, Rev. Dr Samuel W., 19

Ihmels, Bishop, 174
Indian Mission, Durban, 158
Individuals, 67ff, 189
Industrial Christian Fellowship, 79
Ineson, Rev. Percy, 4, 110
Innere Mission, Germany, 98
Inter-Communion, 81
Irish Methodist Conference, 137
Italian Methodist Church, 115, 163

Jackson, Sir Harold, 74
Jackson, Rev. William C., 106, 117
James, Rev. Francis B., 16, 20
Jeremias, Professor Joachim, 103, 127
Jersey, 12ff
Jewitt, Alfred M., 107
Job, Rev. H. Allen, 85
Johannesburg, 138
Johnson, Rev. G. E. Hickman, 16, 117
Jones, Edwin L., 147, 156f
Jowitt, Rev. Dr J. H., 20
Junaluska, Lake, 151, 153ff

Kaehler, Professor, 103, 127
Keeble, Rev. Samuel E., 17, 56
Kempthorne, Right Rev. Bishop, 57f
Kendall, Rev. R. E., 161
Kenya, 161
Kern, Bishop Paul E., 142
King Richard's Road Methodist Church, Leicester, 6f
Kissack, Rev. Reginald, 163

Lambeth Palace, 114
Langland, William, 56
Lardi, Rev. Giacomo, 90, 135f
La Spezia, 116
Lawrence, Rev. H. Jesse, 160
League of Nations, 46ff

Lectures, 27, 36, 121, 151
Legal Hundred, 71
Legal studies, 42f
Leicester, 1, 6, 8, 30, 130
Lester, George Stephen, 109, 123
Lewis, Rev. Dr Douglas W., 16
Lewis, Mrs Mildred C., 129
Leyland, Rev. Dr A. Stanley, 150, 169
Licensed Trade, 47, 49, 51, 78f, 82
Lidgett, Rev. Dr J. Scott, 49f, 57
Life and Work, 17, 57, 171, 175
Lineham, Samuel, 140f
Livingstone, Sir Richard, 189
Lloyd, Rev. A. Kingsley, 169
Lloyd, Right Hon. Selwyn, M.P., 162
Local option, 47, 49
Lofthouse, Rev. Dr W. F., 17f, 56, 86
Long, Rev. Dr Ernest E., 169
Los Angeles, 140
Louisville, Kentucky, 128
Luther, Martin, 100
Lutheran Church, 175, 180, 184

McConnell, Dorothy, 169
McCord, Sister Mary, 64
McNeal, Rev. George H., 35
Makins, Sir Roger M., 157
Maltby, Rev. Dr Russell, 56
Manchester, 106, 116, 122, 124f
Manchester University, 137f
Manson, Rev. Professor T. W., 138
'Manyano', South Africa, 158
Marriage Guidance Council, 191
Martin, Rev. Dr Hugh, 57
Martin, Bishop Paul E., 155, 169
'*Messiah*', Handel's, 37, 103
Methodist Church, The (G.B.), 6ff, 29-44, 129ff, 184ff
Methodist Church, The (U.S.A.), 139ff, 160, 193
Methodist Church Builds Again, The, 118
Methodist Church Music Society, The, 72
Methodist Preaching Houses and the Law, 105, 121
Milan, 92, 136
Mills, John F., 169
Model Trust Deed, 105f, 121
Monod, Pasteur Wilfred, 174
Monte Carlo, 88ff
Montreal, 93
Moore, Bishop Arthur, 133, 162
Morality Council, Public, 191

202   SO APPOINTED

Moral Re-Armament, 190f, 198
Morris, Sir Philip R., 132
Mozart, 102
Musical interests, 4f, 20f, 27, 37, 60, 72, 150, 153

Nairobi, 161
Nall, Bishop T. Otto, 150
Naples, 136
Nashville, U.S.A., 162
Nationalism, 195
Neave, F. G., 43
Newcastle, 129
New Delhi, 179
New York, 92, 152, 156, 164
Niebuhr, Professor Reinhold, 177
North Carolina, 154f
Norway, 57f, 152, 166ff
Nottingham, 9, 40f
Nubia, Archbishop of, 173

Oberammergau, 102f
Odell, Rev. E. W., 129
Olav V, King, 167
Olson, Dr Oscar T., 156
Open-air meetings, 25, 65
Ordination, 27, 29
Orgill, Rev. Canon Harold, 4
Orthodox Churches, 172f, 175, 180, 194
Oslo, Norway, 149, 153, 166ff, 198
Outwood, Wakefield, 37, 39f
Oxford, 147, 169, 175

Paris, 97
Parliamentary, Select Committees and Royal Commissions—
   1917—Premium Bonds, 41f
   1923—Betting Duty, 53f
   1932—Licensing, 82
   1933—Lotteries and Betting, 84f
   1951—Betting, Gaming and Lotteries, 120
Parlin, Charles C., 138, 169
Perkins, A. Elsie, xii, xiv, 30, 32, 36, 46, 55, 62, 86, 97, 115, 135
Perkins, Mary H. (Mrs G. S. Lester), 40, 46, 86, 97, 109, 123
Perkins, E. Benson—
   1881—Home, school, business, church, 2-9
   1903—Candidate for the Ministry, 10f.
   —Jersey, 12-15
   1904—Handsworth College, 15-21
   1907—Helston, 21-8
   1910—Ordination, marriage, 29f
   —Sheffield, 30-7
   1913—Wakefield, 37, 39f
   1914—Chaplain to the Forces
   1916—Nottingham, 40-4
   1920—London, Temperance and Social Welfare Department 45-56
   1925—Birmingham, 61-86
   1935—Sheffield, 61-74
   —Chairman, Sheffield District, 124f
   1939—Manchester, Department for Chapel Affairs, 105-22
   1941—Chairman, Manchester District, 120ff
   1948—President of the Conference
   1952—Secretary, World Methodist Council, 146-168; 1952-4
   —Vice-President, British Council of Churches, 180
   1954—Moderator, Free Church Federal Council, 140-5
   1961—Secretary Emeritus, World Methodist Council, 168
   —Hon. Secretary, Department for Chapel Affairs, 123
Perkins, Edith F. (Mrs P. Ineson), 1, 4, 110, 136
Perkins (George), Father and Mother, 2, 6f, 85f, 130, 137
Perkins, Rev. William, 29
Philadelphia, 128, 150
Phillipson, Rev. W. Oliver, 123, 129
Photios, Archbishop and Pope of Alexandria, 173
Piers the Plowman, The Vision concerning, 36
Portability of church payments, 112f
Portici, 136
Potsdam, 98
Potts, Dr J. Manning, 162
Preaching, 19
Prediger Seminar, Frankfurt, 133
   Gothenberg, 151
Preedy, Elizabeth, 46
Premium Bonds, 41f, 187
Priestley, Arthur, 74

Quadrennial Conference, The Methodist Church, U.S.A., 139ff

INDEX

Question Conferences, 60
Quimby, Dr Karl, 150, 169

Race, 154, 158ff, 165, 197f
Rank, The Right Hon. the Lord, 163f
Rattenbury, Rev. Harold B., 138
Rattenbury, Rev. Dr J. Ernest, 9ff
Raven, Rev. Canon Charles E., 56
Rebuilding Fund, 117, 134
Redundancy, 40
Reformation, 194
Reports, Chapel Department, 118
Reunion, 193
Revival, Cornish, 25f
Richards, Rev. Leyton, 75f
Riches, Right Rev. Kenneth, Bishop of Lincoln, 157
Roberts, Rev. Dr Harold, xi, xiv, 147, 150, 152, 156f, 167ff, 181, 190
Rogers, Rev. Canon T. Guy, 75, 77, 80f
Roman Catholic Church, 114f, 172, 175, 191, 194
Rome, 90f, 135, 163
Royal Navy, Army and Royal Air Force Board, 126, 128
Rupp, Rev. Professor E. Gordon, 132f

St George's, Old, Philadelphia, 151, 156, 164
St Louis, Missouri, U.S.A., 139
St Simon's Island, Georgia, U.S.A., 162
Salisbury, S. Rhodesia, 158, 160
Salisbury, Frank O., 162
Salvation Army, 3, 49
San Francisco, 140
Sangster, Rev. Dr W. E., 129, 141
Santi, Rev. Ricardo, 137
Savannah, 163
Schlink, Professor Edmund, 178
Scholz, Dr Ernst and Luise E., 168, 169
School, Alderman Newtons, 3
  Edgbaston High, 86
  Wyggeston Girls, 4, 30
Seaton, Rev. A. J. G., 7
'Sea Horse, The', 83
Serving the Church, 118
Sexual standards, 188ff
Sharp, Rev. Dr J. Alfred, 47
Shaw, William, 106
Shearer, Rev. W. Russell, 62, 144
Sheffield, 30-7, 59-87, 124f

Sigg, Bishop Ferdinand, 133, 150, 162
Smith, C. Soutter, 74
Smith, Shirley, 74
Snowden, Philip (Viscount), 52
Social conditions, 32, 186ff
Social Service, Wesleyan Methodist Union for, 17, 45, 171
Sociology, 17, 34
Soderblom, Nathan, Archbishop of Sweden, 175
Sommer, Bishop J. W. E., 97, 101, 133, 148, 176
South Africa, 157-60, 180
Sport, 4, 20, 27
Springfield, U.S.A., 147
Spurr, Rev. F. C., 75, 77, 86
Stacey, Rev. Hobart, 57, 88
Statistics, 168
Stockholm, Life and Work Conference, 57, 171
Straube, Elizabeth (Mrs Mattstedt), 86
Strawson, Rev. Dr William, xiv
Sunday, Victorian, 6f
Sweden, 58, 167f, 172ff
Switzerland, 55
Syvret, Phillip, 15

Takoradi, Ghana, 165f
Tasker, Rev. Dr J. G., 16f
Temperance, 47, 81f, 188
Temperance Council of the Christian Churches, 48f, 52, 81f
Temple, Most Rev. William—
  Bishop of Manchester, 56
  Archbishop of York, 84
  Archbishop of Canterbury, 175, 180
Theological differences, 174f, 178f
Theological Institute, 169
Thomas, George T., M.P., 162
Thomas, Sir Percy, 119
Thompson, Rev. Douglas, 161
Tonga, Queen of, 154
Topping, Sister Lilian, 169
Toronto, 92ff, 138, 163
Towlson, Dr Clifford W., 72
Trier, 102
Trott, President Norman L., 163f
Truman, F. C., 47
Trustees for Methodist Church Purposes, 120
Tune-Book, Methodist, 72
Tuttle, Dr Lee F., 168

Unemployment, 33, 65f, 77, 95f
Union, 144, 192
Union, Methodist, 72, 147
United Church of Canada, 94f, 138
Unity, Church, 9, 80f, 176, 192, 195
Upper Room Chapel, 162

Versailles Treaty, 98f, 101, 197
Victoria Hall, Sheffield, 30f, 35, 59
Visser 't Hooft, Dr W. A., 167, 181

Wade, Rev. Wilfred, xiv, 148, 169
Wakefield, 37, 39f
Wakerley, Arthur, 5
Waldensian Church, 136, 163
Wand, Right Rev. J. W. C., Bishop of London, 113, 115
War, 98f, 101, 174f, 183, 197
War Damage Act, 111ff
Commission, 113f
Committee, 116f
War Office, 108
Washington, 156, 163f
Weatherhead, Rev. Dr Leslie, 4, 98
Webb, Rev. Dr J. B., 157, 160
Welfare State, 32, 187f
Welsh Assembly, 135
Wesley, Charles, 149f, 153, 162
John, 13, 41, 76, 100, 105f, 146, 150, 153, 157, 161f, 195
Wesley Guild, 7, 13f, 72f, 166

Wesley Historical Society, 121
Wesley Theological Seminary, 163f
Westbrook, Rev. Dr Francis B., 72
Whithead, Rev. Sylvester, 16
Wiseman, Rev. Dr F Luke, 9, 20
With Christ in the Bull Ring, 65, 79f
Wittenberg, 99
Women in the Ministry, 131
Wood, Sir Kingsley, 111
Woods, Right Rev. F. T., Bishop of Winchester, 173
Woodward, Rev. Max W., 168
World Alliance for Promoting International Friendship through the Churches, 97ff
World Council of Churches, 56, 81, 132, 175ff, 179, 181
World Federation of Methodist Women, 156, 168f
World Methodist Building, 153
Conference, 153ff, 166ff
Council, 147, 154, 156, 168, 171, 198
Executive, 148, 156, 162, 168
Hymn-Book, 153
Wunderlich, Bishop Friedrich, 86, 150, 162

Yorke, Rev. Albert J., 16
Youth Conference, 149, 174f

Zürich, 162

www.ingramcontent.com/pod-product-compliance
Lightning Source LLC
Chambersburg PA
CBHW071437150426
43191CB00008B/1156